SPEECH AND THEOLOGY

God is Infinite, but language finite; thus speech would seem to condemn him to finitude. In speaking of God, would the theologian violate divine transcendence by reducing God to immanence, or choose, rather, to remain silent? At stake in this argument is a core problem of the conditions of divine revelation. How, in terms of language and the limitations of human understanding, can transcendence ever be made known? Does its very appearance not undermine its transcendence, its condition of unknowability?

Speech and Theology: Language and the Logic of Incarnation posits that the paradigm for the encounter between the material and the divine, or the immanent and transcendent, is found in the Incarnation: God's voluntary self-immersion in the human world as an expression of his love for his creation. By this key act of grace, hinged upon Christ's condescension to human finitude, philosophy acquires the means not simply to speak of perfection, which is to speak theologically, but to bridge the gap between word and thing in a general sense. Responding to the works of Augustine, Husserl, and Heidegger through the lens of contemporary French phenomenologists such as Derrida, Levinas, and Marion, *Speech and Theology* reconsiders the perennial theological challenge of speaking of God, as traditionally reflected by devotional poles of predication and silence and of confession and praise. In the process, it passionately asserts two central truths: first, that God demands the effort of speech – that we are compelled to speak of God because he, in the Incarnation, *has first spoken* – and, consequently, that theology cannot properly choose silence in the pursuit of worship in view of its urgent need of words to make God visible. From the revolutionary assertion that God's incarnation is the condition of possibility not only for theological language but for language generally, James K. A. Smith creates a new Christian phenomenology where divine love ultimately functions as the ground for an affirmation of embodiment and materiality, and in which Christ's bodily endowment of worldly signs with the full reality of his own infinitude signals the basis for an entirely new theology of the arts.

James K. A. Smith is Associate Professor of Philosophy at Calvin College in Grand Rapids, MI, and the author of *The Fall of Interpretation: Philosophical Foundations for a Creational Hermeneutic* (2000).

RADICAL ORTHODOXY SERIES
Edited by John Milbank, Catherine Pickstock
and Graham Ward

Radical orthodoxy combines a sophisticated understanding of contemporary thought, modern and postmodern, with a theological perspective that looks back to the origins of the Church. It is the most talked-about development in contemporary theology.

SPEECH AND THEOLOGY

Language and the logic of incarnation

James K. A. Smith

London and New York

First published 2002
by Routledge
11 New Fetter Lane, London EC4P 4EE

Simultaneously published in the USA and Canada
by Routledge
29 West 35th Street, New York, NY 10001

Routledge is an imprint of the Taylor & Francis Group

© 2002 James K. A. Smith

Typeset in Baskerville by
BOOK NOW Ltd
Printed and bound in Great Britain by
MPG Books Ltd, Bodmin

British Library Cataloguing in Publication Data
A catalogue record for this book is available from the British Library

Library of Congress Cataloging in Publication Data
A catalog record for this book has been requested

ISBN 0-415-27695-0 (hbk)
ISBN 0-415-27696-9 (pbk)

For Mom,
who now knows that of which I speak

CONTENTS

ACKNOWLEDGEMENTS

Augustine would often quote the Pauline maxim, "What do we have that we have not received?" (1 Cor. 4:7). That never becomes more apparent than in the completion of a work such as this in which I have incurred many debts, of which I can mention only a few here.

First, I am grateful to Jack Caputo, for his shepherding hand and encouragement throughout these early stages of my career. His own groundbreaking work has cleared a path which has made this study possible, and his insights have provided important directions for not only this work, but many of my labors. I am also thankful that I can count Jack a friend in addition to a mentor. James McCartney and Anthony Godzieba both read the manuscript in its entirety and offered both helpful criticisms and encouraging support. Robert Dodaro and Tom Martin (re)introduced me to Augustine at a critical phase of my research, for which I am grateful. Jim Olthuis continues to be a treasured mentor and important dialogue partner for me, and Merold Westphal has been a generous source of support, exemplifying the model of a Christian scholar. And John Milbank and Graham Ward, whose work has provoked my own, have provided both encouragement and critical engagement which, I hope, have improved the book.

My colleagues and students at Loyola Marymount University aided me in honing these ideas and provided a receptive environment for my work. Thanks especially to Bil Van Otterloo and Shannon Nason for their help with the manuscript in its various stages. I would also like to thank Kenyon Chan, Dean of the Bellarmine College of Liberal Arts, and Joseph Jabbra, Academic Vice President, for their tangible support of my research, including a Summer Research Grant which enabled me to complete the book. I would also like to thank my new colleagues at Calvin College for welcoming me into the rich heritage of philosophy at Calvin – the heritage which spawned this book.

The bulk of this manuscript was penned during our time in the Philadelphia area, where we were blessed to be part of a wonderful church community at Cornerstone Christian Fellowship. I would especially like to thank Pastor Ron Billings for his warm encouragement and persistent interest in my work. David and Stephanie Burton, our Youth Pastor and Music Director, have also been sources of inspiration and have become cherished friends for us. Our Friday nights together with the "Magnificent Seven" kept me – and Deanna – sane and grounded.

My family, my parents and in-laws, have all been a part of this process and project for a number of years. And I couldn't have done it without them. The book is dedicated to my mother, to whom I owe so much, especially a confidence born of her praise and encouragement. But those who have borne the heaviest load throughout this project have been my own family: my wife, Deanna, and the kids, Grayson, Coleson, Madison, and Jackson. Now that I have finished this project, which has too often stolen their father's attention, I am most happy for them. And I am most grateful for their patience and forgiveness – models that I can follow.

This book grapples with the question of how words can do justice to that which cannot be said. In thanking Deanna, I meet this very problem: What can be said? My debt to Deanna, her support and encouragement, exceeds words. But the very project of this book is to also affirm that we can say *something*. Thank you.

Some of this research has appeared in a nascent form in several articles. My thanks to the editors and publishers for their permission to include this material here: Chapter 2 includes material from "Respect and Donation: A Critique of Marion's Critique of Husserl," *American Catholic Philosophical Quarterly* 71 (1997), pp. 523–38 and is included with the permission of Robert Wood, Editor. A version of the first sections of Chapter 3 was originally published as "Taking Husserl At His Word: Towards a New Phenomenology With the Young Heidegger," *Symposium: Journal of the Canadian Society for Hermeneutics and Postmodern Thought* 4 (2000), pp. 89–115, and is reprinted here with the permission of the editor. The final section of the chapter includes material from "Liberating Religion From Theology: Marion and Heidegger on the Possibility of a Phenomenology of Religion," *International Journal for Philosophy of Religion* 46 (1999), pp. 17–33 and is included with the permission of Kluwer Academic Publishers. A version of the first half of Chapter 4 was published as "Between Predication and Silence: Augustine on How (Not) To Speak of God," *Heythrop Journal* 41 (2000), pp. 66–86 and is reprinted with the permission of Blackwell Publishers. The second part of the chapter first appeared as "How (Not) To Tell a Secret: Interiority and the Strategy of 'Confession' in Augustine" in a special issue of the *American Catholic Philosophical Quarterly* 74 (2000), pp. 135–51 devoted to the work of Saint Augustine. It is reprinted with permission.

ABBREVIATIONS

The following is a list of abbreviations for frequently cited works in the text below.

SAINT AUGUSTINE

C   *Confessiones/Confessions*, trans. Henry Chadwick (Oxford: Oxford University Press, 1991).

DC   *De doctrina christiana/Teaching Christianity*, trans. Edmund Hill, O.P. (New York: New City Press, 1996).

DM   *De magistro/The Teacher*, trans. Peter King in *Against the Academicians and On the Teacher* (Indianapolis: Hackett, 1995).

DV   *De vera religione/ Of True Religion*, trans. Burleigh in *Augustine: Earlier Writings* (Philadelphia: Westminster, 1953).

Sol   *Soliloquies*, trans. Burleigh in *Augustine: Earlier Writings* (Philadelphia: Westminster, 1953).

JACQUES DERRIDA

HAS   "How to Avoid Speaking: Attestations," trans. John P. Leavey, Jr. in *Derrida and Negative Theology*, eds. Harold Coward and Toby Foshay (Albany: SUNY Press, 1992).

VM   "Violence and Metaphysics: An Essay on the Thought of Emmanuel Levinas," in *Writing and Difference*, trans. Alan Bass (Chicago: University of Chicago Press, 1978).

MARTIN HEIDEGGER

GA 20   *History of the Concept of Time: Prolegomena*, trans. Theodore Kisiel (Bloomington: Indiana University Press, 1985).

GA 29/30   *Fundamental Concepts of Metaphysics: World, Finitude, Solitude*, trans. William McNeill and Nicholas Walker (Bloomington: Indiana University Press, 1995).

GA 56/57   *Zur Bestimmung der Philosophie: 1. Die Idee der Philosophie und das*

Weltanschauungsproblem, 2. *Phänomenologie und tranzendentale Weltphilosophie*. GA 56/57, ed. Bernd Heimbüchel (Frankfurt am Main: Klostermann, 1987).

GA 59   *Phänomenologie der Anschauung und des Ausdrucks: Theorie der philosophischen Begriffsbildung*, GA 59, ed. Claudius Strube (Frankfurt am Main: Klostermann, 1993).

GA 60   *Phänomenologie des religiösen Lebens*. 1. *Einleitung in die Phänomenologie der Religion*, 2. *Augustinus und der Neuplatonismus*, 3. *Die philosophischen Grundlagen der mittelalterlichen Mystik*, GA 60, eds. Matthius Jung, Thomas Regehly, and Claudius Strube (Frankfurt am Main: Klostermann, 1995).

GA 63   *Ontologie (Hermeneutik der Faktizität)*, GA 63, ed. Käte Bröcker-Oltmanns (Frankfurt am Main: Klostermann, 1988).

JPW   "Comments on Karl Jaspers's *Psychology of Worldviews*," in *Pathmarks*, ed. William McNeill (Cambridge: Cambridge University Press, 1998).

PIA   "Phänomenologische Interpretationen zu Aristoteles: Anzeige der hermeneutischen Situation," ed. Han-Ulrich Lessing in *Dilthey-Jahrbuch für Philosophie und Geschichte der Geisteswissenschaften* 6 (1989): 235–74. "Phenomenological Interpretations with Respect to Aristotle: Indication of the Hermeneutic Situation [1922]," trans. Michael Baur in *Man and World* 25 (1992): 355–93.

SZ   *Sein und Zeit*, GA 2, ed. Friedrich-Wilhelm von Herrmann (Frankfurt am Main: Klostermann, 1977). *Being and Time*, trans. John MacQuarrie and Edward Robinson (New York: Harper & Row, 1962).

EDMUND HUSSERL

CM   *Cartesian Meditations: An Introduction to Phenomenology*, trans. Dorion Cairns (Dordrecht: Kluwer, 1993 [The Hague: Nijhoff, 1950]).

Id   *Ideas Pertaining to a Pure Phenomenology and to a Phenomenological Philosophy*, First Book: *General Introduction to a Pure Phenomenology*, trans. F. Kersten (The Hague: Nijhoff, 1983).

LI   *Logical Investigations*, trans. J. N. Findlay (New York: Humanities, 1970).

Ps   *Phenomenological Psychology: Lectures, Summer Semester 1925*, trans. John Scanlon (The Hague: Nijhoff, 1977).

EMMANUEL LEVINAS

BPW   *Basic Philosophical Writings*, eds. Adriaan Peperzak, Simon Critchley, and Robert Bernasconi (Bloomington: Indiana University Press, 1996).

GP   "God and Philosophy" in BPW.

TI   *Totality and Infinity*, trans. Alphonso Lingis (Pittsburgh: Duquesne University Press, 1969).

JEAN-LUC MARION

GWB *God Without Being*, trans. Thomas A. Carlson (Chicago: University of Chicago Press, 1991).

Int "The Final Appeal of the Subject," trans. Simon Critchley in *Deconstructive Subjectivities*, eds. Simon Critchley and Peter Dews (Albany: SUNY Press, 1996), 85–104.

SP "Le phénomène saturé," in *Phénoménologie et théologie*, ed. Jean-François Courtine (Paris: Criterion, 1992), 79–128. "The Saturated Phenomenon," trans. Thomas A. Carlson, *Philosophy Today* 40 (1996): 103–24.

RD *Réduction et donation: Recherches sur Husserl, Heidegger et la phénoménologie* (Paris: PUF, 1989). *Reduction and Givenness: Investigations of Husserl, Heidegger, and Phenomenology*, trans. Thomas A. Carlson (Evanston: Northwestern University Press, 1998).

Part One

HORIZONS

In Part One we establish the horizons of expectation for the question: How should one speak of that which is incommensurate with language? The first horizon is theological; thus, we situate this formal, phenomenological question within a theological history of the challenge of "naming" God. The second horizon to be established (or better, uncovered) is phenomenological: in particular, it will be necessary to effect a certain "formalization" of this theological question in order to demonstrate its affinity with a central problematic in contemporary French phenomenology as embodied in the work of Levinas, Derrida, Marion, and Janicaud.

1

INTRODUCTION

How to avoid not speaking

. . . one can . . . think . . . the concept of concept otherwise . . .[1]

The violence of concepts and the possibility of theology

Theology is a discourse attended by constant prohibition, just as injunctions to worship are invariably haunted by the temptation to idolatry.[2] But to avoid the lure of brazen images it will not suffice to cease worship – for then we find ourselves only in another idolatry. So also, theology will not resist failure by silence.

In a seminal essay which functions as a horizon for this book, Jacques Derrida raises the question of the (in)adequacy of concepts within the context of a theological discussion.[3] Fending off charges that his deconstruction is simply a reproduction of negative theology,[4] Derrida concedes that both are concerned with a similar challenge: how to speak of that which resists language, which is otherwise than conceptual. Negative theology, he notes, "has come to designate a certain typical attitude toward language, and within it, in the act of definition or attribution, an attitude toward semantic or conceptual determination."[5] The negative theologian is faced with the challenge of how to speak of a God who exceeds all categories and transcends all conceptual determination; "by a more or less tenable analogy," Derrida remarks, deconstruction grapples with a similar problem, which is precisely why he constantly has recourse to apophatic strategies and a "rhetoric of negative determination" when attempting to describe "this, which is called X (for example, text, writing, the trace, differance, the hymen, the supplement, the pharmakon, the parergon, etc.)." While insisting that this X is neither this nor that, neither being nor non-being, neither present nor absent, such strategies remain insufficient, precisely because "this X is neither a concept nor even a name; it does not *lend itself* to a series of names, but calls for another syntax, and exceeds even the order and the structure of predicative discourse. . . . It is written completely otherwise."[6]

In his analysis, Derrida effects a formalization[7] of the problematic of negative theology, raising the broader question of how it will be possible to speak of that which is transcendent, that which is beyond language and exceeds conceptual determination. The project of this book is to push this formalization even further, to locate this problem at the very foundations of philosophical and theological method. Thus, I will initially follow Derrida's project of formalizing the problem of negative theology, in order to open up new a dialogue with phenomenology, particularly the phenomenology of the young Heidegger as a lens for then returning to the proto-phenomenology of Saint Augustine. However, my ultimate goal is to then *return* to the theological challenge which first initiated the project. In other words, the movement of the book is from (negative) theology, to phenomenology, *and back again*. Unlike Derrida, the *telos* of my project is a philosophical reflection on the possibility of theology – the possibility of speaking of God. In addition, my goal is to make space for an experience of the transcendent within phenomenology itself – to provide an account of how phenomenology can recognize religious experience and the appearance of transcendence.

Method and the question of justice

First, a formalization of the problem: If the very topic of philosophy is *experience*,[8] and if we appreciate that experience is *pre*theoretical, then how will it be possible to theoretically describe this pretheoretical experience? Already, however, we have been confronted by three different challenges, three different instances of phenomena that are incommensurate with language: God, *différance*, and factical experience. For each, that which exceeds conceptualization is different: in the first instance, we are confronted by a radical transcendence which cannot be conceived, an "Other" which exceeds conceptual determination. Here we would include the face of the Other in Levinas, Marion's Gxd, and the God of Augustine. In the second case of *différance*, it is not so much a matter of transcendence in a Levinasian sense of plenitude and excess, but rather a "quasi-transcendence," a phenomenon which is not quite a phenomenon, and thus cannot be named. Finally, in the case of factical experience, we find a phenomenon which resists expression in language, not because of its distance, but rather because of its proximity and interiority, a depth to the self which cannot be expressed because it is a mode of being incommensurate with cognitive conceptualization. "Case studies" of the final category would include Augustine and Kierkegaard's account of subjectivity, and Heidegger's notion of facticity.

However, despite their differences, when we formalize the problem we find that all three confront a similar challenge – a methodological challenge: how will it be possible to speak? Or as Derrida asks, *Comment ne pas parler?* How not to speak? How to avoid speaking in a certain manner which in fact denies and conceals? How is it possible to speak and yet not grasp (*con-capere*) in a concept, enframing and thereby stilling that which is spoken of and reducing it to the order of predicative discourse? How can one speak without betraying the object of speech, giving it up and delivering it over to be manhandled by the interlocutor as something present-at-hand? How can language, and more particularly theoretical *concepts*, communicate without doing violence to the "object" which is exterior to language? Do not concepts always already signal the violation of radical alterity?

This concern regarding the violence of concepts is a distinctly postmodern matter, in the simple sense that it is only a "modern" concept which makes claims to totalization, which is precisely why Hegel is Levinas's most significant foil. Indeed, throughout the history of the tradition – particularly in its most theological moments (Dionysius, Augustine, Anselm, Aquinas) – we see a persistent awareness of the *inadequacy* of concepts. Language constantly fails, these premoderns confess, precisely because of the inadequacy of language in the face of God's infinity. From the heart of the tradition, Aquinas confesses that all of the names we would predicate of God "fall short of representing him," and while they signify the divine substance, they necessarily do so in an "imperfect manner."[9] In many ways, I will be attempting to retrieve those aspects of the tradition which recognize the inadequacy or "failure" of the concept to comprehend the transcendent. In modernity, however, philosophy attempts to make up for this failure by reducing the phenomenon to the measure of the concept. In other words, while the medievals accept, even celebrate, the inadequacy of the concept, moderns cannot tolerate it. They refuse the inadequacy of concepts and guarantee their adequation by reducing the object to the measure of the concept. And it is precisely this "cutting-down-to-size" which constitutes what I am describing as the "violence" of the concept.

My concern and object of critique, then, is precisely the "modern"[10] development of the concept in its post-Cartesian form, finding its perfection in Hegel. In modernity, the concept becomes a means of domination, seizure, encompassing, such that one who has the concept of the thing *has the thing*, "in one's grasp," as it were.[11] In modernity – and marking a significant break from the late ancients and medievals – knowledge and comprehension are no longer distinguished; rather, knowledge is only knowledge *insofar as* it comprehends (and thereby guarantees "certainty"). "Absolute knowledge" represents the ideal of appropriation, the institution of *identity* and the erasure of *difference*. And it is just this modernity that gives birth to distinctly modern theologies which must include both neo-Scholasticism and fundamentalisms of varying strains (my concern is its Protestant variety),[12] what Levinas describes simply as "rational theology" (GP 129), or what I would label "theological positivism." Inheriting the modern penchant for comprehension and certainty (what of faith?), modernist (and, unwittingly, anti-modernist) theology is marked by an employment of language and concepts which seeks to define the divine, to grasp the essence of God (and to employ such knowledge to marginalize any who disagree). The *Westminster Catechism* (1647), for instance (both *Larger* and *Shorter*, and the *Confession*), are completely comfortable asking the question, "What is God?," and provide an answer – with straight face and without apology: "God *is* . . . "[13] And it will be precisely this definition which will mark the boundaries of the community of faith.[14] In other words, what Heidegger decried as "ontotheology" is a distinctly modern phenomenon. But it is precisely within a theological context that the violence of such concepts is appreciated: when construed this way, the concept violates transcendence, reducing and "cutting down to size" the Infinite.

The violence of the (modern) concept raises the question of whether language and concepts are inherently reductive and violent. In short, is theory possible? Or rather, is it possible to do theory and employ theoretical concepts without doing violence to that which is "seen?" If the "object" of theoretical articulation is in some way radically exterior to language (God, *différance*, pretheoretical experience), then every unveiling of it within language will fail to produce the object: the phenomenon will fail to appear, precisely because of the failure of the concept to grasp that which necessarily exceeds its comprehension. Or rather, the object will be forced to appear otherwise than itself, forced to play by the rule of the concept and thus suffering the violence of conceptualization. We inherit this concern from Levinas's suggestion that "*theory* also designates comprehension [intelligence] – the logos of being – that is, a way of approaching the known being such that its alterity with regard to the knowing being vanishes" (TI 21). To this we must relate his understanding of violence as "making them [others] play roles in which they no longer recognize themselves" (ibid.). Thus the theoretical disciplines – philosophy and theology included – are faced with the methodological question of how to speak, or how not to speak. And in an important way, this methodological question is fundamentally a question of *justice*: how do we do justice to that which is other (where "doing justice" means respecting the other as other, rather than reducing it to a relation of identity[15]), particularly in our theoretical descriptions and articulations? It would seem that either one treats all objects as present-at-hand (a positivist kataphatics), thereby denying their alterity and unwittingly engaging in violence; or, one gives up any possibility of non-violent description and thereby gives up theory (an apophatics which ends in silence).

Unless, perhaps, there is a "third way" out of this aporia: what if, recognizing the violence and failure of theoretical concepts which treat all phenomena as present-at-hand, but at the same time appreciating the imperative of description, one were to develop and work with a *new* kind of concept or different set of categories? Could there be a kind of concept, and therefore a kind of theory, which does not treat objects as present-at-hand, but rather both honors transcendence and answers the call for reflection? That is, could the violence of the (traditional) theoretical concept signal the development of a new kind of concept and set of conceptual categories, precipitated by a fundamental redirection of philosophy to pretheoretical experience? Could we, as Derrida suggests, think the concept of the concept otherwise? The construction (or recovery) of just such a third way is precisely the task of this book: to provide an alternative interpretation of concepts which do not claim to grasp their object, but rather signal the phenomenon in such a way that respects its transcendence or incommensurability rather than collapsing the difference and denying otherness. Such a reinterpretation of concepts will open a philosophical space for a reconsideration of theological method.

At stake here is the very possibility of both philosophy and theology – the *ethical* possibility of philosophy and the possibility of an *ethical* philosophy.[16] This philosophical consideration of concepts will then function as the foundation for a theological employment of concepts which "do justice" to God. In particular, I will attempt to develop the possibility of a "new" phenomenology which is attentive to this methodological question of justice, since it has been precisely phenomenology which has been the object of critique as a philosophical method which denies alterity and levels transcendence. When formalized, the provocation of transcendence in God and the Other, the quasi-transcendence of *différance*, and the inexpressibility of factical lived experience all pose a methodological challenge to phenomenology: the *incommensurable* – phenomenology's "impossible." How could the incommensurate appear? And further, how could we speak about the incommensurable? If phenomenology effects a return to experience as the fund for reflection, how will it be possible to give a philosophical or theoretical description of experience, which is itself pretheoretical and resists theoretical articulation? Is it not precisely the fullness of experience which cannot be "put into words"? Is not factical experience precisely that which is incommensurate with conceptual, philosophical thought? After passing through this formalized version of the challenge of speaking (with Husserl, Levinas, Marion, Derrida, and Heidegger), I will then return to the more specific theological question of how (not) to speak of God (with Augustine, Aquinas, and Kierkegaard).

Phenomenology's other: the French challenge to phenomenology

It is precisely the "other" of philosophy – "its death and wellspring" (VM 79) – which challenges the very possibility of philosophy. And yet it is precisely the "paradoxical revelation of Transcendence" – the other of philosophy's immanence – "in a source at the heart of phenomenality" which has challenged phenomenology's first and defining trait: its reduction to "immanent phenomenality."[17] Thus the "trait" which distinguishes contemporary phenomenology from "the first reception of Husserl and Heidegger," Dominique Janicaud suggests, is a "rupture with immanent phenomenality" and an "opening of phenomenology to the invisible."[18] The horizon of the question which I am pursuing here is found in these developments in contemporary French phenomenology. Recent movements in French thought, particularly in the work of Jean-Luc Marion and Emmanuel Levinas, have sought to challenge phenomenology's gaze as one that denies alterity, reducing the phenomenon to the constituting ego (for Levinas, the concern is the reduction of the ethical alterity of the face; for Marion, at issue is the reduction of God's infinity to the finite ego). Throughout this study, the "religious" site will continually resurface as a privileged case of incommensurability, and more specifically, transcendence, in Marion and Levinas, but also Heidegger and Augustine. The religious phenomenon, or the phenomenon *of* religious experience, is something of a limit case or exemplary instance of the incommensurability of conceptual thought and pretheoretical experience.[19] As that which constitutes the phenomenon, the phenomenological ego denies and violates the transcendent other, reducing it to the sphere of the same, to its *Eigenheitssphäre*. For Marion, this is a denial of the phenomenon's "right of appearance," such that the phenomenon appears in phenomenological description only insofar as it measures up to the ego's criteria; rather than giving itself, the phenomenon must give up its transcendence in order to make a showing.

On Levinas and Marion's accounting, the very project of phenomenological description is unjust: by attempting to conceptualize or theoretically describe that which is transcendent, phenomenology reduces and violates the phenomenon. As that which attempts to grasp the other, the concept reduces the alterity of the phenomenon. In order to challenge this order, Levinas and Marion both, in different ways, attempt to locate a "giving" or "donation" which undoes the self, which overwhelms the ego, which saturates the intention and thus exceeds the concept. This "saturated phenomenon" is a giving for which phenomenological description – as conceptual – is both inadequate (because the phenomenon exceeds conceptual grasp) and unjust (because the concept, as an operation of the immanence, violates and reduces the transcendence of the phenomenon). Thus, in the name of phenomenology, we are given a "new phenomenology" (harking back, as Janicaud suggests, to *la nouvelle théologie*[20]).

Here we are left with two questions to be pursued in Part One ("Horizons"): first, is the "new" phenomenology of Levinas and Marion in fact phenomenology "as such"? Should we not be suspicious of claims regarding "absolute experience" and "pure givenness"? "All of Levinas' discourse," Janicaud suggests, "is suspended on this presupposition:"[21] "The absolute experience is not disclosure but revelation" (TI 61/65–6). But "how can exteriority be pure, if it is present?"[22] If the reduction is displaced by revelation, immanence by transcendence, "why keep playing along at phenomenology?" So also with Marion, who proposes a (phenomenological!) reduction which distills transcendence, "pure givenness": how can the "pure" be given to be experienced? "Is not this experience, slimmed down to its *apriori* sheathe, too pure to dare pass itself off as phenomenological?"[23] How could there be an experience of the "unconditioned"? And if such is impossible, how could we give a *phenomenological* account of it? What, in the end, does the *new* phenomenology have to do with *phenomenology*? And more critically, are its claims admissible? Does their strategy solve the paradox of transcendence for phenomenology, or does it rather remain intact by an evasive strategy which proposes a *coincidentia oppositorum* as the solution to a paradox?

Second, can we find resources *within* phenomenology (even within Husserl) for grappling with the challenge of transcendence on phenomenology's own terms? Could it be the case that phenomenology is in fact rigorously attentive to the matter of doing justice to transcendence? Do we perhaps find in Husserl an implicit or latent answer to the challenge of incommensurability? Could we not draw out such implicit trajectories in the formulation of an alternative "new" phenomenology? Would this not be to take up and productively repeat the project of the young Heidegger? And do we not find an impetus for that project in the strategies of a young Augustine?

Could we not think the concept of "concept" *otherwise*?[24] Is not the challenge of transcendence/incommensurability precisely an impetus to develop a new (non-objectifying) concept of the concept, and so a new phenomenology?[25] Attentive to the concerns of Levinas and Marion, though critical of their response, could we not envision something of an "ethical" concept – a concept of the concept which does justice to the incommensurable?

Towards a new phenomenology

In the face of that which is "other," the concept both violates and fails: failing to grasp this excess, the concept reduces it to its own measure, cuts it down to the size of theoretical thought, and thereby undoes its dynamism and fullness. This violence and failure can be located in a number of examples: the other person (Levinas), God (Marion, Augustine), my own self (Augustine, Heidegger). All of these are, in a sense, instances of *incommensurability* – cases where theoretical description is at a loss, where the tools (concepts) of phenomenological description are confronted by something or someone which exceeds their grasp. In a formalized sense, Levinas' Other, Marion's Gxd, Derrida's *différance*, and Heidegger's facticity are all phenomena which are incommensurate with conceptual thought and language: they are *otherwise than*[26] conceptual, appearing on a completely different register. There is a qualitative difference – an abyss – between the order of thought and that of experience, for example. In other words, as incommensurate, they have nothing in common, no common point of overlap; it is a radical difference of order. The incommensurate is precisely that which is wholly other, and any account of the incommensurate – if it is going to do justice to that difference – must preserve this difference. Any account of the incommensurable which makes it commensurate with, for instance, cognitive knowing or conceptual language, fails to do justice to the incommensurate *as* incommensurate.

How, then, will it be possible to speak? How can we avoid not speaking? Are we, if we are concerned about methodological justice, consigned to silence? "To give an account," it would seem, would be to already domesticate the incommensurate in the order of language. As we will discover, the matter of language is central here: concepts are linguistic, whereas the phenomenon we are concerned with, particularly the religious phenomenon, is not. Thus, what is at stake is a certain account of language. For instance: if concepts (as finite) violate transcendence (as infinite), then can we *speak* about that which is transcendent? Can we speak about God? Or can we share our experiences, since the dynamics and fullness of factical experience cannot be reduced to language and words? Can we describe our experience of a poem, or another person, or a mystical vision? Is there any way to "say" that which exceeds and resists language? Or are we doomed to silence? Are our only options either a reductionistic, conceptual language – or silence? Does silence do justice to our experience? Are there not situations where speaking is imperative, perhaps in the name of justice? The question then becomes: how not to speak? *Comment ne pas parler?* How to speak in such a way that does justice to that which exceeds description? How is it possible to put transcendence into words? How can one express the inexpressible? And this challenge, I am arguing, does not apply only to limit cases such as God, or *différance*; it is a challenge which persistently confronts a phenomenological philosophy which takes experience as its topic, since such experience is pretheoretical while the tools of phenomenological description are theoretical in character.

What this challenge demands is a new concept of the "concept," a revisioning of the concept, and of phenomenology itself. Thus, I will attempt to think the concept otherwise – to locate the possibility of a non-objectifying, even nonviolent, "concept" (which is not a concept[27]) which both sketches and indicates its topic, but at the same time respects its alterity and incommensurability. Thus, I will suggest that I am at the same time offering a new phenomenology – understanding phenomenological appearance as a matter of "incarnation" and phenomenological method as a struc-ture of *respect* or *praise*.[28] My goal, systematically sketched in Part Three, is to outline an understanding of philosophical (and theological) "concepts" as "incarnational" (following Augustine) "formal indications" (following Heidegger). By this, I mean to suggest that such revisioned "concepts" are able to indicate that of which they speak, without claiming to make them objectively present. This notion of the "concept" is grounded in an alternative account of phenomenological appearance: against the criticisms of Levinas and Marion, I mean to show that the transcendent pheno-menon is not reduced to the sphere of ownness; rather, within Husserl's account of the appearance of the Other, we see an appearing which is at the same time a withholding, such that the Other is both present and absent. I will describe this as "incarnational"[29] insofar as it bears analogy to the appearance of God within humanity, such that the Other appears within the sphere of immanence without giving up its transcendence. And as Augustine suggests (in Sermon 119), words (and "concepts") can operate in a similar manner: that which is otherwise than linguistic or conceptual can nevertheless be sketched or indicated with the use of language. I will concede that my employment of the notion of "incarnation" draws on a theo-logical understanding, rather than a merely philosophical notion of "embodiment" (as found, for instance, in Merleau-Ponty). By describing my account as "incarnational," I mean to invoke the analogy of the Incarnation, of the appearance of God within humanity in the person of the God-man, Jesus of Nazareth (particularly as sketched in Kierkegaard's *Philosophical Fragments* – a text which will appear persistently throughout this study). This is an instance of the transcendent appearing within the immanent, without sacrificing transcendence. In the Incarnation, the Infinite shows up within the finite, nevertheless without loss. My task, however, in no way involves the defense of a Christology, though it perhaps presupposes one. I invoke the Incarnation as a metaphor, bracketing strictly christological questions, but nevertheless pursuing a question about the philo-sophical possibility of theology itself.

What would this incarnational account of concepts mean for the possibility of philosophy? In what sense does this inform a philosophical method which is concerned with doing justice to that which is otherwise than philosophical or theoretical? My claim (to be demonstrated in what follows) is this: that by understanding "concepts" as what Heidegger describes as "formal indications," it will be recognized that that which philosophy (and/or theology) attempts to describe, even conceptualize, cannot be grasped as present-at-hand, cannot be made present within a concept. There is an incommensurability between pretheoretical, factical experience, and the theoretical descriptions of both philosophy and theology.[30] Nevertheless, with such an "incarnational" account of language, such incommensurability does not consign us to silence; rather, it remains possible to speak, to point to that which is other without pretensions of grasping.

And what, ultimately, will these methodological analyses mean for the possibility of theology? Returning from a formalized consideration of incommensurability and developing a linguistic, conceptual strategy in response to that challenge, I will then go back to the more specific instance of God's transcendence, developing an incarnational account of theological language. In other words, the phenomenological analyses are intended to open space for the philosophical possibility of theology, indicating that my project might be considered within the classical project of fundamental theology or what might simply be described as a philosophical theology.

In order to reach this systematic goal, in Part Two I will turn to two important historical resources: the young Heidegger (Chapter 3) and Augustine (Chapter 4), both of whom were very attentive to the problem of conceptualization or theoretical description of pretheoretical or factical experience. For Heidegger, it is precisely the relocating of phenomenology as a science of pretheoretical factical experience (an explication of the "natural attitude") which demands methodological revisions. Confronted by the incommensurability of factical life in relation to theoretical thought, predicative assertions (*Aufzeigen*) become not only insufficient, but violations of that experience. Thus in order to honor or do justice to this otherness, Heidegger proposes a new conceptuality: the formal indication (*formale Anzeige*), which is an oblique concept, one which points rather than grasps, which respects the transcendence or incommensurability of the phenomenon but nevertheless is able to indicate its appearance. (At the conclusion of Chapter 3, however, I will critically analyze the way in which the traditional concept returns in the neo-Kantian project of *Sein und Zeit*.)

The subsequent turn to Augustine is by no means an arbitrary one; rather, Augustine is one of the primary sources which provided an impetus for the young Heidegger's methodological reflections. In his 1920 course which offered a "Theory of Philosophical Concept Formation"[31] (GA 59), he chose his motto from Augustine's *De civitate dei*:

> For philosophers are free in their choice of expressions, and are not afraid
> of offending the ears of the religious when treating of subjects very hard to
> understand, while we Christians are in solemn duty bound to speak in
> accordance with a fixed rule, for fear that a looseness of language might
> give rise to a blasphemous opinion about the realities to which the words
> refer.[32]

My task in Chapter 4 will be to determine just what it was that Heidegger found in Augustine which provided a fund for methodological considerations, though my analyses certainly go beyond Heidegger's published engagements with Augustine on these methodological questions. But his debt to Augustine will be the springboard and lens for a fresh reading of Augustine against this horizon. As we will see, Augustine grappled with the same methodological challenge: how will it be possible to put into words that which exceeds and resists language? How can one say that which is unsayable? This challenge is located in two sites: first, the incommensurability between *signa* and *res*, which finds its analogy in the problem of the Incarnation and the problem of how one can speak of God. In this case, *sacramentum* is a structure of respect, that which points or indicates without making fully present: a "veiling/unveiling, in a degree proportionate to its object's transcendence."[33] In the face of the Incommensurable, Augustine takes up the laudatory strategy of "praise." Second, the incommensurability between the radical interiority of the soul and its expression in language poses a second challenge; here, the strategy of *confession* is taken up as a mode of expression which obliquely indicates the interiority of the self, yet is attentive to the impossibility of making the secret life of the soul objectively present.[34]

These historical resources will then provide the fund for a systematic construction of a philosophical method which is attentive to the challenge of incommensurability. I will first outline an understanding of phenomenological appearance as "incarnational" (providing an account of both transcendence and immanence), which will then form the basis for an incarnational interpretation of philosophical and theological concepts, drawing on Heidegger's notion of concepts as formal indicators, and Augustine's account of the use of language in "praise" (*laudare*) and "confession" (*confiteri*). The goal is an interpretation of concepts as non-objectifying, non-reductive "icons" which signal transcendence without violating such transcendence and reducing it to immanence. The employment of such iconic concepts signals the possibility of a philosophical method which does justice to its other, and hence the possibility of an "ethical" theology.

Notes

1 Jacques Derrida, "Afterword: Toward an Ethic of Discussion," *Limited Inc*, trans. S. Weber (Evanston: Northwestern University Press, 1988), 117.

2 As Jean-Luc Marion suggests, "theological writing always transgresses itself" and thus "renders its author hypocritical" (GWB 9–10/1–2).

3 Jacques Derrida, "How to Avoid Speaking: Attestations," trans. Ken Frieden in *Derrida and Negative Theology*, eds. Harold Coward and Toby Foshay (Albany: SUNY Press, 1992), 73–142.

4 For an account of Derrida's protests – that *différance* is not the God of negative theology – see John D. Caputo, *The Prayers and Tears of Jacques Derrida: Religion Without Religion* (Bloomington: Indiana University Press, 1997), 1–57. The primary difference, which Derrida emphasizes in "How to Avoid Speaking," is that the God of negative theology is characterized by a "hyperessentiality," whereas *différance*, rather than being "beyond being," doesn't quite measure up to being.

5 Derrida, "How to Avoid Speaking," 74.

6 Ibid., 74. For a lucid discussion of Derrida's relationship to negative theology and the apophatic tradition, see Kevin Hart, *The Trespass of the Sign* (Cambridge: Cambridge University Press, 1989) and Thomas A. Carlson, *Indiscretion: Finitude and the Naming of God* (Chicago: University of Chicago Press, 1999).

7 On this methodological process of formalization, see Derrida, "Sauf le nom," in *On The Name*, ed. Thomas Dutoit (Stanford: Stanford University Press, 1995), 76. I have

discussed this methodological strategy in Derrida's later work in "Determined Violence: Derrida's Structural Religion," *Journal of Religion* 78 (1998): 207–10.

8 This book locates itself within the phenomenological tradition of Husserl, and operates on the basis of this assumption.

9 *Summa Theologica*, trans. Fathers of the Dominican Province (New York, Benzinger, 1947 – henceforth *ST*), 1.13.2, and *passim*. We will return to Aquinas and the central category of analogy in Chapter 5.

10 Having noted this, however, I would ask whether even patristic concepts became "totalizing" in this sense. Consider, for instance, the role that the concept *homoousion* came to play in early ecclesiastical debates. (Could not Marion's chosen icon of "love" also become an idol?) Perhaps we ought to say that the origin of all concepts may be "iconic" or heuristic, but through sedimentation can also become idolatrous (as conciliar history would seem to indicate). And such idolatrous sedimentations also tend to be accompanied by an *institutional* violence. For a historical consideration of the way in which theological concepts evolved into idolatrous constructions, see Edward Farley, *Ecclesial Reflection: An Anatomy of Theological Method* (Philadelphia: Fortress, 1982), 83–127 and 179.

11 Sartre refers to this as a "digestive" theory of knowledge, which seems particularly appropriate for its Hegelian form (one would also have to consider here the devouring Hegelian *SA* in Derrida's *Glas*), where knowledge is a matter of appropriation and possession, making the object enter the "dark stomach" of knowledge. For a discussion, see Maurice Natanson, *Husserl: Philosopher of Infinite Tasks* (Evanston: Northwestern University Press, 1973), 151–3.

12 For a discussion of the modernity of fundamentalism, see James K. A. Smith and Shane R. Cudney, "Postmodern Freedom and the Growth of Fundamentalism: Was the Grand Inquisitor Right?," *Studies in Religion/Sciences Religieuses* 25 (1996): 35–49.

13 For the definitive study of Protestant scholasticism, which gave birth to contemporary "evangelical" theology, see Richard A. Muller, *Post-Reformation Dogmatics*, Vol. 1: *Prolegomena to Theology*, Vol. 2: *Holy Scripture: The Cognitive Foundation of Theology* (Grand Rapids: Baker, 1987, 1993). For my own critical account of the scholasticism of evangelical theology, see James K. A. Smith, "The Closing of the Book: Pentecostals, Evangelicals, and the Sacred Writings," *Journal of Pentecostal Theology* 11 (1997): 49–71.

14 In many ways, it is the ecclesial (communal) effects which, for me, are of gravest concern in my critique of theological positivism. For a sketch, see James K. A. Smith, "Fire From Heaven: The Hermeneutics of Heresy," *Journal of TAK* 20 (1996): 13–31. In this sense I am continuing to raise concerns regarding the "ethics of interpretation" first discussed in my *The Fall of Interpretation: Philosophical Foundations for a Creational Hermeneutic* (Downers Grove, IL: InterVarsity Press, 2000), 175–8. See also Edward Farley's critique of "classical criteriology," or what he describes as the "house of authority" in *Ecclesial Reflection*, 83–169.

15 This is why Levinas thinks that "mysticism" in fact represents a violation of alterity because it closes the space of "separation" and difference in its quest for "union" (identity).

16 I do not intend to construct an "ethics," to offer yet another framework for moral philosophy or philosophical ethics; rather, my topic is the possibility of a philosophy which does justice to its topic – a topic which exceeds and resists philosophical description and articulation. For me, the question of philosophical *method* is a question of *justice*. And it seems that it was also such a question for (at least the later) Husserl when he asked: "How are we to do justice systematically – that is, with appropriate scientific discipline – to the all-encompassing, so paradoxically demanding, manner of being of the life-world?" See Husserl, *Crisis*, 131.

17 Dominique Janicaud, *Le tournant théologique de la phénoménologie française* (Paris: Éditions de l'éclat, 1991), 8, 13. (Throughout I have employed the translation of Pruzak, forthcoming

from Fordham University Press.) In this first section of Janicaud's essay, he documents the way in which the "problem" of transcendence is an unresolved problem which is part of "the Husserlian legacy" handed down to Sartre and Merleau-Ponty, neither of whom resolved the paradox. Janicaud's account is considered in more detail below.

18 Ibid., 8, 15. In the end for Janicaud, however, it is Merleau-Ponty who offers the slogan of phenomenology's approach to transcendence: "not an absolute invisible . . ., but the invisible *of* this world" (p. 22).

19 By "pretheoretical experience," I mean only a mode of being-in-the-world which is not characterized by the reflexivity of the theoretical attitude. In other words, factical life is characterized by first-order immediacy, not second-order reflection. It is not to suggest that such experience is "pre-linguistic."

20 Janicaud, *Le tournant théologique*, 51–2.

21 Ibid., 31.

22 Ibid.

23 Ibid., 49.

24 While I will locate such a project in Augustine and the young Heidegger, along with my own constructive proposal, Peter Cook has recently suggested that such is also the project of Deleuze, quite outside phenomenology. See Peter Cook, "Thinking the Concept Otherwise: Deleuze and Expression," *Symposium: Journal of the Canadian Society for Hermeneutics and Postmodern Thought* 2 (1998): 23–35. From yet another standpoint, C. S. Peirce considered the "ethics of terminology" to be central to his "pragmaticism." For an extensive discussion, see John Deely, "The Ethics of Terminology," *American Catholic Philosophical Quarterly* 72 (1998): 197–243.

25 Insofar as phenomenology, as theoretical, must therefore be conceptual. I do not question the assumption, Husserlian in spirit, that phenomenology is "rigorous science." (I will question Heidegger's notion of phenomenology as a "pretheoretical originary science" [GA 56/57], suggesting that by this he must mean a science *of* pretheoretical, factical experience, since the notion of a pretheoretical science, on my accounting, is a contradiction in terms.) What will require revision will be the concept of "science" we employ; here I agree with Janicaud's proposed "reorientation" (*Le tournant théologique*, 75–9). What is required is a broadening of the idea of a "science" as a theoretical *attitude* as such, rather than a body of unrevisable knowledge, as Husserl assumed. Apodicticity as the scientific ideal is precisely that which is called into question in post-Kuhnian philosophy of science. Science is not to be defined by apodictic judgments, but rather a theoretical, reflective attitude. (While this will receive further consideration below, I must here acknowledge my debt on this score to Herman Dooyeweerd, *In the Twilight of Western Thought: Studies in the Pretended Autonomy of Theoretical Thought*, Collected Works, B/4, ed. James K. A. Smith [Lewiston: Edwin Mellen Press, 1999], 7–10.)

26 My employment of this construction is intended to mark an analogy with the Levinasian analysis of the *autrement qu'être*. The status of the "otherwise" is not simple negation ("not" being, "not" lingual, etc.); such negation maintains the priority of that which is negated and thinks the "other" in terms of its opposite. The thematics of *autrement*, however, indicates a difference of *order*, a completely different register or paradigm. For instance, the religious experience is not simply not-rational, let alone ir-rational. To think it in terms of rationality at all, even as non-rational, still maintains the hegemony of the rational order. While not without problems, the strategy of employing "otherwise" is an attempt to appreciate the radical difference of order.

27 I will generally refer to the traditional (objectifying and violent) concept without quotation marks, and will surround the "new" (non-objectifying and non-violent) concept (as formal indication) with just such quotation marks, in order to mark its distinction from its homonymic counterpart.

28 Here I follow Derrida's reading of Husserl in "Violence and Metaphysics" (VM). For a

more detailed discussion, see below, Chapter 2, section entitled "Incommensurability and transcendence," and James K. A. Smith, "Respect and Donation: A Critique of Marion's Critique of Husserl," *American Catholic Philosophical Quarterly* 71.4 (1997): 523–38.

29 The centrality of this theme in contemporary French phenomenology is indicated by Graham Ward in "Kenosis and naming: beyond analogy and towards *allegoria amoris*," in Paul Heelas, ed., *Religion, Modernity, and Postmodernity* (Oxford: Blackwell, 1998), 233–57, and Phillip Blond, "The Primacy of Theology and the Question of Perception," in ibid., 285–313. My account, however, will differ from their approach (see Chapter 5 below).

30 The *telos* of this conception is an ethical one: once we recognize that our concepts do not grasp or comprehend that which is transcendent, then our conceptual descriptions must be attended by a certain humility. In 1919, Heidegger himself indicated (in a letter to Elizabeth Blochmann) that philosophy is "humility before the mystery," a reserved awe before the *mysterium tremendum*. (Martin Heidegger and Elizabeth Blochmann, *Briefwechsel, 1918–1969*, ed. Joachim Storck [Marbach: Deutsche Schillergesellschaft, 1989], 14. For further discussion, see John van Buren, "The Ethics of *Formale Anzeige* in Heidegger," *American Catholic Philosophical Quarterly* 69 [1995]: 157–70.) I am most interested in this ethical *telos* with respect to theological method; this will mean that our theological descriptions and formulations must be relativized. Our concepts can neither comprehend the mystery, nor deliver to us what God thinks. As I have suggested elsewhere, this will demand a rethinking of the categories of "orthodoxy" and "heresy." See James K. A. Smith, "Fire From Heaven: The Hermeneutics of Heresy," *Journal of TAK* 20 (1996): 13–31.

31 The full title is *Phänomenologie der Anschauung und des Ausdrucks: Theorie der philosophischen Begriffsbildung*.

32 GA 59 1, citing Augustine, *De civitate dei*, 10.23 (following the translation of Henry Bettenson, *City of God* [New York: Penguin, 1984], 404).

33 Luigi Alici, "Sign and Language," included as an Introduction in DC, 44.

34 I first suggested that an analogy to this is found in Kierkegaard's strategy of indirect communication in James K. A. Smith, "Alterity, Transcendence, and the Violence of the Concept: Kierkegaard and Heidegger," *International Philosophical Quarterly* 38 (1998): 369–81; this suggestion is pursued in detail in Chapter 4 below.

2

PHENOMENOLOGY AND
TRANSCENDENCE
Genealogy of a challenge

Transcendence in early phenomenology

Three phenomenological reductions: an heuristic

Writing something of a sequel to Vincent Descombes's *Le même et l'autre*,[1] Dominique Janicaud offers the notion of a "theological turn" as an heuristic to understand developments in French phenomenology in its post-Merleau-Ponty and post-Sartre era. Presenting what he describes as an "interpretive intuition,"[2] Janicaud argues that recent French phenomenology's preoccupation with "transcendence" constitutes a "rupture with immanent phenomenality" – the latter being the mark of distinction which is characteristic of rigorous (orthodox?) phenomenology.[3] And yet, such a departure was latent in the initial reception of Husserl in France via Sartre and Merleau-Ponty in whom he finds initial methodological insufficiencies regarding the very possibility of phenomenology as eidetic description – a difficulty "handed down to us by Husserl" (p. 13). Sartre, he suggests,

> masks real difficulties, of which the most serious is how the method of "eidetic description" is going to enable us to find and to reconstitute the "concrete," in particular the affective domain, without falling into essentialism. *The affective life is animated by a dynamism that lends itself poorly to the* grasp *of the* eidos; what's more, this dynamism is not wholly monolithic.[4]

And Merleau-Ponty, despite attentiveness, also suspends the question to a certain extent, partly because of the continued egology of Merleau-Ponty's thought, and partly due to the "strange game of sacralizing the reference to Husserl."[5] (In addition to the problematic of transcendence handed down from Husserl and infecting Sartre and Merleau-Ponty, Janicaud also points to the late Heidegger as an inspiration for the theological turn. The notion of a "phenomenology of the inapparent" [offered in the Zähringen seminars in 1973] is, phenomenologically speaking, a contradiction in terms. But "this enigmatic formula raises difficulties less on account of the 'inapparent' than in its maintaining of the reference to phenomenology."[6] Aside from the biographical matter of Heidegger's need to continue, even in 1973, to associate himself with phenomenology, Janicaud sees Heidegger's *Kehre* as the condition of possibility for the later French *tournant*.)

Ultimately, the problem passed on to later phenomenology is "the paradoxical revelation of Transcendence in a source at the heart of phenomenality."[7] This problem gives birth to two kinds of solutions or phenomenological accounts of transcendence: the "intertwining" explanation of Merleau-Ponty and what Janicaud describes as Levinas's account of the "aplomb" – indicating a challenge from "on high." For Merleau-Ponty, the transcendent is intertwined with the immanent: horizon involves excess, the visible points to an *in*visibility even as the very condition of seeing.[8] Levinas's "aplomb" is the antithesis, the "categorical affirmation of the primacy of the idea of infinity, immediately dispossessing me."[9] The infinite is that which challenges (*aplomb*). Here Janicaud emphasizes: "The goal [of both Merleau-Ponty and Levinas], let us underline, is the same (at least at first): overflowing the intentional horizon."[10] Even the strategies are similar: both open phenomenology to the "invisible." What is it, then, that distinguishes them? It is the difference between "the unconditional affirmation of Transcendence [Levinas] and the patient interrogation of the visible [Merleau-Ponty]," which issues in a difference of method.[11]

A common theme throughout Janicaud's analysis of contemporary French phenomenology is his admonishment regarding the possibility of philosophy *outside* phenomenology. "Phenomenology is not all of philosophy," he will say. One then gets the impression that he only means to guard phenomenology's turf; he does not question the validity of the projects of Marion, Levinas, *et al.*: "Our challenge will not bear on these works' spiritual intention," he remarks.

> To the contrary, maintaining phenomenology in its methodological limits, clearly defined and assumed, without losing from sight the ideal and constraints of scientificity, can only facilitate the taking up, by hermeneutics or another mode of 'thought' finer still, of those fundamental questions which, overflowing the phenomenal field, give rise to philosophic thought no less.[12]

He only wishes they would stop calling it "phenomenology." So too with the late Heidegger: we can affirm his notion of "thinking," but please don't call it phenomenology, Janicaud implores, since such notions of unconditioned transcendence fall outside the pale of orthodox phenomenology which, on the basis of the reduction, is committed to immanence as the condition of knowing. In other words, a reduction to the sphere of immanence – the subjective horizons of the ego – constitutes the phenomenological condition of possibility for knowledge; hence, the incommensurate would be precisely that which can never be "known."

But could there be *another* reduction – a reduction which would disclose absolute givenness? In other words, while it is the *reduction* which is a necessary component of phenomenology,[13] is this necessarily a reduction to the sphere of immanence – the sphere of the *cogito* and its constitution of the world? Could there be a reduction to *transcendence*, to pure givenness, disclosing a phenomenon which is not constituted by the ego but in fact constitutes the ego, making a claim upon the cogito and calling it to responsibility? Such a reduction *qua* reduction would retain its phenomenological filiations, but at the same time would break with (or go beyond) the conditions of knowing established by Husserl's phenomenological reduction. Husserl's reduction, first to the sphere of consciousness, then to the sphere of ownness (*Eigenheitssphäre*), establishes the possibility of knowledge only within the sphere of immanence, the sphere of "transcendental subjectivity" opened by the *epoché*. Here we can understand immanence simply in terms of horizonality: in order for the phenomenon to be constituted by the ego, it must appear within the horizon *of the ego* (CM 44–6). This is, as Husserl confesses, inherently egological and begins from the subject. A reduction which would disclose pure transcendence, however, would reverse the intentional aim, would disclose the way in which the subject is constitut*ed*. Rather than granting being or constituting objects, the *I* of this other reduction would be grant*ed* being, called into being by that which is other. It would be the subject of a claim placed upon it (RD 297–302/198–202).

It is this other reduction – a reduction to transcendence – that Jean-Luc Marion offers in his revisioning of phenomenology in the name of phenomenology. Phenomenology picks up, in a sense, where metaphysics left off; that is, it arrives (after Nietzsche) at the end of metaphysics (RD 7/1). Indeed, phenomenology is the end (*telos*) of metaphysics.[14] The question asked at the end of metaphysics is this: "Can the conditions of presence be extended to the point that all beings reach it, beyond the limits fixed by previous states of metaphysics [Kant, Leibniz[15]], or even by any metaphysics at all? Can the givenness [*donation*] in presence of each thing be realized without any condition or restriction [*réserve*]?" (RD 7/1). By thinking the possibility of such a givenness without condition, phenomenology might be described as "postmetaphysical" (ibid.): "In undertaking to free presence from any condition or precondition for receiving what gives itself as it gives itself, phenomenology therefore attempts to complete metaphysics" (ibid. 8/1). Thus Marion reads the impetus of phenomenology as the "liberation of presence" – liberating the phenomenon from restrictions placed upon presence in earlier metaphysics (esp. Kant). What phenomenology will (or should!) locate is a givenness *without condition*.

But this "breakthrough" (RD 8/1) – located by Marion in Husserl's investigations of 1900/01 – is jeopardized and even denied by Husserl's re-establishment of limits and conditions in the notion of "objectivity." The emphasis on objectivity runs counter to the first impetus of phenomenology above, viz. the liberation of presence from conditions and restrictions. "Does not the reestablishment, or better the irrepressible consecration of objectivity by Husserl indicate the extreme difficulty that phenomenology has in remaining faithful to its own endeavor?" (RD 8/2). In requiring objectivity, Husserl lost his faith, strayed from the first faith of phenomenology in sheer givenness. Thus, the objective of phenomenology shifted from a donation without restriction to the disclosure of objective Being, from showing the things as they give themselves, to disclosing things as given "in the form of their constituted objectification" (ibid.).

But this is precisely where we might locate the debate between Husserl and Heidegger, Marion suggests: for Heidegger, "the objective of phenomenology does not coincide with objectivity" (RD 8/2). Thus, what we find in Heidegger (particularly GA 20) is "a critique of the ideal of objectification pursued by Husserl." For Heidegger, the return to the things themselves is not a return to their objectivity but to their Being; it is a reduction not to the transcendental I but rather to Dasein.[16] But did Heidegger retrieve the initial endeavor of phenomenology? Did Heidegger save the faith? In Heidegger, do we find a disclosure of things as they give themselves, a donation without condition or restriction? Not quite, Marion argues, since "*Dasein* still remains haunted by the *I*" (RD 9/2).[17] Further, the phenomenon of Being never shows itself and thus never gives itself; Being (in Heidegger) remains yet another *condition*, as objectivity in Husserl (ibid. 9/3).

But if phenomenology is to survive as a philosophical discipline, it must "admit that its method . . . does not have to depend on the question of Being any more than it was previously able to limit itself to the objective of objectivity" (RD 9/3). And this is precisely Marion's goal: to "free the phenomenological way of thinking [as expressed in the initial breakthrough] without confusing it with its successive, and, in a sense, provisional objectives [objectivity, Being]" (RD 9–10/3). Thus Marion seeks to go "beyond" phenomenology "as actualized" (in Husserl and Heidegger) in the name of a more originary phenomenology, remaining faithful to its original endeavor. Marion thus offers another heuristic for considering the poles of immanence and transcendence in phenomenology, a sketch of three "reductions" as found in Husserl, Heidegger, and Marion (and Levinas).[18] Since it is "the conditions of the reduction [which] fix the dimensions of givenness" (RD 303/203), an interrogation of these conditions (which, he is arguing, are variable) will raise the question of the possibility of a radical givenness – a donation *without condition*. The *first* reduction is "transcendental ('Cartesian,' 'Kantian,' 'phenomenological,' it matters little here)" (RD 304/204), and allows phenomena to appear only under the conditions of objectivity (i.e. as constituted by the ego). The *second* reduction is "existential" (that of Heidegger) and does "broaden" the conditions and thus opens the space for phenomena not glimpsed by Husserl (such as equipmentality and "the world"). But it still retains conditions in the continued "autarchy" of Dasein and the horizon of Being (RD 304/204). Thus, Marion argues, it is only the *third* reduction which locates a givenness without condition: "The originary absence of conditions and determinations of the claim [*la revendication*] allow it to appeal, without any limit, as much to what is not objectivated as to what is objectivated, as much to what does not have to be as to what must be" (RD 305/204–5).

To reformulate this in terms of the poles of transcendence and immanence: the first and second reductions both privilege immanence (of the *I*) as the condition for knowing or appearance. In other words, that which is transcendent, in order to appear, must show up within the horizon of immanence. As such, the transcendent is reduced to the immanent and cannot appear on its own terms, as it gives itself. The possibility of the latter, however, is seen in the third reduction, which discloses a call or appeal which proceeds from the other.[19] In this chapter, I will employ Marion's heuristic notion of three reductions in order to consider the way in which transcendence is approached in Husserl and Heidegger, and then critiqued by Levinas and Marion. I will then schematize this debate in the final section of the chapter and offer Derrida's reading in "Violence and Metaphysics" as a mediator, which will also provide an opportunity for a first sketch of my constructive proposal for an incarnational phenomenology.

First reduction: the possibility of transcendent knowledge in Husserl

The question of the other: the challenge of phenomenology

In the fifth of his *Cartesian Meditations*, Husserl finally raises the question that has haunted phenomenology since *Ideen* I:[20] if we have effected the transcendental reduction – the *epoché* – then what does phenomenology tell us about the "objective" world (CM 89–90)? Isn't this just Kant, or Descartes, all over again? Is not the intentional object a kind of "appearance" or phenomenal object, which is distinguished from the thing-in-itself or noumenal object, from which we are barred access?

> When I, the meditating I, reduce myself to my absolute transcendental ego by phenomenological epoché do I not become *solus ipse*; and do I not remain that, as long as I carry on a consistent self-explication under the name phenomenology? Should not a phenomenology that proposed to solve the problems of Objective being, and to present itself actually as philosophy, be branded therefore as transcendental solipsism? (CM 89)

Is Husserl's phenomenology a simple repetition of Kantian idealism (CM 86)? Or is this Berkeley? Are appearances all we have? Does thing = perception?

To address this problem, Husserl takes the other ego as a case[21] of transcendence *par excellence*. "But what about other egos," he asks, "who surely are not a mere intending and intended *in me*, but, according to their sense, precisely [transcendent] *others?*" (CM 89, cf. 90). The issue is this: can we have "actually transcend*ent* knowledge"(CM 90)?[22] Can we have knowledge *of* transcendence? "Above all," he asks, can we know other egos, who are "not actually in me"? Does not the transcendental reduction preclude this? Have we not reduced our sphere of knowledge to the transcendental realm of the ego, thus denying the possibility of transcend*ent* knowledge? As Quentin Lauer formulates it, "[t]he difficulty is that to be subject means to have experiences; to be experienced as subject is to be experienced as having experiences. Somehow, then, the experiences of others must form part of my intentional life, without at the same time being my experiences."[23] Formally, then, the question is how that which is *other* (transcendent) can be known.

Phenomenology happens precisely within the phenomenological reduction of the *epoché*, which is a reduction to the ego as a field of consciousness.[24] As such, it moves within the field of a transcendentally reduced ego; hence phenomenology is an egology. But when the ego is reduced to the phenomenological ego by the *epoché*, do I not become *solus ipse*, and would that not make phenomenology a solipsism instead of a philosophy which would solve the problems of objective, transcendent being? By this reduction to my pure consciousness, it would seem that others are eliminated, leaving me alone as a solipsistic self. As Husserl argues, however, solipsism is distinct from egology inasmuch as it is a question of *existence*: solipsism posits that nothing exists outside of the self; the phenomenological ego makes no such conclusion, precisely because the phenomenological reduction does not *deny* existence, it only *brackets* existence. And finally, as Husserl will now go on to suggest, others *do* appear or present themselves within the transcendental field of inquiry, and this "experienced Other" functions as a "transcendental clue" (cf. CM §21), something that comes to me from beyond the reach of my transcendental experience. That is, I do not experience the world as a private world but rather as an intersubjective one (CM §43).

In order to address the question of transcendent knowledge, Husserl will undertake a constitutional analysis of the alter ego (CM 90).[25] For our part, we begin with the *experience* of the other "in straightforward consciousness." When we undertake an analysis of this experience, I find that I experience the other ego *as* actually existing, and *as* a "world Object" (CM 91). However, I do not experience the other ego as a mere physical thing, though I do experience him or her as a thing in a certain sense. Thus, they are experienced as being "'in' the world" like other objects, but also as "subjects for this world" (ibid.) – that is, as others who also experience the world as I experience it. I experience the other as a thing that also experiences (CM 90). So then, I do experience "within myself" – i.e., within the transcendental sphere of the phenomenological ego – the world. I *experience* the world; I experience *the world*, which includes *others*. I experience the world not as something that I have invented as though it were my own "private synthetic formation," but "as other than mine alone, as an intersubjective world" (CM 91). I experience it as a world that others experience, whose experiences will differ from my own, but whose experiences are nevertheless *of the same world*. "[T]he experienced world exists in itself over against all experiencing subjects and their world phenomena" (ibid.).

At this juncture Husserl reminds us that what is at stake in the explication of how transcendental knowledge is possible is not just knowledge of other people, but of all that is other than the ego (CM 92). "*How* can my ego, within his peculiar ownness, constitute under the name, 'experience of something other,' precisely something *other*?" (CM 94) That, in this phenomenological inversion of Hamlet, is the question.

The primacy of immanence: reduction to the sphere of ownness

In order to *found* a transcendental theory of the objective world (CM 92) that is valid for everybody, we must first, within the phenomenological reduction, perform another reduction: the reduction to the transcendental sphere of ownness (*Eigenheitssphäre*) or to my transcendental concrete I-myself.[26] In this reduction, we bracket all that is alien (*Fremde*), such that the sphere of ownness may be characterized negatively as all that is non-alien. This is done by bracketing or disregarding all those objects or constitutional effects which relate to other subjectivities (CM 93). It is, as such, a "thematic exclusion of the constitutional effects produced by experiencing something other, together with the effects of all the further modes of consciousness relating to something other" (CM 95). This will exclude, for instance, all cultural constitutions, and in fact, all that might be characterized as "objective," there-for-everyone. What is left is what is peculiarly my own, what is actually present to me as given originarily. As a result, a substratum remains which Husserl describes as "Nature" or "mere Nature" (CM 96), in contrast to the objective nature investigated by the natural sciences – and it is this stratum which *founds* the experience of the other (ibid.).[27] In other words, the ego's own experience is the condition of possibility for knowledge of the other. The other will show up *like* the ego, or at least according to the ego's own determination of experience. "I" comes before others; others will "appear" on the basis of my experience, and according to my experience.

Now, within this sphere I perceive bodies, but only *my* body is singled out as an *animate organism*, because the subjectivities of the other bodies are bracketed in the sphere of ownness, precisely because they are not – and *cannot* be[28] – actually present to me as my own consciousness (CM 97). Therefore, all others appear only as material objects. My body is a presumptive unity such that I perceive embodiment as the embodiment of myself; I experience myself as the subject "incarnated" in my body, *acting* in my body. That is, my body is co-given or co-intuited as *motivated*. However, precisely what is *inaccessible* to me is the subjectivity of the other ego – its consciousness. It admits of no possible future presentation; while I can go to the back of the house (spatial), or wait for the next stock car race (temporal), the subjectivity of the other is *genuinely* transcendent because it admits of no intuition or original presentation (it cannot be experienced *originaliter*). Thus Steinbock describes the other ego as "an inaccessible being-for-itself."[29] Thus, all that I perceive of the other ego is its *body* which, at this point of the meditation, appears only as a physical body, not as a lived body, like my animate organism.

The question of how the other is known *as other* is made difficult – made a question – by the fact that "every *consciousness of* what is other, every mode of appearance of it, belongs in the [sphere of ownness]"(CM 100). It is within and by means of this ownness that the other is constituted as other. But is it then other? Has it not been reduced to the same? Has not the other been constituted by the ego "in its own likeness"? Does not the constitution of the other within the ego's sphere of ownness undo the alterity of the other?[30]

Appearances of transcendence: the analogical apperception of the other

As Husserl suggests, when we speak of another being before us "in person," we do not mean that his or her *Erlebnisse* or stream of consciousness is present to me as my own. If this were the case, the other would not be other but only the same as myself (CM 109). Further, if the other were *only* a body constituted in my primordial sphere – by me – then the other would be another material object but not another *ego*. Thus, the other, as more than body and yet appearing "in person," appears by means of *appresentation* – the (co)appearance of that which is not, or cannot be made present along with what appears.[31] There are, however, two kinds of appresentation: (1) an appresentation of external perception of physical things (e.g. the back of a house); and (2) the appresentation of another subjectivity (or "original sphere"). They are markedly different, however, because the appresentation of the back of a house can be verified through a fulfilling presentation (I can walk to the back of it), whereas verification of the latter is excluded apriori, because the other's *Erlebnisse* can *never* be present to me, whereas the back of the house can (CM 109). The *Erlebnisse* of the other can never be given; there is a structural lack (or rather, withholding) of intuition – an essential secret. "What is *appresented*," Husserl emphasizes, "can never attain to actual presence, never become an object of perception proper" (CM 112).

What is it, then, that "moves" me to constitute the other as another *ego*? This appresentation of another subjectivity is a non-originary making present *motivated* by an originary presentation, viz. a body over there. However, having made the reduction to the sphere of ownness, only *my* body is present as an animate organism; thus, the other body appears only as a material object (an immanent transcendency, CM 110). But the *similarity* of the body with my own body *motivates* an "analogizing" apprehension of the other body *as* an animate organism (CM 111).[32] This analogical apperception, however, is not an inference or thinking act; instead, the result is an "analogical transfer." As analogical, it accounts for otherness on the ground of sameness. Thus, the other is both given and withheld: "that component of the Other which is not accessible originaliter[33] [the other's subjectivity] is combined with an original presentation (of 'his' body as part of the Nature given as included in my ownness)" (CM 114). By "original," Husserl means "present," "immediately given" – in this case, speaking of the body of the other ego. Note, then, that it is the subjectivity of the ego (its *Erlebnisse*) which is given only *mediately*, non-originarily, precisely because of the transcendence of the other which cannot be made present. Thus the appearance of the other is a combination of presence and absence, giving and withholding.

"Pairing" is a primal form of the kind of passive synthesis described as association (CM §39), in contrast to identification (CM §18). It indicates a primitive givenness of two phenomena together; having a unity of similarity, they are given *as a pair*. Such is the case with the ego and the alter ego: they are always and necessarily given in an original pairing. Thus the other body given, as similar to mine, is paired with my own and appresented as an alter ego. Further, it is demonstrably an alter ego because, although similar to mine, its conscious life is not accessible *originaliter*, and hence it cannot be my animate organism (i.e. it maintains its otherness).

Unlike the confirmation of appresentation of physical objects, whereby the *ap*presentation is confirmed by later *present*ations, the verification of the appresentation of the other can only be accomplished by later appresentations – because the other as ego can never be present *originaliter*. Thus the appresented animate organism proves itself to be another original sphere in its later (n.b.

temporal) *harmonious* behavior – continuing behavior which confirms the appresentation. This behavior, as carried out by the body of the other, provides an originary presentation which motivates this verification. The (bodily) behavior of the other is an accessible means of verification for that which is inaccessible (CM 114).

My animate organism is reflexively "here," whereas the other's body is over "there." However, I can imagine my position as if it were "there" and not "here." By this variation, I realize that the other is not simply a duplication of myself, for reflexively my experience revolves around my "here," not the "there" where I perceive the other body. Further, the other experiences its place as a "here," one distinct from my own – confirming, we might say, the otherness of the other body.

From the perspective of the constituting ego, the other's subjectivity is genuinely transcendent, and thus in a sense structurally "absent" – never able to be present within the sphere of ownness which Husserl describes as the "core of presentation" presupposed by appresentation. Thus, it is on the basis of that which is present – the body of the other (*Körper*) paired with my animated body (*Leib*) – that the ego *posits* that which is absent. That which is absent is appresented on the basis of that which is present. "Thus every perception of this type," Husserl remarks, "is transcending: it posits more as itself-there than it makes 'actually' present at any time" (CM 122).[34] The other's body, as present, "signals" or "indicates" the subjectivity of the other, which can never be made present. Or to put it conversely, the subjectivity of the other is manifested or incarnated in her or his body, constituting "the 'irreal' intentional reaching of the other into my primordiality" (CM 129). The other *qua* other can never be present, can never be "seen" or "show up" within the sphere of ownness, which is the very condition for knowledge in Husserl's phenomenology. But would this not mean that phenomenology, when it comes to the other, is operating "in the blind"? And if appresentation is characteristic of *all* perception,[35] would this not mean that there is a certain blindness at the heart of phenomenology? For that which is appresented, we lack intuition, lack sight. But insofar as intuition is the condition of possibility of knowledge, might we not conclude that we do not *know* the other but only *believe* the other body to be an ego (though with good reason)? Would this signal a faith at the heart of phenomenology (surprising those who thought phenomenology had no *kardia*)? *Je ne sais pas; il faut croire.*[36]

Second reduction: Heidegger's critique of Husserl

Recalling that Marion's schematic of three reductions serves as our heuristic framework for opening the question of transcendence in phenomenology, it is important, at least briefly, to indicate the main lines of his account of Heidegger's critique of Husserl as outlined in *Sein und Zeit*.[37] As Marion recounts, the heart of the debate between master and pupil revolved around the question of the being of the subject – a question that continues to haunt us: who or what will follow the subject? Marion argues that this is an urgent challenge confronting phenomenology, answered in one of two ways: (1) those who would proclaim the abolition of the subject and any possible heir (i.e. Nietzsche), or (2) a repetition of the function of subjecti(vi)ty (Int 85). In order for phenomenology to answer the question, we must first sketch the way in which phenomenology could go beyond or after the subject, outside metaphysics, as it were. If the Husserlian transcendental ego fails to escape such metaphysical strictures, does Heidegger's Dasein perhaps meet this requirement? "To what extent," Marion asks, "does the existential analytic exceed the problematic (and thus also the abolition) of the metaphysical [i.e. transcendental] subject?" (Int 85). Does Dasein, which finds its authentic existence in "anticipatory resoluteness [*vorlaufende Entschlossenheit*]," surpass the metaphysical subject, or must we wait for another?

Dasein certainly *subverts* the (transcendental, phenomenological) subject, indeed, revolutionizes it. Subjectivity, for Dasein, is not located in the objectivization of the object, since its instrument – intentionality – has been broadened to encompass not simply the constitution of objects (Husserl) but rather an opening of a "world." In other words, being-in-the-world is a mode of intentionality broader than the constitution of objects; objective constitution is only one, even peculiar, mode of being-in-the-world.[38] Thus we have "Dasein" rather than a "subject" – not a "spectator" constituting objects, but a worker involved in the world. And rather than the *Eigenheitssphäre*, Heidegger provides an account of *Jemeinigkeit*. Dasein, as that one involved in the world, and as that being for whom its own being is at stake, is also that one for whom the Being of all other beings is at stake – *not* because the being of objects is constituted by the subject, but rather because Dasein is that being which is in-the-world, as always already involved, and cannot escape its worldliness (Int 87). This represents the "impossibility on the part of Dasein acceding to Being otherwise than placing itself in play *in the first person* – in risking itself as it is exposed to death" (Int 87, emphasis added). Thus the "mineness" (*Jemeinigkeit*) of being does not represent an unshakable subjectivity but rather a fundamental "exposedness" and risk of Dasein. And Dasein "attains its proper being" only when it seizes this risk (in anticipatory resoluteness) (Int 87).

Thus it is Dasein who "takes over" from the (objectively constituting Husserlian) subject. But here we find the need of a new interrogation: "On what condition does Dasein accomplish the 'mineness' that is characteristic of its proper way of Being?" (Int 88). Since the answer is "anticipatory resoluteness," we can ask this differently: "What does resoluteness resolve?" This is fixed in the three-pole constellation of *anxiety*, the *guilty or indebted conscience*, and *Being-towards-death*. However, all three of these components point to what might seem a hollow answer: resoluteness resolves precisely *nothing*: "the three phenomena which determine the Being of Dasein as care only define anticipatory resoluteness as an open extasis towards nothing" (Int 89). However, it is precisely this openness to nothingness which distinguishes or "isolates" Dasein as that being which differs from all other innerworldly beings. Dasein is that "being without any possible substitution" (Int 89). This constitutes the *ipseity (Selbstheit)* of Dasein; in other words, Dasein exists "qua itself." Resoluteness is simply a *constancy* of the self of Dasein (SZ §64, S. 322). There remains a self which is constant and permanent in its resoluteness. This, on Marion's accounting, is yet one more "subject":

The analytic of Dasein thus rediscovers, in a way that is familiar, but is yet derived from the care which is distant from familiarity, the metaphysical avatar of constitutive subjectivity. Thus arises the prodigious paradox of 1927: the extasis of care, which radicalizes the destruction of the transcendental subject in Descartes, Kant, and Husserl, nonetheless leads to a miming of the subject by reestablishing an autarky of Dasein, identical to itself through itself up to the ponit where this ipseity stabilizes itself in a self-positing. (Int 90)

Having noted the "autarky" of Dasein, Marion asks two questions: (1) "[T]o what extent does Dasein still 'destroy' the metaphysical project of a transcendental *I* which is unconditioned because it is self-constituted? And (2) how might this autarky be concerned with the question of Being in general?" (Int 90).

(1) While Dasein certainly displaces the transcendental ego and the permanency of the *ousia* or *res cogitans*, can we still distinguish the "self-presence" of these earlier egos from the self-constancy of Dasein? Can we distinguish constant "presence-at-hand" from the constancy of the self (Int 91)?[39] Does not Dasein at least "function" in a manner analogous to the transcendental subject? Does Dasein require *Destruktion* as yet another element of the history of ontology? In Dasein, rather than that which follows the subject, do we not find "the last heir of the subject itself" (ibid.)? Rather than "overcoming" the subject, does not Dasein represent the "final appeal of the subject," indeed its completion?

(2) The question of Being is a question which Dasein poses to itself. Dasein questions; Dasein is not question*ed* by another, is not called into question. The call of conscience is not a call to responsibility for the other, but rather summons to oneself (SZ 273/252). Nothing calls Dasein (ibid.); that is, "Dasein calls only to itself" (Int 92). No "claim" (*revendication*) is placed upon it, and therefore its subjectivity is not interrupted by anything other. The call of conscience is only a self-disturbance, a disturbance from within rather than a disruption from without. At no point does alterity disrupt Dasein; and therefore at no point does transcendence impose itself upon the immanent autarky of Dasein. While displacing the primacy of theoretical consciousness, the second reduction (the existential analytic) in no wise disturbs the phenomenological hegemony of immanence and the sphere of the same.

The violence of immanence: the French critique

A third reduction to unconditioned givenness

Both Husserl's and Heidegger's reductions, Marion argues, entail a privileging of immanence over transcendence. In both, immanence – the finite horizon of the constituting ego – is the condition for knowing, and thus the phenomenon is forced to appear under conditions established by the finite ego. In other words, the phenomenon is not permitted to give itself from itself (*kath'auto*, Levinas would say); rather, the phenomenon must give itself within limits. But at this juncture Marion asks "whether a phenomenological reduction would achieve a step back that allows one to consider givenness as such" (RD 63/39). His "third" reduction, he concludes, discloses this givenness "as such," pure givenness: "Apparition is sufficient for Being only inasmuch as, in appearing, it already perfectly *gives* itself; but it thus gives itself perfectly by the sole fact that it appears only inasmuch as it is *reduced* to its givenness for consciousness" (RD 303/203). The reduction to "pure" givenness (a notion to be interrogated below) opens the space for a *revelation*, a pure, perfect giving of the phenomenon without condition or limits.[40] This alone, according to Marion, permits the appearance of transcendence as such.

And here Levinas and Marion are in agreement:[41] what needs to be displaced in phenomenology is the privileging of immanence over transcendence. As such, both seek to locate an unconditioned phenomenon which is wholly other (*tout autre*), a case of transcendence *par excellence*. For Levinas, this is located in the ethical apparition of the face; for Marion, it is primarily the revelation of God *sans l'être*. The goal of this section is to provide an exposition of their critique of Husserl; a more critical evaluation of their positions will be taken up in the final section of this chapter.

The same and the other: Levinas

Knowledge and comprehension

Levinas's critique revolves around the problematic which we have discussed, particularly in relation to the Fifth of Husserl's *Cartesian Meditations*: the problem of *transcendence*. How can we *know* that which is genuinely transcendent? Does not knowledge itself – as conceptual thinking – reduce what is transcendent to the *immanent* conditions of the ego? In other words, if we are to *know* something, must it not be "reduced" to concepts by which the ego "makes sense" of it, or as Husserl would say, *gives* it sense or meaning (*Sinngebung*)? Is this not a reduction of what is *other* (transcendent) to the sphere of the *same* (immanent)? And would this not preclude *knowledge* of transcendence? Wouldn't we always only know immanence, the same rather than the different? Would this not mean that infinity is always reduced to the finite? This charge is leveled against phenomenology in an acute way; indeed, is it not precisely Husserl's phenomenology which represents the pinnacle of such reduction? Does not phenomenology found itself on the very principle that what is known must be *constituted by the ego*, must be given sense by the ego? As we saw in the Fifth Meditation, Husserl maintains that what can be known must present itself in the sphere of ownness – the sphere of the "same" of the ego's constitution. Anything that cannot "show up" within this sphere cannot be known.[42]

For Levinas, this is not just an epistemological problem. It is a question of *ethics*, of "doing justice" to the other *as* Other, as different, rather than reducing it to concepts, to the Same. To effect such a reduction to immanence constitutes, for Levinas, a *violence* – one which has accompanied the history of Western philosophy up to Husserl, and includes also Heidegger. "The philosophical discourse of the West," he comments, "claims the amplitude of an all-encompassing structure or of an ultimate comprehension" (GP 129). And, as he also remarks, "[r]ational theology accepts this vassalage" (ibid.): "as soon as he is conceived, this God is situated within 'being's move' ['*geste d'être*']" (GP 130). In such a rationalist theology, or what I have described above as theological positivism (of which Heidegger's later "Letter on Humanism" would be an example for Levinas), God must be submitted to the condition of Being, such that God is subject to Being. But that is precisely the problem, contends Levinas, because "the God of the Bible signifies the beyond being, transcendence" (GP 130). So also philosophy, construed as conceptual knowing, seeks to "grasp" and "encompass," to acquire and possess its object (BPW 152). The con*cept* (Be*griff*) recalls the concreteness of this metaphor, and "[*t*]*hese metaphors are to be taken seriously and literally*. They belong to the phenomenology of immanence" (BPW 152, emphasis original). Phenomenology, part of the history of philosophy whose story has been "a destruction of transcendence" (GP 130) offers a "theory of knowledge"[43] for which

> [k]nowledge is a relation of the *Same* with the *Other* in which the Other is reduced to the Same and divested of its strangeness, in which thinking relates itself to the other but the other is no longer other as such; the other is already appropriated (*le propre*), already *mine*. Henceforth, knowledge is without secrets or open to investigation, that is to say, it is a *world*. It is immanence. (BPW 151)

This is why, as suggested above, Levinas sees the phenomenological ego as a reproduction of the Platonic soul, since in this phenomenology of immanence "one only learns what one already knows, . . . nothing absolutely new, nothing other, nothing strange, nothing transcendent, could either affect or truly enlarge a mind committed to contemplating everything" (BPW 151).

We must appreciate the sense in which Levinas's posing of the question is a fundamentally *modern* (i.e. post-Cartesian) account of knowledge insofar as knowing is equated with comprehension. Only in modernity, after Descartes's equation of truth with certainty, does knowledge become synonymous with comprehension, abolishing the medieval distinction between the two. We can thus legitimately call into question Levinas's sweeping claim regarding the equation of knowledge and comprehension "in the West." For medieval thinkers such as Aquinas, for instance, one can "know" God without "comprehending" him. Or to put it conversely, just because one does not "comprehend" God (which is impossible) does not mean that one cannot "know" God (which is, indeed, the condition of possibility for salvation).[44] But on Levinas's reading, particularly of phenomenology, to know is to constitute, to give meaning on the basis of the ego, to possess the object, to grasp and comprehend and therefore to reduce to immanence. Thus phenomenology, for Levinas, is a philosophy of immanence *par excellence* – indeed another "Hegelianism" for which "nothing remains absolutely other" (BPW 153). To return to Levinas's discussion of "rationalist theology" noted above, such an equation of knowledge with comprehension means that God either cannot be known, or must be reduced to the measure of the finite concept. The God of Abraham, Isaac, and Jacob must show himself as the God of the philosophers, or fail to show up.[45] God, proclaimed to be incomprehensible, would thus be unintelligible; rather than exceeding being, he would fail to measure up (GP 131).

Knowledge (or what Levinas will also call "theory") is a *totalizing* relation and is thus defined in *Totality and Infinity* as "a way of approaching the known being such that its alterity with regard to the knowing being vanishes" (TI 42).[46] The known being is objectified by means of the concept – "a third term, a neutral term" which deprives the known being of its alterity by forcing the other to appear in terms of "the general" (ibid.). In other words, thought makes sense of the Other by constituting the other as an object; it does this by grasping it in a concept which participates in the generality or universality of language and thereby denies the other of singularity.[47] The known being, if it is to be known, cannot show up on its own terms; its appearance must be made in terms of the same (TI 43). Thus to be known, the other "is somehow betrayed, surrenders, is given in the horizon in which it loses itself and appears, lays itself open to grasp, becomes a concept" (TI 43–4). In phenomenology, he argues, it is the idea of "horizon" which plays the role of the concept in classical idealism: the phenomenon is forced to appear within the horizon of immanence of the constituting ego (TI 45). The transcendence of the phenomenon must be violated in order for the phenomenon to be known.

To be known, the other must give up its transcendence, must become something it is not. This is why phenomenology, according to Levinas, is fundamentally a philosophy of *violence*. War ("politics by another means"), Levinas observes, represents the suspension of morality; that is, in war, I do not respect the other but violate the other. War is characterized by a fundamental violence; however, we must understand violence in its broadest sense: "violence does not consist so much in injuring and annihilating persons as in interrupting their continuity, *making them play roles in which they no longer recognize themselves*, making them betray not only commitments but their own substance" (TI 21, emphasis added). War seeks to eliminate otherness, it "does not manifest exteriority and the other as other" (ibid.), but rather betrays a penchant for *totality*. It is this same penchant, and the same war, which has characterized Western philosophy: the desire to reduce all that is other than thought to the sphere of thought. All individuals are "given sense" from out of this totality, from the Same. It attempts to reduce all that is otherwise than philosophical to the philosophical concept (*Begriff*). In contrast to this "politics" stands a "prophetic eschatology" which is open to the future, open to the other, open to surprise.

For Levinas, this epistemological issue is also an *ethical* issue:[48] "ontology," which reduces the other to the same (TI 42), is a form of domination (45), exploitation (46), and tyranny (47):

> The relation with Being that is enacted as ontology consists in neutralizing the existent in order to comprehend or grasp it. It is hence not a relation with the other as such but the reduction of the other to the same. Such is the definition of freedom:[49] to maintain oneself against the other, despite every

relation with the other to ensure the autarchy of an I. Thematization and conceptualization, which moreover are inseparable, are not peace with the other but suppression or possession of the other. (TI 45–6)

This is why phenomenology, as a philosophy which privileges immanence and the sphere of the same, is at root "a philosophy of injustice" (TI 46).

Enclosure, disclosure, and manifestation

As I have suggested in our discussion of Husserl's Fifth Meditation (though it is not something Husserl himself considered), *language* plays a crucial role in maintaining a relationship with the other which both establishes a relation and respects its transcendence (this will also be important for our account of Augustine's strategy of "confession" considered below). The "relation" which rests on language is precisely a relation "in which the terms *absolve* themselves from the relation, remain absolute within the relation" (TI 64). *Knowledge*, however, is different: "the knowledge of objects does not secure a relation whose terms would absolve themselves from the relation" (ibid.). Rather, within this paradigm, truth is understood as *disclosure*, and so always disclosed relative to the knower/discloser.[50] Rather than giving itself from itself (*kath'auto*), the object is disclosed against the horizon of the ego. The other becomes "thematized," "predicated;" as such, to *dis*close something is to *en*close it in the Same. The other no longer speaks, is no longer present face-to-face; denied its voice, the other no longer speaks for itself (TI 65). Husserl's theory of horizonal constitution, as well as Heidegger's account of interpretation, both represent violations of the other in which the other is not "manifested" *kath'auto* (from itself), but rather disclosed on the basis of the ego's intentional aim. The "gaze" of the ego dominates the object (ibid.).

In contrast to a disclosure – which is "controlled," in a sense, or determined by the ego – Levinas points to a "revelation" (TI 66), a "manifestation" in which a being "speaks" to us "independently of every position we would have taken in its regard, *expressing itself*" (TI 65).

> Here, contrary to all the conditions for the visibility of objects, a being is not placed in the light of another but presents itself in the manifestation that should only announce it; it is present as directing this very manifestation – present before the manifestation, which only manifests it. (Ibid.)

In expression, in "saying" (*dire*), the other is present: "a coinciding of the expressed with him who expresses" (TI 66). "The face," Levinas continues, "speaks." (Here, Levinas should have recalled Husserl's own account of "expression" in the First of his *Logical Investigations*.) In expression, the other *manifests* itself, rather than being disclosed by the knowing ego. Thus, it challenges and confronts the Same as Other. This presenting of oneself in expression/language is what Levinas calls "meaning" or "signification" and what founds "discourse"(TI 66). Thus, "to signify is not to give"

– by this, Levinas means that expression or signification is not a kind of intuition or donation which can be appropriated or possessed by the perceiving ego; instead, discourse is "an original relation with an exterior being" (ibid.). It is a relation which is at once "more direct," but in which the other is also "more remote", viz. Other. In manifestation, the other appears "without slipping away and without betraying itself" (TI 65). What is unique about language/expression, and unlike "action," is "the coinciding of the revealer and the revealed in the face" (TI 66–7).

In "disclosure" (as in Husserl, but esp. Heidegger), the other appears "on the basis of a subjective horizon" (TI 67), whereas in expression, the other discloses *itself* – it "enters into a relation while remaining *kath'auto* . . . whose *way* consists in starting from himself, foreign and yet presenting himself to me" (ibid.). It is precisely this freedom of the absolutely other which is precluded by both Heidegger and Husserl (TI 68–9). At the core of Levinas's critique, then, is the Husserlian doctrine of intentionality, and more particularly, constitution; his goal, however, is to jettison the latter while retaining the former in a "more fundamental" sense,[51] without privileging representation (TI 122). It is precisely in "the Husserlian thesis of the primacy of the objectifying act" and his "excessive attachment to theoretical consciousness" (TI 123)[52] that Levinas locates phenomenology's first violence – the violence of constitution. On Levinas' reading, this leads to the affirmation "that the object of consciousness, while distinct from consciousness, is as it were a *product of* consciousness, being a 'meaning' endowed by consciousness, the result of *Sinngebung*" (ibid., emphasis added). This, however, means that the object, "which is first exterior, is given, that is, is *delivered over* to him who encounters it as though it had been entirely determined by him." As such, "the exterior being presents itself as *the work of* the thought that receives it" (ibid., emphasis added). The object, exterior to thought, in being given to consciousness is delivered over to be grasped, forced to play a role chosen by the constituting ego. Indeed, the *telos* of constitution is "total adequation" which is in fact "a mastery exercised by the thinker upon what is thought in which the object's resistance as an exterior being vanishes" (TI 123–4).[53] Thus is the object (always other) rendered "intelligible," having been "given meaning" (*Sinngebung*) by the ego which determines it. The incommensurability between the other and the same is collapsed; the transcendent is reduced to the immanent; it is "without mystery" (124). And that, Levinas says, means war.

But if knowledge is relegated to immanence – to comprehension and conceptualization – can transcendence or alterity be "intelligible"? Would transcendence be something we could "know"? What this calls for, Levinas suggests, is "another phenomenology" (BPW 153), an-other phenomenology which differs from Husserl's phenomenology, and also differs from the philosophical tradition which has privileged "knowledge," particularly theoretical knowing. What Levinas is looking for is an account (a description, hence the retained title of "phenomenology"[54]) of a relation to transcendence which is not one of "knowing" in the sense of grasping – a relation which is otherwise than knowledge, "a *spiritual intrigue wholly other than* gnosis" (BPW 154, emphasis original). This will be a relation which is not a relation in the sense of adequation, "a relation without relation" (TI *passim*) – such that the other term is not reduced to the sphere of the same, but is related to *as Other*. This would not be thought or knowledge, but could only be indicated as "thought" or "knowledge" in a different sense, a non-conceptual knowing by which the transcendent appears, reveals itself, but is not reduced to concepts or the conditions of the constituting ego. It would be "a thinking which does not bring all transcendence back to immanence and does not compromise transcendence in understanding it" (BPW 155): "An impossible demand!" (ibid.)

Levinas sees intimations of this in the history of philosophy, notably Kant's notion of the Categorical Imperative, and even more importantly in Descartes's account of the *idea of the Infinite* in the Third Meditation – an "idea" which exceeds thought, an idea which cannot be contained by the finitude of the *cogito*. It is a thought which cannot be reduced to immanence, cannot be grasped in a concept, and cannot be submitted to correlational analysis. Here we have an "appearance" – a "revelation" – in which the other who appears remains Wholly Other. Here Levinas uses the important metaphor of *surplus* or *excess* to describe his project, casting it in terms of the phenomenological theme of *fulfillment* and displacing the primacy of adequation in Husserl's account of transcendence (TI 22–3). For Husserl, the intention always exceeds its fulfillment; there is always a surplus of "mean-ing" without intuition. What Levinas is looking for is an intentional relation (albeit "an intentionality of a wholly different type") wherein there is a surplus of *intuition*, an excess of *donation* which overwhelms the intentional gaze, which "dazzles" it. This surplus or excess would be exterior to, lying outside of, the sphere of immanence or the same. It would be an exteriority, a "beyond," an "infinity" (TI 23), which is nevertheless "reflected within" the totality.

Consistently, Levinas turns to Descartes's "idea[55] [not 'concept'] of the infinite within us" as a site for this kind of intuition, a donation which undoes the phenomenologically constituting ego (TI 25). Indeed, the infinite is precisely that which the ego cannot constitute, but rather constitutes the ego. It is precisely a thought which cannot be contained, cannot be *thought*, properly speaking, because it "overflows" thought (BPW 156). Thus, "[t]he relation with infinity will have to be stated in terms other than those of objective experience; but if experience precisely means a relation with the absolutely other, that is, with what always overflows thought, the relation with infinity accomplishes experience in the fullest sense of the word" (TI 25). So in the "idea of the infinite" we find a "revelation" of transcendence *within* the sphere of the same: "the improbable feat whereby a separated being, fixed in its identity, the same, the I, nonetheless contains in itself what it can neither contain nor receive solely by virtue of its own identity" (TI 27). The subject is ruptured by an Other who invades its sphere of ownness, marking the revelation of a genuine transcendence.

The "Saturated Phenomenon": Marion's critique of Husserl

As Husserl and Levinas both considered the other person or subjectivity as something of a "limit case" for the question of knowing transcendence, Marion looks to the "the religious phenomenon" (God) as just such a test case for phenomenology. Can we "know" – in the phenomenological sense – God? Is it not the case that "the field of religion" is precisely that which "philosophy excludes or, in the best case, subjugates?" (SP 103). Is it not precisely such a transcendence which is excluded by phenomenology – a transcendence which is inaccessible and cannot be known, precisely because it cannot be made present, cannot be encompassed by a horizon? Thus, a "philosophy [or phenomenology] of religion" – "if there were one" – would be confronted by a double-bind: *either* it would involve the conceptualization of the religious phenomenon, in which case its transcendence would be denied by being encompassed; *or*, its field would be phenomena which cannot be conceptualized, in which case it would be silent. It would be a question of describing the *in*visible. "The religious phenomenon thus amounts to an impossible phenomenon" (SP 103).[56]

And so the question becomes: could God appear in phenomenology, this science of light (*phôs*), this logos of what shines (*phanei*) in the darkness (cf. John 1:4–5)? Does God have a right to appear (*un droit à paraître*) in phenomenology? What laws would govern the appearance of God as a phenomenon, or what would make such an appearance possible? Would God refuse to appear, or perhaps be *unable* to appear, signaling a divine impotence? Would God fail to show up in phenomenology, and would this be God's fault, or would phenomenology be compelled to bear responsibility for this absence? If we are asking whether God appears in *Husserl's* phenomenology, the answer appears to be evident: God appears only to be excluded, shining (as "ground") in the sweeping project of phenomenology for the blink of an eye in order to be bracketed by the transcendental reduction (Id 133–4). God, we might suggest, has no right to appear in Husserl's phenomenology.

But is Husserl phenomenology? Could the question of God's appearance perhaps bring to light the criteria of phenomenality in general – the question of the possibility of phenomena – pushing phenomenology to its limit? Would not the consideration of the (non-)appearance of God require a careful analysis of the conditions and laws that govern the appearance of phenomena, offering an occasion to develop a more radical phenomenology, a phenomenology which is not only after Husserl but beyond Husserl, even transgressing Husserl? And would not such a radical phenomenology in fact liberate phenomena from oppressive conditions, restoring their "right to appear" (*droit à paraître*)? Thus the question of the (im)possibility of the religious phenomenon (as an "index") raises the more general question of "phenomenality" itself: What are the "criteria" of phenomenality? What is it that makes it possible for a phenomenon to "appear"? What are the conditions for its "visibility"? Why is the impossible phenomenon invisible? What are the rules and regulations of appearance? And who establishes these laws?

Conditions of the phenomenon

At least since Kant, Marion argues, the phenomenon, in order to appear, has had to measure up to certain standards or criteria of phenomenality; that is, its right to appear has been established by conditions or laws which govern appearance. In Kant, for instance, the possibility of the phenomenon's appearance is determined in advance by "formal conditions," viz. the coupling of intuition and the concept. In Leibniz, the law is Sufficient Reason, or rather Sufficient Reason is the law which governs phenomena. In both, there are appearances which would be impossible, realities which cannot measure up to this standard of phenomenality and thus are denied the rights of phenomena (SP 80–1/103–4). In both cases, the phenomenon is conditioned by the finitude of the knower: the "formal conditions" or "power of knowing" (Kant), and the law of Sufficient Reason (Leibniz). For both Kant and Leibniz, the "possibility [of the phenomenon] does not follow from the phenomenon, but from the conditions set for any phenomenon" (SP 81/103). Thus, in such "metaphysical" systems, "the possibility of appearing never belongs to what appears, nor phenomenality to the phenomenon" (SP 83/104); rather, the law of appearance is determined by the knowing ego: "Any phenomenon is possible that grants itself to the finitude of the power of knowing and *its* requirements" (SP 81/104, emphasis added). The object/phenomenon does not appear on its own terms, but under conditions established by the ego.

We can appreciate Marion's argument if we keep returning to our limit or test case: the religious phenomenon. Within a "metaphysical" system, God must be conceptualized, made an object (objectified), which can only happen in terms of the formal conditions of knowing determined by the experiencing ego. Thus, the infinite is reduced to the finite; the transcendent is absorbed into the immanent; the "impossible" is forced to appear within the realm of possibility, under certain conditions and laws.

In contrast to such "metaphysical" systems,[57] Marion suggests that phenomenology's "principle of all principles," or at least a certain reading of it, offers a phenomenality *without condition*, providing liberation and deliverance (*relève*) from the law (*le droit*) of phenomenality and at the same time restoring the phenomenon's rights with its *own* justification (SP 84/105). This unconditioned giving is signaled in the "principle of all principles," which states

> that *every originary presentive intuition is a legitimizing source of cognition,* that *everything originarily* (so to speak, in its "personal" actuality) *offered* to us in *"intuition" is to be accepted simply as what it is presented as being,* but also *only within the limits in which it is presented there.* (Id I 44)

In contrast to external conditions imposed upon the phenomenon (as in Kant and Leibniz), Marion argues, in phenomenology it is the phenomenon *itself* which sets the rules for appearance, which determines its own appearance and is its own source of legitimation or justification. The phenomenon appears on its own terms, "on the basis of itself [*à partir de soi-même*] as a pure and perfect appearance of itself, and not on the basis of another than itself which would not appear (a reason)" (SP 84/105). As such, it appears without horizon or background or presupposition: it is a *donation*, an originary giving.

Now the problem, according to Marion, is that Husserl said too much: within the space of a typically long German sentence the Law (condition) returns in order to govern phenomena; the Revolution which procured the freedom of phenomena is quickly followed by a Reign of Terror which restores their oppression. The "first trait" of intuition, as the unconditional donation of phenomena, is undone by a second and third trait which restore conditions of appearance and deny phenomena their rights. Thus Marion wants to suggest that

> the principle of donating intuition does not authorize the absolutely unconditioned appearance, and thus the freedom of the phenomenon that gives itself on the basis of itself. To be sure, this is not because the intuition as such limits phenomenality, but because it remains framed, as intuition, by two conditions of possibility, conditions which themselves are not intuitive but are nevertheless assigned to every phenomenon. (SP 85/105)

The "second trait" of intuition is its essential *limitation*: everything is to be accepted as it is presented, "but also *only within the limits in which it is presented there*" (Id 44). Every phenomenon *must* – it is the law – appear within the horizon of an intentional aim by which it is meant; that is, there is a background against which things appear for me, which forms a horizon of possibility for that which will be seen (which Heidegger translated by the notion of a "totality of involvements" by which the thing gains significance). Thus the horizon, which is always *my* horizon, is at once a limitation and yet the very possibility of appearance of the phenomenon. The donation, then, is not quite as pure or unconditioned as first suggested by the first trait of donation; instead, the second trait of horizonality contradicts the first, asserting that there are rules which govern the appearance of phenomena and even deny the right of appearance to those realities which resist the law, or perhaps are too lowly for the law, unable to appear before the law or stand up before the tribunal of horizonality.

The undoing of unconditioned donation continues within the principle of all principles, however, when Husserl declares that the originary donation is nevertheless offered *to us*; that is, the phenomenon, in the end, remains a *constitution* of the ego, which, for Marion, means that the *I* is the judge and tribunal who determines what can and cannot appear. Rather than the phenomenon appearing on its own terms, as the principle of donation suggests, in the end the phenomenon must answer to the ego as perceiver (a structure enforced by the phenomenological reduction). The right of appearance is not something the phenomenon has "of itself" (*soi-même*); rather, that right must be conferred or bestowed upon it by the ruling ego which constitutes it as a phenomenon. The rights of the phenomena are not inalienable or absolute, but rather granted by the kingdom of the *I*, and thus contingent.

Intuition, for Husserl, gives fulfillment to our intentions or meaning-acts, *gives* the object *itself* – and it is this "seeing" which is "the ultimate legitimizing source of all rational assertions" (Id 36). The ego's meaning or intending of the object is fulfilled by the giving of intuition; thus a very important distinction is made between "merely positing" ego acts and intentions which are fulfilled by intuitive donation, or what

Husserl describes in the sixth Logical Investigation as the difference (and relation) between "meaning-intention" and "meaning-fulfillment" (LI 668). Meaning is an act of pointing, of intending, but such pointing would be empty without a "percept" or what is given by intuition (LI 683–4). The object *meant* becomes the object *seen* or known by the fulfillment of intuition: "The fact that our meaning-intention is united with intuition in a fulfilling manner, gives to the *object* which appears in such intuition, when it primarily concerns us, the character of a thing known" (LI 696). Further, intuition gives objects "more or less" adequately; that is, fulfillment admits of degrees or a "graded sequence" such that meaning-intentions may only be "partially" fulfilled.[58] With regards to transcendent objects, such as physical things (though in a sense "it holds good for *all realities* without exception"), fulfillment is *always* inadequate because experience of them is given only "onesidedly" and never – it is the law – "allsidedly" (Id 8). Thus for Husserl, intention always exceeds fulfillment. Nevertheless, inadequate fulfillment still *gives* the object *itself*; that is, inadequate perception nevertheless "reaches" the object, in contrast to a merely positing meaning-intention. Intuition of the transcendent object, though one-sided, is nevertheless a donation and a "having", a reaching rather than a pointing, a seeing "in person" rather than an intending from afar. As Levinas comments, "[t]o say that intuition actualizes the mere intention which aims at the object is to say that in intuition, we relate directly to the object, we reach it. That is the entire difference between aiming at something and reaching it. A signifying intention does not possess its object in any way; it only thinks it."[59]

Marion marks three "traits" of this principle of all principles, which are also three fundamental traits of phenomenology: (1) *Donation*: intuition is a "pure giving," "without background," in which the phenomenon "shows itself on the basis of itself," rather than against the horizon of a determining ego (SP 84/105). It appears "on the basis of itself," on its own terms, not under the conditions of another, the ego or Reason. Thus the phenomenon does not submit itself to conditions which are imposed upon it. The appearance is precisely *un*conditioned, absolute. "Nevertheless," Marion continues, "it still remains to be verified whether the 'principle of all principles' in point of fact ensures a right to appear for *all* phenomena, whether it indeed opens for them an absolutely unconditioned possibility – or whether it renders them possible still only under some condition" (SP 85/105, emphasis added). It turns out to be the latter: the second and third "traits" are precisely conditions which limit and restrict the pure and unrestricted giving indicated by the first trait of donation. (2) *Horizonality*: as the principle of principles states, "everything that offers itself to us originarily in intuition is to be taken quite simply as it gives itself out to be, but also *only within the limits* in which it is given there" (Id 44). Thus there are limits to its donation: the limits of perception which require that everything appear against the background of a "horizon" of the perceiver. The phenomenon must be "inscribed . . . within the limits of a horizon" (SP 86/105). Recall that for Husserl, horizonality is one of the fundamental characteristics of consciousness (along with intentionality and constitution). This horizon is precisely a *condition* of appearance: anything that would be possible as a phenomenon must be constituted against the horizon of a finite, projecting ego. Thus the second trait of the principle of all principles contradicts the first trait of *un*conditioned donation. (3) *Reduction*: the principle also states that "everything that offers itself *to us*" is to be taken as given. Here is yet another condition, Marion argues: in order to appear, in order to measure up to the criteria of phenomenality, the phenomenon must be "led back, and therefore reduced, to the 'I'" (SP 88/106). This is what is effected by the phenomenological reduction: the world of phenomena is reduced to that constituted by the ego. And "if every phenomenon is defined by its very reducibility to the 'I,' must we not exclude straightway the general possibility of an absolute, autonomous – in short, irreducible – phenomenon?" (88/106). Would it not, for instance, be impossible for God to appear as God, on God's own terms, in an irreducible manifestation? Would not the infinite God always be reduced to the horizon and constitution of a finite ego?

So despite the centrality of the phenomenon's unconditioned donation in Husserl's "principle of all principles" (and even in the *Logical Investigations*, Marion argues), the traits of horizonality and reduction undo the principle of donation as unconditioned, restoring the law and denying rights in such a way that the appearance of an absolute, autonomous, irreducible phenomenon becomes, by right, impossible. Such a phenomenon could never appear, lying beyond the horizon of possibility and resisting reduction to the *I*. And the problem with that, on Marion's accounting, is that God would never show up, would never show his [*sic*] face in phenomenology, could never appear. For if there is a God (not that this is a question for Marion), he is certainly absolute, unconditioned, and irreducible. A God that could be reduced to the perception of the ego or encompassed by the horizon of a creature or constituted by the *I* would be no God at all for it would not be wholly other (*tout autre*) and thus only an idol. If intuition limits the giving of the phenomenon by a horizon of possibility and reduction to the ego, such that phenomena cannot be purely given and always fall short by reason of a "logic of shortage" (SP 85/105), then God would fail to appear as a phenomenon precisely because he *exceeds* the limits of a horizon and refuses to be reduced to the ego's constituting glance. Under these conditions, God would either be forced to appear within the rules and regulations established by the finite creature, or could not show up at all. Either God would be absent, or compelled to appear on terms established by the perceiving ego. Such is the essence of the problem for Marion.[60]

The finitude of intuition

Within what Marion describes as the metaphysical tradition of Kant, Leibniz, and Husserl (as maintaining the conditions of the ego), the phenomenon can only appear insofar as it is "lacking" intuition – that is, only insofar as its intuition remains finite. A non-lacking, complete intuition is, for Husserl, an impossible ideal, a regulative ideal for which we strive but which is impossible to achieve. Such an intuition would be "adequate": the intentional aim would be completely or adequately "fulfilled." However, since this is a regulative ideal, the phenomenon only appears less than adequately. For Husserl, intention or meaning always exceeds fulfillment; there is always an excess of meaning, "attendant mean-ings" which remain unfulfilled.

This is the case in Husserl's phenomenology, Marion proposes, because of "the most metaphysical definition of truth as *adaequatio rei et intellectus*" as indicated in the notion of adequation as the highest form of phenomenality possible, that ideal toward which all phenomena strive (SP 89–95/107–9). However, the ultimate fulfillment of adequation remains always and only a regulative ideal: meaning always exceeds intuition and intention always surpasses the givenness of the phenomenon, signaling intuition's structural poverty and thus precluding the possibility of a saturated phenomenon where intuition would in fact *exceed* meaning (SP 99/110). This structural lack, Marion goes on to argue, is due to the *finitude* of intuition; since the phenomenon is constituted by the finite *I*, its givenness remains encompassed by a finite horizon. "Phenomenality is indexed according to intuition," and "if intuition alone gives objects, there falls to human finitude only an intuition that is itself equally finite" (SP 99/110). "Intuition's failure," therefore, is due to the "finitude of intuition":

> This radical lack has nothing accidental about it, but results from a phenomenological necessity. In order that any phenomenon might be inscribed within a horizon (and there find its condition of possibility), it is necessary that that horizon be delimited (it is its definition), and therefore that the phenomenon remain finite. In order for a phenomenon to be reduced to an obviously finite *I* who constitutes it, the phenomenon must be reduced to the status of finite objectivity. In both cases, the finitude of the horizon and of the *I* is indicated by the finitude of the intuition itself. (SP 101–2/111)[61]

In order for an irreducible, unconditioned, absolute phenomenon to appear, then, Marion must locate instances of "non-finite intuition" as the condition for its possibility (SP 102/111).

"Why," Marion asks, "does adequate evidence most often remain a limit case, or even an excluded case? . . . Answer: because the equality that Husserl maintains *de jure* between intuition and intention remains for him in fact untenable. Intention (almost) always (partially) lacks intuition, just as meaning almost always lacks fulfillment" (SP 93/108). Thus Marion sees a lack, deficit, and structural impoverishment to intuition because of the limits imposed by the experiencing ego. The ego denies the phenomenon of its rights, does not allow it to appear in its fullness. What is common to Kant, Leibniz, and Husserl – common, then, to both metaphysics and (Husserl's) phenomenology – is that the phenomenon is reduced to the finitude of the perceiving ego, circumscribed by a horizon and reduced to an "I." The phenomenon is thus conditioned and reduced through "de-*finition*: the phenomena are given by an intuition, but that intuition remains finite, either as sensible (Kant), or as most often lacking or ideal (Husserl)" (SP 101/111). Phenomena thus suffer from a "deficit" or "shortage" – a lack, Marion argues, that is caused by the ego's denial of the phenomenon's excessive givenness, the restrictions placed upon the donation of intuition. The phenomenon is thus "reduced to the status of finite objectivity" (SP 101/111); that is, the phenomenon can only be objectively (conceptually) determined insofar as it is constituted as finite. "In both cases," he continues, "the finitude of the horizon and of the 'I' is indicated by the finitude of intuition itself" (SP 102/111). Therefore, following from the hypothesis suggested earlier, an absolute, irreducible phenomenon could only be possible "if *a non-finite intuition* ensured their givenness" (ibid.). But could this even be "envisaged"?[62]

The saturated phenomenon

In phenomenology, phenomena can only appear insofar as they *lack* intuition, insofar as the "amount" of givenness can be contained within the horizon of finitude. The phenomenon is only possible, then, insofar as it can be encompassed by the intentionality of the finite ego. Lack of intuition becomes the criterion of phenomenality, the condition under which the object must "appear" or be "visible." Marion's "hypothesis" seeks to invert this conditioning: based on the criteria of finitude/lack, would it be possible for a phenomenon to appear whose givenness *exceeded* or "saturated" the intentional aim of the ego (SP 102–3/112)? Would such a phenomenon be *possible*? While phenomena, for Husserl, always appear inadequately, in the sense that they cannot fulfill intentional meaning and thus admit of infinities of experience, Marion wants to consider another possibility:

> what would occur, as concerns phenomenality, if an intuitive donation were accomplished that was absolutely unconditioned (without the limits of a horizon) and absolutely irreducible (to a constituting I)? Can we not envisage a type of phenomenon that would reverse the condition of a horizon (by surpassing it, instead of being inscribed within it) and that would reverse the reduction (by leading the I back to itself, instead of being reduced to the I)? (SP 89/107)

Such a phenomenon would be given excessively, more than adequately, exceeding meaning, overflowing the intention of the ego, leaving, instead of an excess of meaning, an overabundance of donation; in short, it would be a "phenomenon par excellence" (SP 89/107). If complete or adequate fulfillment is the regulative ideal for the phenomenon's donation in Husserl, then such a giving without reserve, which saturates and overflows intentionality, would signify the most excessive phenomenon.

Glimpses of such a donation can be seen, Marion suggests, in Kant's "aesthetic idea," Anselm's (wrongly described) "ontological argument,"[63] and (as in Levinas) Descartes's "idea of the infinite."[64] For a first sketch he turns, perhaps ironically, to Kant's "aesthetic idea." Let us recall an important distinction here: for Kant, knowledge is possible only by a coupling of intuition on the one hand, and concepts on the other. Intuition without concepts is blind; concepts without intuition are empty. There are two ways to "fall short" of this kind of conceptual knowledge: (1) to have a concept without intuition, which is what Kant calls a "rational *idea*" (as opposed to a concept). Such an object would not meet the criteria of phenomenality because of the lack of an adequate intuition (SP 103/112); (2) one may have an intuition for which no adequate concept can be found. This is what Kant calls the "aesthetic idea" (ibid.). Rather than lacking intuition, it is the concept which cannot measure up to an excess of intuition, "a failure of the (lacking) concept that leaves the (overabundantly given) intuition blind." Thus we encounter a phenomenon which is not a phenomenon, not because it cannot measure up to the law of appearance (above), but because it exceeds and overwhelms such conditions. Thus it struggles to "appear" because it gives itself too much, excessively, more than the ego can handle. It gives itself more than any concept can "expose" (SP 104/112).

Having outlined the (non-)conditions of its appearance, Marion undertakes a description (as a "radical phenomenology") of the "saturated phenomenon," outlining four characteristics:

1   *Invisability.* By this neologism, Marion means that the saturated phenomenon is something that "cannot be *aimed* at [*ne peut se viser*]" or predelineated – cannot be constituted by an intentional aim, but rather overpowers intentionality. It issues in what Descartes describes as *amazement* [*l'étonnement*], a being confronted, an imposition (SP 106–7/113–14) – an experience which, at the conclusion of Descartes's encounter with the Idea of the Infinite, issued only in praise.[65]

2   *Unbearability.* Since the saturated phenomenon is given without limit or restriction, perception is overwhelmed by its intensity and cannot bear it (*ne peut se supporter*): "intuition, which is supposed to be 'blind' in the realm of impoverished phenomena, proves to be, in a truly radical phenomenology, much rather blind*ing*" (SP 109/114). This issues in *bedazzlement.* This is a seeing which is not a seeing, a seeing which sees too much and thus cannot constitute what is appearing. Overwhelmed by light, the ego is blinded. Thus the saturated phenomenon is perceived "by the gaze only in the negative mode of an impossible perception, the mode of bedazzlement" (SP 109/114). Thus bedazzlement marks a seeing without constituting.

3   *Absolute* (SP 112–13/115–16). By this, Marion means to emphasize that the "saturated phenomenon" bears no analogy to any other phenomenon or experience (*contra* CM §50). It is absolutely *singular*: "a pure event" (SP 113/116). Incommensurate with any other term, "this phenomenon would escape all relations because it would not maintain any common measure with these terms" (SP 115/117). It is not something that can be constituted by association, predelineated in terms of prior experience, or apprehended by analogical strategies; it is radically singular.

4   *Irregardable.*[66] The saturated phenomenon is "incapable of being looked at" precisely because it cannot be constituted as an object – not because of lack of intuition but because of its excess. Therefore, not being constituted, it cannot become an "object." It is a "non-objectivizable object" which "refuses to let itself

be looked at as an object, precisely because it appears with a multiple and indescribable excess that suspends any effort at constitution" (SP 120/119). To indicate it as irregardable, however, "in no way implies that absolutely nothing appears here: intuitive saturation . . . imposes itself in the capacity of a phenomenon that is exceptional by excess, not by defect" (ibid.). It is not that nothing appears, but that something appears which overwhelms the perceiver, which cannot be constituted because of its imposition and a deluge of givenness.

The saturated phenomenon, Marion argues, is not a rare or limit phenomenon: rather, it is a more rigorous understanding of the phenomenon in general, the phenomenon of a "radical phenomenology" which goes beyond Husserl himself (SP 123–4/120). It is a reading of Husserl against himself, dropping the second and third limiting traits of the principle of all principles (as returning metaphysical criteria) and grounding the phenomena in pure donation; it is, he suggests, "the coherent and conceptual completion of the most operative definition of the phenomenon: it alone truly appears as itself, of itself, and starting from itself" (SP 124/120, alluding to Heidegger). It is an understanding of the phenomenon as a *revelation* (cf. Levinas's "manifestation"). In short, if one has the faith to believe it,[67] the saturated phenomenon is God, the "being-given par excellence" who "gives himself and allows to be given more than any other being-given."

> That he is the given par excellence implies that "God" is given without restriction, without reserve, without restraint. "God" is given not at all partially, following this or that outline, like a constituted object that nevertheless offers to the intentional gaze only a specific side of its sensible visibility, leaving to appresentation the duty of giving further that which does not give itself, but absolutely, without the reserve of any outline, with every side open. (MP 588)

God's donation is precisely that giving which challenges the second and third traits of the "principle of all principles," viz. the enframing of a horizon and the reduction to the ego's intention. God, indeed, is a cheerful giver who happily gives himself, diffuses himself, and thereby gives himself all the more, to the point that he risks abandonment and makes himself vulnerable to the possibility of not appearing. "The phenomenon par excellence," Marion suggests, "exposes itself, for that very excellence, to not appearing – to remaining in a state of abandon" (MP 589). The saturated phenomenon would not fail to appear because of lack of givenness, but because of an excess which bedazzles the intentional aim; in short, it would be "a phenomenon saturated to the point that the world could not accept it. Having come among its own, they did not recognize it – having come into phenomenality, the absolutely saturated phenomenon could find no room there for its display" (SP 118). Such are the risks of revelation.

Incommensurability and transcendence:
the violence of the concept

A formalization of the question

In this final section of Chapter 2 (and the conclusion of Part One), my goal is (a) to formalize or broaden the question of transcendence as a methodological problem for phenomenology, indeed, for philosophical theory; and (b) to offer something of a preliminary defense of phenomenology's "respect" for transcendence, responding to Marion and Levinas by drawing on Derrida's critical reading in "Violence and Metaphysics." This preliminary sketch of an alternative, even "new" phenomenology will open space for a return to Heidegger's own project for a new phenomenology (Chapter 3), and the impetus for that project in Augustine (Chapter 4).

The challenge of phenomenology revisited

Several times I have previously referred to the challenge for phenomenology which is the problem of transcendence or alterity, viz. how can transcendence "appear," and how can we speak of that which exceeds description? We have encountered this challenge in several locales: (1) as we defined phenomenology early on, it is a philosophical method for describing experience. But this then raised a question: how will it be possible to give a *philosophical* or *theoretical* description of experience, which is itself pre-theoretical and thus resists theoretical articulation? Is it not precisely the fullness of experience which cannot be "put into words"? Is not factical experience precisely that which exceeds and eludes conceptual, philosophical thought? This, as we will see, is the problem as confronted by Heidegger in the notion of "facticity."[68] (2) For both Husserl and Levinas, it is the subjectivity of the other which is taken as a limit case for phenomenological knowledge, raising the question of the possibility of transcendent knowledge. For Husserl, the other subjectivity is necessarily inaccessible, cannot be made originally present and thus cannot be reduced to an intentional object of consciousness. For Levinas, the other is an infinity which exceeds the horizons of the same. (3) For Marion, it is primarily the "religious phenomenon" (God) which plays the role of the utterly transcendent, that which exceeds and resists phenomenological or conceptual description.

While these three instances of challenge are different, I would like to consider what is common to the three of them, with the goal of sketching the general problematic of the challenge we are grappling with.

Incommensurability and transcendence

In all three of the "cases" above, we find a situation where thought is inadequate for its task – what from a modern perspective would be a certain "failure of the concept," insofar as it cannot *grasp* its object. Or perhaps we should speak of the "violence of the concept" which reduces that which exceeds it to its own terms. In any case, the three cases above – factical lived experience, the other subjectivity, and God – all point to sites where theoretical description is at a loss, where the tools (concepts) of phenomenological description are confronted by something or someone which exceeds their grasp. I would like to refer to this as the formal problem of *incommensurability*. All of the alterities considered are incommensurate with conceptual thought and language: they are *otherwise than* conceptual, appearing on a completely different register. There is a qualitative difference – an abyss – between the order of thought and that of experience, for example. In other words, as incommensurate, they have nothing in common, no common point of overlap. It is a radical difference of order. To speak of transcendence *in terms of* immanence is always to reduce it, to make it something other than itself, to translate it into terms which are not its own. This general problematic of *incommensurability* is found in all three cases above: (1) lived experience is not theoretical but pretheoretical; as such, it has a "quality" and "knowing" which are its own, and which cannot be reduced to theoretical or phenomenological concepts. There is an irreducibility of non-cognitive ways of being which cannot be reduced to representational consciousness. In sum, the heart has reasons of which reason knows nothing.[69] (2) The other subjectivity is precisely inaccessible, alterior to thought, particularly *my* thought. It is an essential secret which is incommensurate with the consciousness of another. And (3) God is precisely that infinity who exceeds conceptual categories, who cannot be thought, but nevertheless can be known. What I have referred to as the "challenge of phenomenology" is precisely the *problematic of incommensurability*.

What is at stake, first of all, is an account of how that which is incommensurate would even make a showing. In other words, how can that which is transcendent "appear" *as transcendent*, given the phenomenological conditions of knowing? As Marion and Levinas correctly observe, within phenomenology it is a reduction to the (immanent) sphere of the constituting ego which is the condition of possibility for knowing – a reduction which would seem to preclude the appearance of a genuine transcendence, since the transcendent would have to show up *in terms of* the ego's horizon, rather than on its own terms. Marion's strategy for grappling with this problem is to displace the phenomenological conditions of knowing (which I will critique below); my strategy, sketched here and then developed in Part Three ("Trajectories," Chapter 5), will be to rethink the means of appearance while retaining the phenomenological conditions.

Putting transcendence into words: the question of language and concepts

The second question will then be: how will it be possible to speak of that which is incommensurate? As I have suggested above, the matter of *language* is central here: "concepts" are linguistic; thus what is at stake is a certain account of language. If "concepts" violate transcendence, then can we even speak about that which is transcendent? Can we speak about God? Can we share our experiences? Can we describe our experience of a poem, or another person, or a mystical vision? Is there any way to "say" that which exceeds and resists language? Or are we doomed to silence? Are our only options either a reductionistic, conceptual language, or silence? Does silence do justice to our experience? Are there not situations where speaking is imperative? The question then becomes: how not to speak? *Comment ne pas parler?* How to speak in such a way that does justice to that which exceeds description? How is it possible to put transcendence into words? How can one express the inexpressible? It is in the face of this challenge that I will make a turn to Augustine, who, of course, knew nothing of Husserl or phenomenology, but nevertheless was confronted by the same problematic of incommensurability, the challenge of expressing the inexpressible. And it is precisely Augustine who develops very careful analyses of language in this regard. Thus we turn to Augustine to see his repetition – or rather, first development – of this problematic. But further, we turn to him for an account of how to speak, of how (not) to tell the secret of the self.

Let me just briefly anticipate what it is that we are looking for at this point. Marion frames the "double-bind" rather well at the beginning of "The Saturated Pheno-menon:" it seems that we either reduce the transcendent to conceptual language, or we give up the possibility of speaking altogether. It seems our choice is either metaphysics or silence. But what we are looking for is a "third way," a mode of speaking which is non-conceptual, non-objectifying, and non-predicative – and therefore, non-reductive and non-violent. It will be what we might describe as "praise" (Augustine, Marion) or "de-nomination" (Marion), "prayer" (Derrida), or Augustine's strategy of "confession." But in order to mark out this "third way," it is necessary to first grapple with the critique of phenomenology offered by Levinas and Marion. For if phenomenology is inherently violent in this regard, then we are forced to choose between the first two options: reduction or silence. A third way will only be possible insofar as we are able to provide an account of phenomenological appearance which is able to do justice to transcendence. In order to open the space for such an account, I will provide an exposition of Derrida's critique of Levinas's posing of the problem.

Phenomenology as respect: Derrida

Philosophy and its other

The "other" of philosophy – the non-philosophical (religion? literature? facticity?) – is philosophy's "death and wellspring" (VM 79). The experiences which are other-wise than philosophy are both that on which it is nourished, and that on which it is shattered. The other-than philosophy is that which philosophy desires and that which it cannot have; that which drives philosophy and that which displaces philosophy. The problem is that philosophy is not always wont to admit this weakness or lack, this dangerous liaison with non-philosophy. Thus we are bequeathed, from the Greeks, a myth of philosophy's purity. For both Husserl and Heidegger,[70] Derrida comments, "the entirety of philosophy is conceived on the basis of its Greek source . . . and it would not be possible to philosophize, or to speak philosophically, outside this medium" (VM 81). "No philosophy," Derrida suggests, "could possibly dislodge [this Greek dominion] without first succumbing to them, or without finally destroying itself as a philosophical language" (VM 82).[71] In other words, any critique of philosophy must speak Greek. (This will be the dilemma for Levinas – and the limit that Derrida will point out.) It is here, Derrida suggests, "that the thought[72] of Emmanuel Levinas can make us tremble," for he, "in Greek . . . summons us to a dislocation of the Greek logos" (VM 82).

The initial "departure from Greece" (VM 84) was sketched in Levinas's early *Theory of Intuition in Husserl's Phenomenology*. Here the young Levinas was bothered by "the imperialism of *theoria*" in Husserl, though at this point the critique remains timid (VM 85-6). Further, Levinas is attentive to the fact that, for Husserl, "theory is correctly distinguished from objectivity in general" (VM 85). He is also "attentive to everything in Husserl's analyses which tempers or complicates the primordiality of theoretical consciousness" and acknowledges "that the primacy of objectivity in general is not necessarily confused, in *Ideas I*, with the primacy of the theoretical attitude" (VM 86). There are nontheoretical acts and corresponding objects. So here we already find a movement in Levinas, repeated in *Totality and Infinity*, where he contests the letter of Husserl with the spirit of Husserl (VM 86 n.14). Nevertheless, in the final analysis, Levinas "takes his leave" from the primacy which continues to be accorded to cognition as the primary mode of life for Husserl's phenomenology (VM 86-7).[73] (For a brief while, Heidegger is a partner and source for this project. Later, he becomes its target [VM 87-92].)

In sum, for Levinas there is a complicity between philosophies of light and philosophies of domination: to see is to know, to know is to grasp, to grasp is to control. "Everything given to me within light," for Levinas, "appears as given to myself by myself" (VM 91-2). But the question is, how can one escape a philosophy of light, or the language of light? "How, for example, will the metaphysics of the face as the *epiphany* of the other free itself of light?" (VM 92) Can the Other show up in phenomenology?

Conceptual violence

In *Totality and Infinity*, the early critique is repeated with blistering force in terms of the relation between the Same and Other. "The alterity or negativity interior to the ego, the interior difference, is but an appearance: an *illusion*, a 'play of the Same'" (VM 93). (Later Derrida suggests that "if one is not convinced by these initial propositions authorizing the equation of the ego and the same, one never will be" [VM 94].) In contrast, the "encounter with the absolutely-other" is "[n]either representation, nor limitation, nor conceptual relation to the same" (VM 95), but a "relation without relation" (*rapport non rapport*). And this "first of all because *the concept* (material of language), which is always *given to the other*, cannot encompass the other, cannot include the other" (ibid.). Therefore, the encounter cannot be conceptualized, because it is "resistant to all categories" (ibid.):

Concepts suppose an anticipation, a horizon within which alterity is amortized as soon as it is announced precisely because it has let itself be foreseen. The infinitely-other cannot be bound by a concept, cannot be thought on the basis of a horizon; for a horizon is always a horizon of the same. (Ibid.)

Thus the encounter with the other is "being-together as separation," a relation without relation which Levinas describes as "religion" – "the only incarnated nonviolence in that it is respect for the other" (VM 96). The face-to-face, then, "eludes every category" (100). The face, Levinas suggests, does not signify; the other is not signaled by the face, but rather is present in the face, absolutely present. "The other, therefore, is given 'in person' and without allegory only in the face" (100–1). Here we have the difference between signification and the face's *expression*, its presentation of itself in person: in living speech ("Bonjour!") the other is present, accompanies its expression.[74]

Phenomenology as *respect: Derrida's "Critique"*[75] *of Levinas*

In order to sketch the features of Derrida's critique which are relevant for my critique, I will consider them under three themes:

1 *Subjectivity.* The target of Levinas's critique of the Greek philosophies of light is also a critique of modern philosophies of subjectivity; and despite their common critique of Hegel, Levinas protests against Kierkegaard as well: "It is not I who do not accept the system," he remarks, "it is the other." But would Kierkegaard have heard this distinction? Is it not precisely *as* subjective existence that the other does not accept the system, Kierkegaard would ask? "The philosopher Kierkegaard does not *only* plead for Soren Kierkegaard . . . , but for subjective existence in general" (VM 110). "And is not this essence of subjective existence," Derrida continues, "presupposed by the *respect* for the other, which can be what it is – the other – only as subjective existence?" (ibid.).[76] If this is the case, then the quick collapsing of Ego and the Same must be put into question; in other words, every Other demands respect precisely because the Other is another ego. And does this not raise again the question of the possibility of Levinas's project – "the attempt to achieve an opening toward the beyond of philosophical discourse, by means of philosophical discourse, which can never be shaken off completely, cannot succeed *within language*" (VM 110)?

2 *Exteriority.* Raising this question of language again, Derrida asks why Levinas must employ the notion of "exteriority" to signify what is to be a "nonspatial relationship" (VM 112): "And if every 'relationship' is spatial, why is it necessary still to designate as a (nonspatial) 'relationship' the *respect* which absolves the other?" Is this because we cannot philosophically speak of such a relationship outside the philosophical logos, determined by Inside/Outside? Could we say that Levinas speaks here *sous rature* (VM 112)? "In vain would one

exile any given word ('inside,' 'outside,' 'exterior,' 'interior,' etc.), and in vain would one burn or imprison the letters of light" (VM 113). This is simply to acknowledge that the infinite cannot be stated because of the original finitude of speech (VM 113). But Levinas cannot respond as the negative theologian with a "disdain for discourse" (VM 116), because the encounter of the face-to-face takes place *in language*. Thus he cannot, as negative theology does, "give himself the right to speak . . . in a language resigned to its own failure" (ibid.).

> If, as Levinas says, only discourse (and not intuitive contact) is righteous, and if, moreover, all discourse essentially retains within it space and the Same – does this not mean that discourse is originally violent? And that the philosophical logos, the only one in which peace may be declared, is inhabited by war? (Ibid.)[77]

Thus Levinas remains within an economy of violence, fighting light with light, waging a war for freedom and peace – "a war which he knows is inescapable, except by denying discourse, that is, by risking the worst violence" (VM 117).[78]

3   *Respect.* (a) *Method*: Levinas's metaphysics, in addition to presupposing light and language, "always supposes a phenomenology in its very critique of phenomenology" (VM 118). Can it be distilled as simply a "method," or even later (in 1987 German preface to TI) as an "inspiration" without becoming complicit with its violence? Can one separate this method from its desire to establish itself as rigorous science, i.e. as theory? And if so, why call it phenomenology (cf. Janicaud)?

(b) *Intentionality*. Levinas also purports to retain the doctrine of intentionality, this "essential" aspect of Husserl's teaching, but enlarging it, broadening it, and thereby critiquing it, on two fronts: first, Levinas sees *adequation* as a central aspect of intentionality in Husserl (VM 118–19); further, he views adequation as that which reduces the other to the same: adequation "would exhaust and interiorize all distance and all true alterity" (ibid.). It is precisely the adequation of the object to the subject which reduces the other to the same, the exterior to the interior, infinity to the finite, alterity to the ego. Levinas, however, contends that intentionality *as adequation* does not define consciousness at its fundamental level (ibid.). Thus one could construct an alternative account of intentionality which displaces the role of adequation; indeed, as we have seen above, Levinas's project is to describe an intentional relation which is *reversed* and in which the ego is overwhelmed by a donation which is more than adequate. Second, the "infinity" which does show itself in Husserl is a negative infinity, a "false infinity" (VM 119). But at this juncture Derrida poses the question to Levinas:

> But is there a more rigorously and, especially, a more literally Husserlian theme than the theme of *in*adequation? Of the infinite overflowing of horizons? Who was more obstinately determined than

47

Husserl to show that vision was originally and essentially the inadequation of interiority and exteriority? And that the perception of the transcendent and extended thing was essentially and forever incomplete? (VM 120)

For Husserl, like the Kantian *Idea*, the infinite overflowing of horizons of experience means that the horizon itself can never be constituted as an object (even by a "divine" intuition), which is why "in phenomenology there is never a constitution of the horizons, but [only] horizons of constitution" (VM 120). The ideal of adequation is, for Husserl, an impossible ideal, indeed, *the* impossible. "This impossibility of adequation," Derrida comments, "is so radical that neither the *originality* nor the *apodicticity* of evident truths are necessarily adequations" (ibid.). Does not this insistence on inadequation indicate that Husserl, and phenomenology, guard against the totalization of the object, the reduction of its plenitude and fullness? Does this not indicate phenomenology's respect for interiority of the other? "*Is not phenomenology respect itself?* The eternal irreducibility of the other to the same, out of the other *appearing as* other for the same? For without the phenomenon as other no respect would be possible. The phenomenon of respect supposes the respect of phenomenality" (VM 121, emphasis added). What Levinas accuses Husserl of is not only a false accusation, it is in fact the condition of possibility for Levinas's own account.

(c) *Theoretism.* Can one "think" that which is not an object? Can thought be object-less? Is not phenomenology's central contribution precisely its renewal and enlargement of the concept of "object" and objectivity in general? "No discourse . . . could be meaningful, could be thought or understood. . . ," without drawing upon this notion of the object – and this includes the "thought" of Emmanuel Levinas and the discourse of *Totality and Infinity* (VM 121). In other words, in order for something to be *said, thought,* or *expressed,* it must have a meaning for consciousness "in general," i.e. for others, and thus must participate in a general objectivity. "[E]very determined meaning, every thought meaning, every noema (for example, the meaning of ethics) supposes the possibility of *noema in general*" (VM 122). Thus, we must reconsider Levinas's charge of the primacy of theoretical consciousness: does transcendental phenomenology's emphasis on objectivity reduce all phenomena to theoretical thought? Does it reduce practical phenomena to theoretical phenomena? We must recall here that there are two meanings of the theoretical: (i) the "current meaning" against which Levinas protests, which would reduce all phenomena to "things" for *cognition*; and (ii) "the more hidden sense in which *appearance* in general is maintained, including the appearance of the nontheoretical . . . in particular" (VM 122). If phenomenology is a "theoretism" in this second sense, it is to the extent that "all thought and all language are tied to theoretism, de facto and de jure," insofar as they think, speak, or express – and this would include the discourse of *Totality and Infinity*. But it is not necessary for this to collapse into the first sense: in this second sense, the theoretical can nevertheless respect the non-theoretical "as such": "I have regard for recognizing that which cannot be regarded as a thing, as a facade, as a theorem. I have regard for the face itself" (VM 122), even in speaking of it, when I understand that this of which I speak cannot be made an object of cognition in the strict sense. But there must still be a sense in which the non-theoretical is "known" and thus must "appear" under the conditions of phenomenological appearance.

(d) *Constitution.* The core of Levinas's critique regards Husserl's account of the constitution of the other by analogical appresentation in the fifth of the *Cartesian Meditations.* By making the other appear as an alter ego, Levinas argues, Husserl reduces the other to the same, neutralizing absolute alterity. We must, however, consider this critique in more detail (recalling our analysis of Husserl above): first, Husserl is concerned precisely with understanding how the other appears *as other* (presented as "originary nonpresence" [VM 123]), demonstrating his concern with respecting alterity. The other appears as other, as *irreducible* to the ego, the "phenomenologically inaccessible" (Steinbock) which cannot ever be given to consciousness. Further – and this is critical – we must conclude that

> it is impossible to encounter the alter ego (in the very form of the encounter described by Levinas), impossible to respect it in experience and in language, if this other, in its alterity, does not *appear* for an ego (in general). One could neither speak, nor have any sense of the totally other, if there was not a *phenomenon of* the totally other, or evidence of the totally other as such. (VM 123, emphasis added)

One can only speak of that which is given, of which there is some indication, some appearance; there can be no absolutely other that one could experience. However, there can be an experience *of* the absolutely other – but this other must show up in terms that the ego can understand.[79]

Second, the root of the problem is a misconstrual of the Husserlian notion of "constitution" by Levinas. Constitution is not opposed to encounter; constitution "creates, constructs, engenders, nothing" (VM 315 n.44). "*Constitution is not an invention; hence, the constitution of the other is not an invention of the other*" (VM 316).[80] "Conscious production" does not mean that I invent and fashion this supreme transcendence; it means that the transcendent other – the ego, God – only has *meaning* insofar as it appears within the sphere of the same (VM 132).

Third, the appearance of the other in the fifth CM is an "originary non-phenomenality," emphasizing the "*irreducibly mediate*" nature of the appearance (VM 123). The other is not given, presented, to the ego immediately, but rather obliquely indicated; it is not presented, but *ap*presented, even though "in person." "The necessary reference to analogical appresentation, far from signifying an analogical and assimilatory reduction of the other to the same, confirms and respects separation" (VM 124), since in order for analogy to operate, it requires precisely a *difference.* It is precisely the appresentation which preserves the other as other, which indicates that the other withholds itself in its giving. Appresentation is "respect for the secret" (VM 124) – in other words, *non-violence*.[81] Indeed, appresentation – operating in the blind – can offer only *testimony* of the other, not knowledge. In fact, it seems that Husserl is more insistent about the alterity of things than Levinas: for Levinas, only the other subjectivity is "other;" but for Husserl, all transcendent things are "other," exterior, and thus appresented (though the other ego does not ever admit of presentation, unlike, e.g. the back of the house).

By acknowledging the possibility of *appearance* of this infinitely other *as such*, "Husserl gives himself the *right to speak* of the infinitely other as such" (VM 125), unlike Levinas. Husserl "describes the phenomenal system of nonphenomenality" (ibid.). While Levinas speaks of the infinitely other, he does not have authorization to do so, since he denies that the infinitely other can appear within the sphere of the same. But if it does not appear, how could I speak of it? On the basis of what evidence?

Fourth, with regards to violence: Husserl attempts to see the ego precisely as an *other* ego, an ethical gesture which guards against construing the other as another of myself. Indeed, if the other could be presented in the sphere of ownness, it would *not be other*, as he emphasizes (VM 125). "This economy," Derrida suggests, "is the transcendental symmetry of two empirical asymmetries" (VM 126). In other words, "the other is absolutely other only if he is an ego, that is, in a certain way, if he is the same as I" (VM 127). So it is precisely the symmetry of Husserl's account which guards and respects the alterity of the other.

On predication

We end with questions of language and violence, central to our concerns here. "According to Levinas," Derrida observes, "nonviolent language would be a language which would do without the verb *to be*, *that is, without predication*" (VM 147, emphasis added). Predication, in other words, is the violent employment of language, "the first violence" (ibid.). "Nonviolent language," then, "would be a language of pure invocation, pure adoration," or what we will describe below as a language of "praise." But Levinas, emphasizing that the face is present *in speech and language*, cannot do without language, retreating to the nonverbality of the glance. The face speaks; but "there is no phrase which is indeterminate, that is, which does not pass through the *violence of the concept*. Violence appears with articulation" (VM 147–8, emphasis added). The question is: is all determination violent?[82]

Thinking the concept otherwise: towards an incarnational phenomenology

As Derrida suggests, we can find within Husserl's own account of transcendence a rigorous attention to and respect for alterity. By accounting for the appearance of the other by means of *appresentation*, Husserl is able to maintain both that the other appears, and yet remains transcendent and other. The Other is both present and absent. We can rehearse this slightly differently by returning to Marion's critique of Husserl *vis-à-vis* the reduction of the transcendent other to finite constitution of the ego. It is certainly true that, for Husserl, adequation or perfect fulfillment is rare, perhaps even impossible (as I will suggest momentarily), precisely because there is always a surplus of meaning. But now the question is, *why* is this the case? Is it due to a "failure of intuition" or a structural lack owing to human finitude, as Marion suggested? Is it the ego which deprives the phenomenon of its right to appear? Or is this inadequation instead rooted in the otherness of the phenomenon, in its *transcendence*? If the latter turns out to be the case, then the inadequation of the meant-object and the object-given would not be due to the finitude of the ego, and as such, a "non-finite intuition" (which Marion purports to locate) would still fail to produce an adequate perception of the transcendent object. In short, Marion's proposal would fail to open the space of possibility for a donation which exceeds the intention and horizon of the *I* because the lack of intuition is rooted in the transcendence of the object itself. I will first explore the grounds for inadequacy in Husserl and then go on to explore the implications of this for Marion's proposal.

Inadequation in Husserl

Intuition, as an originary "seeing," can be *adequate*, in the sense that the object-meant corresponds perfectly with the object-given, or it can be an *inadequate* seeing, which simply means that attendant and unfulfilled meanings remain – more of the thing remains to be given. Inadequacy does *not* indicate a false giving or deceptive giving (contra Marion's reading of this deficit as a "deception" [SP 103f]), but rather an incomplete giving where other possible perspectives remain. (Thus an adequate intuition would be the sum of all possible perspectives.) As Husserl emphasizes at the beginning of *Ideen* I, certain kinds of realities or "essences" can never be given adequately but rather, because of their essential structure, can be given only "onesidedly" and never "allsidedly"; that is, one could never have the sum of all possible perspectives. As he indicates,

> This holds good for every essence relating to something *physical*; and it holds with respect to all the essential components of extension or of materiality. *Indeed, as can be seen on closer inspection . . . , it holds good for* all realities *without exception*. (Id 8–9, emphasis added)

Thus in experience we are given "adumbrations" or "profiles" of the phenomenon which draw us into "infinities of experience" such that "every experiential multiplicity, no matter how extensive, still leaves open more precise and novel determinations of the physical thing; and it does so *in infinitum*" (Id 9).

Later analyses then demonstrate that the structurally inadequate givenness of (at least) the physical thing is grounded in the *transcendence* of the object to perception; that is, the object adumbrated in perception nevertheless remains transcendent to the process of adumbrating because there is "a fundamentally essential difference (an incommensurability!) between *being as mental process and being as a physical thing*" (Id 89). Adumbrating, as a mental process, is *immanent*[83] to consciousness, but the physical thing, by right (*de jure*), is that which can never be immanent to consciousness. Because of its "incapacity of being immanently perceived" the physical thing is "in itself, unqualifiedly transcendent" (Id 90). And because it is incapable of being immanent to consciousness, the transcendent physical thing is always and only given by means of adumbrations. Thus Husserl emphasizes that the distinction between being-as-mental-process and being-as-transcendent-thing is a differentiation in *modes of givenness*, a fundamental difference in the "how" of donation (Id 90). The adumbration of an immanent mental process is excluded by the very nature of *cogitationes*; conversely, the physical thing can only be given by means of profiles (Id 94).

What is important to note in the context of our discussion is the reason for the inadequacy of intuition: rather than being due to the finitude of the perceiving ego, the transcendence of the phenomenon is, as underscored by Husserl, the grounds for the surplus of meaning and the inadequacy of givenness. Further, he expressly denies that this structural asymmetry is due to anything like human "finitude":

> It is neither an accident of the own peculiar sense of the physical thing nor a contingency of "our human constitution" that "our" perception can arrive at physical things themselves only through mere adumbrations of them. Rather it is evident and drawn from the essence of spatial physical things . . . that, necessarily a being of that kind can be given in perception only through an adumbration; and in like manner it is evident from the essence of cogitationes, from the essence of mental processes of any kind, that they exclude anything like that. (Id 91)

The inadequacy of donation, which we might suggest is a "withholding," is grounded in the transcendence of the object and not, as Marion suggests, in the finitude of the ego which constitutes it.

At this juncture Husserl addresses a "fundamental error" which lies behind a common assumption, and one that is particularly intriguing against the horizon of Marion's proposal regarding a "non-finite intuition." According to this common proposition, which includes in its legacy every ontology which purports a "thing-in-itself" (which would include Kant *and* Levinas),

> [t]here belongs to any existent the essential possibility of being simply intuited as what it is and, more particularly, of being perceived as what it is in an adequate perception, one that is presentive of that existent itself, "in person," *without any mediation by "appearances."* God, the subject possessing an absolutely perfect knowledge and therefore possessing every possible adequate perception, naturally has that adequate perception of the very physical thing itself which is denied to us finite beings. (Id 92)

But that, on Husserl's view, is countersensical and fails to recognize the fundamental difference between something transcendent and something immanent. In the "postulated divine intuition," a transcendent physical thing, in order to be given adequately, would have to become immanent to the "divine stream of consciousness and divine mental processes generally," which would be quite *unsinnig* (Id 92). Thus, contrary to Marion's suggestion, the transcendent physical thing is given inadequately even to a non-finite perceiver. If the impossibility of adequation were simply due to finitude, then God would have adequate perception of transcendent phenomena. But Husserl argues for just the opposite: not even God would have adequate perception of physical things because the inadequation is rooted in the transcendency of the thing and the essential structure of perception itself. Thus the thing remains transcendent even to God.

> It is shown, therefore, that something such as a physical thing in space is only intuitable by means of appearances in which it is and must be given in multiple but determined changing "perspective" modes and, accordingly, in changing "orientations" *not just for human beings but also for God* – as the ideal representative of absolute cognition. (Id 362)[84]

Thus Marion's attempt to locate a non-finite intuition would not overcome the structural poverty of donation (*Gegebenheit*) and the essential excess of meaning with regards to transcendent phenomenon. In short, the very grounds for the possibility of the saturated phenomenon's appearance as a "non-finite intuition"[85] fails to undo the structural lack of intuition because it misinterprets this lack as one of finitude on the part of the perceiving ego.

As such, it would seem important henceforth to refrain from describing this lack of intuition as a structural "poverty" or "deficit" attributed to the ego's finitude (as Marion does) inasmuch as such language forces the ego to bear responsibility for the phenomenon's lack of givenness, whereas in fact it is the phenomenon itself which does not give itself entirely. The inadequacy of perception does not signify the ego's denial of rights of appearance but rather the phenomenon's assertion of its right to privacy, its right to refuse to appear, its right to preserve itself as transcendent and thereby maintain its identity. Thus, just as Marion suggests, it is the phenomenon which determines its appearance "as a source of right, justificatory of itself" and hence appears "on its own terms" (SP 84f). Rather than a structure of poverty and deficiency, the lack of donation signals a *withholding* of the phenomenon in itself, as itself, of itself – in short, as transcendent Other. While Marion (mis)reads the inadequacy of givenness (*donation*) as an indication of the violent reduction of phenomena to the perceiving I's (finite) horizon – "making them play roles in which they no longer recognize themselves" (TI 21) – in fact, the intentional structure of meaning and fulfillment is precisely that which signals and respects the transcendence of phenomena. The excess of meaning and lack of donation maintains the otherness of the phenomenon such that we might ask with Derrida, "Is not intentionality respect itself?" Here it seems warranted to again cite Derrida's observations:

But is there a more rigorously and, especially, a more literally Husserlian theme of inadequation? Of the infinite overflowing of horizons? Who was more obstinately determined than Husserl to show that vision was originally and essentially the inadequation of interiority and exteriority? And that the perception of the transcendent and extended thing was essentially and forever incomplete? (VM 121, 120)

Rather than violating the phenomenon's right of appearance, the phenomenological structure of intentionality secures it as inalienable, as grounded in the object's transcendence.

The *scope* of this structure, however, remains to be considered. In *Ideen* I, the archetypical transcendent phenomenon for Husserl is the physical object, as all of his examples suggest. For instance, a house can never be adequately given because the back and the front could never be originarily given at the same time; when I am looking at the front, the back is appresented. In other words, the physical object, as transcendent, can never be given "allsidedly" (Id 8). However, a number of parenthetical remarks by Husserl would seem to suggest that the scope of this structure of transcendence (and hence inadequacy) is wider than just physical objects, perhaps even universal. Thus early in *Ideen* I he suggests that "it holds good for *all realities* without exception" (Id 9). Later he remarks that it at least pertains to objects of which we have changing perceptions:

> One and the same shape (given "in person" *as* the same) appears continuously but always "in a different manner," always in different adumbrations of shape. *That is a necessary situation, and obviously it obtains universally.* Only for the sake of simplicity have we taken as our example the case of a physical thing appearing in perception as unchanging. The application to cases involving changes of any kind is obvious. (Id 87)

To the physical thing and indeed "to any reality in the genuine sense . . . there belongs essentially and quite 'universally' the incapacity of being immanently perceived," which is the condition of "unqualified transcendence" (Id 90). Only an "ideal" object can be adequately given (Id 342–3); all transcendent objects, "no matter what its genus may be, . . . can become given only in a manner analogous to that in which a physical thing is given, therefore through appearances. Otherwise it would be precisely a being of something which might become immanent; but anything that is perceivable immanently is perceivable *only* immanently" (Id 95).[86] On the basis of the above distinction between immanence and transcendence, it must be concluded that, for Husserl, the transcendent phenomenon – not just physical objects – can only be given inadequately.

A phenomenology of incarnation

Could God appear in phenomenology? If God is to be transcendent – wholly Other – then, Marion argued, his appearance must be one that is not conditioned by horizons or reducible to an *I*; it must be a giving *par excellence*, a donation which is not only adequate but excessive, saturating and overflowing intentionality. But, as we have discovered, for God to be given more than adequately he must be given at least adequately, which would require that God be given immanently – thereby undoing his transcendence. Thus Marion's proposal, which seeks to maintain God's transcendence, would seem to fail to allow God to appear, or unwittingly consign God to the same conditions he seeks to displace.

However, Husserl himself emphasizes that God's transcendence is precisely that which excludes God from phenomenology, for "this [divine] being would obviously transcend not merely the world but 'absolute' consciousness. It would therefore be . . . *something transcendent in a sense totally different* from that in which the world is something transcendent" (Id 134). Now, it is precisely because Husserl conceives of God as a "principle" or *arche* which stands as an origin, that it "could not be assumed as something transcendent in the sense in which the world is something transcendent" (Id 116) – it is "a transcendency standing in polar contrast to the transcendency pertaining to the world" (Id 133). Since, on the one hand, God cannot be simply immanent to consciousness, and since, on the other hand, "a worldly God is evidently impossible," God is denied the right to appear in phenomenology.

But what if a "worldly God" were all we had, all that was expected to appear? What if, in contrast to a god immanent to consciousness *and* a god which merely functions as a "theological principle" (*arche*), a "worldly God" is all that is possible? Would that not in fact be a rigorously phenomenological appearance in accordance with the "principle of all principles" inasmuch as God would appear "in person" (Id 44)? Is it not in fact the case that God does not appear and cannot be seen apart from an appearance "in person," "in flesh"?[87] Is it not this quite "worldly God" who came to his own but was not received? And rather than finding "no room there for its display," was not the problem a matter of finding room in the inn (contra SP 118f)? Instead of being overwhelmed by a saturated phenomenon, is it not in fact this quite "worldly God" who "bedazzles" and "amazes" with a certain "fullness"?[88] Is not our only "revelation" (SP 124f) of God an appearing of this one whom we have seen with our eyes, whom our hands have touched and our ears have heard (1 John 1:1–3)? And rather than giving himself to the point of perceptual abandonment, does not this "worldly God" give himself to the point of death, *thanatou de staurou* (Phil. 2:8)?[89]

Is not a worldly God, "evidently impossible," the only possibility for God's appearance (which has always been a bit of a *skandalon* because of its impossibility)? Evidently so. And as such, God, as transcendent, appears, like all transcendent realities, in a manner analogous to the physical thing, viz. by means of adumbrations or profiles (i.e. incarnationally), an experience which "draws us into infinities of experience" and produces a plurality of perspectives and accounts (Id 9).[90] But as transcendent, God's appearance is perceived with dubitability, with a certain undecidability (*Ideas*, 100–4), which is to say, by faith. In other words, the incarnational appearance of God is structurally similar to the "incarnation" of the other ego, whose body moves me to posit another subjectivity different from my own. But that subjectivity can never be given or present, but rather only indicated and signaled by the body which *is* present and given. Apperception, as I have argued above, involves a moment of fundamental *faith* – I don't "know" the other ego; I *believe* the other to be an ego. *Je ne sais pas; il faut croire.*[91] So also with the incarnational appearance of God: God's "divinity," as it were, is structurally transcendent and thus cannot be present or given – it cannot become immediately manifest. However, it can be manifested in a mediated, incarnational manner. But in that case, it would not be "perceived"; it would be a matter of faith. But against Husserl, who assumes that a "worldly God" is impossible, an incarnational account does open the space for God's appearance. If the other person can show up in phenomenology, why can't God?

Notes

1 Vincent Descombes, *Le même et l'autre: Quarante ans de philosophie française* (Paris: Éditions de minuit, 1979) (*Modern French Philosophy*, trans. L. Scott-Fox and J. M. Harding [Cambridge: Cambridge University Press, 1980]). Janicaud might have entitled this sequel, *L'immanance et le transcendance*.

2 Which, he also claims, is not intended to imply "any value judgment" (*Le tournant théologique*, 8). One quickly perceives, however, that the theological turn is just what is *wrong* with contemporary French philosophy (at least *vis-à-vis* "method"). How would this not be a "value judgment"?

3 Ibid., 8, 13.

4 Ibid., 9, emphasis added. My project is to show that the young Heidegger was attentive to *just* this problem: factical life resists theoretical description and articulation in concepts, demanding a new kind of concept, the formal indication. And as we will discover in Chapter 3, it was precisely the Augustinian heritage which enabled him to appreciate the fundamentally *affective* character of factical life, in contrast to the primacy of cognition in Husserl.

5 Ibid., 11.

6 Ibid., 16.

7 Ibid., 13.

8 For a relevant discussion of Merleau-Ponty on this point, see Jacques Derrida, *Memoirs of the Blind: The Self-Portrait and Other Ruins*, trans. Pascale-Anne Brault and Michael Naas (Chicago: University of Chicago Press, 1993), 51–2.

9 Dominique Janicaud, *Le tournant théologique de la phénoménologie française* (Paris: Éditions de l'éclat, 1991), 14.

10 Ibid., 15.

11 At this point, Janicaud chides Levinas's move as a theological one: "faith rises majestically in the background. The reader confronted by the blade of the absolute, finds him or herself in the position of a catechumen. [...] Strict treason of the reduction that handed over the transcendental I to its nudity, here is theology restored with its cortège of capital letters" (pp. 15–16). While perhaps missing the formalization of theological and religious thought in Levinas (on this see Jill Robbins, *Prodigal Son/Elder Brother: Interpretation and Alterity in Augustine, Petrarch, Kafka, Levinas* [Chicago: University of Chicago Press, 1991], 100–32), we must also ask Janicaud: what exactly does he mean by "theology"? Does he collapse the "religious" and the "theological"? What is "theology" and/or the "theological"? What, for that matter, is the "philosophical"? To these questions Janicaud never provides answers, indicating what appears to be a lack of rigor (for which he so often scolds those advocates of the theological turn).

12 Ibid., 21.

13 In *Basic Problems of Phenomenology*, Heidegger emphasizes that the reduction is necessary for any method which would describe itself as phenomenological, but the reduction is "not the only basic component of phenomenological method." See Heidegger, *Basic Problems of Phenomenology* [GA 24], trans. Albert Hofstadter, rev. ed. (Bloomington: Indiana University Press, 1988), 21. As we will see, Marion also retains the rhetoric of reduction in his "phenomenology." But Janicaud would maintain that this is simply retaining the family name while auctioning off the family heirlooms.

14 On this point, cf. Marion's other essays, "Metaphysics and Phenomenology: A Relief for Theology," and "The End of the End of Metaphysics," trans. Bettina Bergo, in *Epoché* 2 (1994): 1–22.

15 On the "conditions" imposed upon the concept by Leibniz and Kant, see SP, 80–3/103–4.

16 What was at stake here, Heidegger would emphasize, is that Husserl failed to call into question the Being of the being which constitutes the world.

17 This is the focus of Marion's essay, "The Final Appeal of the Subject [*L'interloqué*]," which I will consider in detail below.

18 Note, however, that Marion only takes this third reduction as a retrieval or return to the original impetus of phenomenology as seen in the "breakthrough" of 1900/01, or as found in the first trait of the "principle of principles" in Id §24.

19 While this is offered of Marion, he would argue that the same structure is found in Levinas. This will be considered in more detail in the section below, "The same and the other."

20 And continued to haunt Husserl into the last stages of his work, including the *Krisis* texts (esp. *Krisis* IIIa).

21 Below I will suggest that Levinas and Marion utilize similar strategies of locating "cases" of transcendence. For Levinas and Husserl, it is the subjectivity of the other which is taken as a limit case for phenomenological knowledge, raising "the very question of the possibility of actually transcendent knowledge" (CM 90). For Marion, it is the "religious phenomenon" which plays the role of the utterly transcendent, that which exceeds and resists phenomenological or conceptual description (SP 79/103). Below, in the section "Incommensurability and transcendence," I will consider the general problem which these three strategies are grappling with, despite their different sites and solutions.

22 I follow Anthony Steinbock in his reading of the Fifth Meditation, which calls into question the traditional interpretation which suggests that the *fil conducteur* of the Fifth Meditation is (1) to establish objectivity by recourse (2) to a multiplicity of egos. The latter, Steinbock demonstrates, is addressed by an eidetic approach; and the question of objectivity is addressed "by elucidating a mode of transcendence, that is, the sense of an alter ego in relation to me." See Anthony J. Steinbock, *Home and Beyond: Generative Phenomenology After Husserl* (Evanston, IL: Northwestern University Press, 1995), 65. Husserl's project, he is arguing, is entirely taken up with how transcendence is given: "The turn to the subject, in other words, is only one (initial) consequence of this basic concern with *transcendence*. *Transcendental phenomenology is a phenomenology of transcendence*" (p. 14). I am here trying to show that the consideration of the *other* subject is also only an instance of a broader concern with transcendence in general. On the originality (and religiosity) of this concern for Husserl, see Rudolf Schmitz-Perrin, "La phénoménologie et ses marges religieuses: la correspondance d'Edmund Husserl," *Studies in Religion/ Sciences religieuses* 25 (1996): 481–8.

23 Quentin Lauer, "The Other Explained Intentionally," in Joseph J. Kockelmans, ed., *Phenomenology: The Philosophy of Edmund Husserl and Its Interpretation* (Garden City, NY: Doubleday, 1967), 172. Anthony Steinbock provides a more recent crystallization: "How can phenomenology account for the originality of the other subjectivity that transcends my own experience and yet whose sense as other is constituted in and from my intentional life? How can another ego (transcendence in the true sense) that is not merely intended as an object in my experience be constituted as precisely other?" See Steinbock, *Home and Beyond*, 65.

24 For a succinct exposition in this context, see CM, Meditation II.

25 It is important to realize, however, that the transcendence which is characteristic of the alter ego *par excellence* also applies to all physical (i.e. transcendent) objects. We must recall that, for Husserl, transcendence consists in "being non-really included" (CM 26) – being extrinsic to consciousness. On this score, we must also recall Husserl's consistent, though parenthetical remarks in *Ideen* I, where he suggests that "as can be seen on closer inspection…, [the mode of appearing inadequately] holds good for *all realities* without exception" (Id I 8–9). For further discussion, see James K. A. Smith, "Respect and Donation: A Critique of Marion's Critique of Husserl," *American Catholic Philosophical Quarterly* 71 (1997): 529–36. See also Phillip Blond, "Emmanuel Levinas: God and Phenomenology," in *Post-Secular Philosophy: Between Philosophy and Theology*, ed. Phillip Blond (New York: Routledge, 1998), 203–5.

26 Note that for Husserl, this is undertaken to unveil the structure; thus it remains a static analysis (CM 95).

27 Steinbock argues that the account of the alter ego sketched in the Fifth Meditation is part of the "progressive procedure" which characterizes Husserl's static and genetic analyses. As a progressive procedure, it starts from a foundation which is given in order to account for that which is not immediately given. As such, it is also a foundational procedure. Steinbock's project is to locate a "regressive" and "nonfoundational" procedure in Husserl's later work. These analyses are described as "generative" rather than genetic. See Steinbock, *Home and Beyond*, Introduction and Section 4.

28 This is precisely the reason that other egos are the exemplary site of utter transcendence. If we were to describe this in Kierkegaard's terms, the conscious experience of the other is, to me, an *essential* (rather than a merely accidental) *secret*. See Søren Kierkegaard, *Concluding Unscientific Postscript to Philosophical Fragments*, ed. and trans. Howard V. Hong and Edna H. Hong (Princeton: Princeton University Press, 1992), 79–80. For Kierkegaard, this is an incommensurability of my own subjective experience and its possible expression. This thematic will be analogous to Augustine, which we will consider below in Chapter 4, in the section "Silence and secrets."

29 *Home and Beyond*, 67.

30 This line of questioning – which is Levinas's – will be pursued in the section "The same and other" below.

31 For a lucid discussion of appresentation in a theological context, see Edward Farley, *Ecclesial Reflection: An Anatomy of Theological Method* (Philadelphia: Fortress Press, 1982). While not extensively engaged here, I would like to acknowledge my debts to this text as a seminal work in my pursuit of these matters.

32 The simple physical resemblances, however, are insufficient; if this were sufficient, the most convincing wax statues or mannequins would be constituted as other *egos* (which, of course, does happen when I am initially "surprised" by one in a museum). The body must also exhibit activity and behavior which is in harmony with expressions of free subjectivity (CM 114). (What seems left unconsidered by Husserl is the role that language would play in this regard: when the other body speaks – says *Bonjour!* – the other is present in that speech. We will consider the role of language below in our discussions of Levinas and Augustine.)

33 "The 'inaccessibility' of the 'phenomenological in-itself,'" Steinbock observes, "will be the mode in which the other is given to me. The other is accessible through embodiment *as inaccessible*." In what I will describe below as an incarnational gesture, he remarks that "the other's *Erlebnisse* are *indicated* to me corporally" (66–7, 70, emphasis added). We will return to the semiotics of these considerations the section "Incommensurability and transcendence" below.

34 This is characteristic of every external perception (CM 122; cf. Id I §44). Husserl then "applies" this to "the case of experiencing someone else."

35 I have catalogued a number of passages from *Ideen* I which suggest this in my "Respect and Donation," pp. 535–6 (see esp. Id I 90).

36 I am alluding here to Derrida's analyses of intuition in *Memoirs of the Blind*.

37 Heidegger's critique in the early Freiburg period (unaddressed by Marion) will take up the whole of Chapter 3 below. Here we note the contours of his "second reduction" (during his Marburg tenure, it should be noted) *vis-à-vis* Husserl and as suggested by Marion. Throughout RD, Marion is at pains to demonstrate that "as early as 1925" (RD 72, 73/45) this line of interpretation can be found. What I will seek to demonstrate in the final section of Chapter 3 is that 1925 is already too late.

38 See SZ §69(b), where Heidegger offers something of an archaeology of the "theoretical attitude" as a derivative way-of-being.

39 Marion here notes Janicaud's observation that "subjectivity is neither destroyed nor emptied of content by Heidegger. It is metamorphosed, but nevertheless preserved and even revived through the fundamental role of the *Selbst*."

40 I note here two points: (1) from Husserl and Heidegger, Marion culls the principle that appearance is sufficient for being; that is, the phenomenon *is* inasmuch as it *appears*. As such, and against a long metaphysical tradition, "appearing is sufficient for the accomplishment of Being" (RD 303/203). This is the case only because in appearing, the phenomenon is *given*; or more strongly, Marion argues, "in appearing, it already perfectly *gives* itself." That which appears gives itself: here I agree. Indeed, my central thesis is that in formal indication there is an appearance of transcendence such that the other does "show up," is given. So in this I agree with Marion: that to appear is to be given. (2) Where I *dis*agree is with Marion's hyperbolic qualifier which claims that the phenomenon is *perfectly* given. On my accounting, the formal indication is precisely an appearance with absence, a giving *and* a withholding (cf. GWB 23–4). And it is precisely this aspect of absence or withholding which preserves the transcendence of the phenomenon; in the formal indication, transcendence is indicated, pointed to, but not made present nor "perfectly given."

41 It must be noted that Levinas does not speak of a "third reduction"; for him, it is precisely the reduction which is the problem and he does not employ the rhetorical strategies of Marion to maintain his phenomenological pedigree. At this juncture, Levinas is happy to leave home, so to speak, while Marion seeks to retain the family name. Levinas does not locate the "spirit" (let alone "essence"!) of phenomenology in the notion of the reduction. For his discussion of this and his relationship to phenomenology, see the Preface to the German translation of *Totalité et l'infini* (included in *Entre Nous: On Thinking-of-the-Other*, trans. Michael B. Smith and Barbara Hashav [New York: Columbia University Press, 1999], 197–200).

42 There is a certain restaging of the Learner's Paradox at work here, considered in both Plato's *Meno* and Kierkegaard's *Philosophical Fragments*. On Levinas's account, Husserl remains within the Platonic tradition which "solves" the paradox by denying otherness and novelty. The self-sufficiency of the soul receives nothing from others, is not interrupted by alterity. In a certain way, Levinas would align himself with Kierkegaard's strategy which is a *revelational* account. The other (the Unknown) is *given*. But what Levinas misses, I will argue, is that for Kierkegaard this is also an *incarnational* giving. The Wholly Other (the god, the Unknown) appears *within* immanence, condescends to finitude. Why? Because it (i.e. finitude) is the condition of possibility for the self to know the Wholly Other. The Other must show up in terms which the self can understand, which are finite. God reduces *himself* to the sphere of immanence. (I will take up a more sustained analysis of this Kierkegaardian account in the final section of this chapter and again in Chapter 5.)

43 Levinas uses this (rather neo-Kantian) heuristic in his first exposition of Husserl in *The Theory of Intuition in Husserl's Phenomenology*, 2nd ed., trans. André Orianne (Evanston: Northwestern University Press, 1995), lvii–lviii.

44 Aquinas, *ST,* Ia.12.1. (Does this mean Aquinas does not offer us a "rational theology" [per ibid.]? For a suggestion in this regard, see John Martis, "Thomistic Esse – Idol or Icon? Jean-Luc Marion's God Without Being." *Pacifica* 9 (1996): 55–67.)

45 Gilson's move, of course, is to show that these two "Gods" are identical. Marion's project, considered below, is to re-emphasize their discontinuity, freeing Yahweh from the constriction of Latin *esse,* which is already a subjection. Levinas offers a similar criticism in this regard: "The problem which is thus posed . . . is whether the meaning that is equivalent to the *esse* of being, that is, the meaning which is meaning in philosophy, is not already a restriction of meaning" (GP 131).

46 Levinas suggests that a "first" or originary notion of "theory" or knowledge designates "a relation with being such that the knowing being lets the known being manifest itself while respecting its alterity and without marking it in any way whatever by this cognitive relation" (TI 42). This would be "theory understood as a respect for exteriority" (TI 43). This alternative, originary notion of theory or knowledge is precisely what Levinas seeks to recover – and it is my aim as well. My critique of Levinas resides in the fact that (1) he fails to see this element of respect inherent in Husserl's phenomenology (see "Incommensurability and transcendence" below), and (2) his account of an "absolute" or "pure" intuition represents an impossible ideal which would, in fact, preclude knowledge of transcendence (see Chapter 5 below).

47 A similar account of the universality of language and the impossibility of expressing singularity can be seen in Kierkegaard, *Fear and Trembling,* Problema III (pursued in Chapter 4 below).

48 Unlike for Derrida, it seems, for whom a "preethical violence" is a "necessity" (VM 128). Is this not an "essentialization" of violence? (On this notion of "essentialization," see John D. Caputo, *Demythologizing Heidegger* [Bloomington: Indiana University Press, 1993], 119–30.) For my critique of Derrida's notion of violence, see James K. A. Smith, *The Fall of Interpretation* (Downers Grove, IL: InterVarsity Press, 2000), ch. 4.

49 For Levinas, "freedom" is opposed to (ethical) "responsibility."

50 Cf. SZ §44.

51 Levinas will describe "enjoyment" as a form of intentionality in opposition ("in an opposite direction") to Husserl's representational understanding of intentionality.

52 Levinas's critique of the primacy of theoretical consciousness in Husserl is detected already in *The Theory of Intuition in Husserl's Phenomenology,* 61–2. What he calls into question is Husserl's assertion that *representation* forms the basis of every kind of intention, even non-theoretical intentions. (Here, Levinas is in league with Heidegger.)

53 Already in 1930, Levinas remarked: "We believe that this idea of 'adequation' is the source of all difficulties and problems" (ibid., 84).

54 "The presentation and the development of the notions employed owe everything to the phenomenological method" (TI 28). Janicaud, as we have noted above, questions this confession.

55 This is why Levinas will also locate an analogous "manifestation" in the primacy of practical reason in Kant's second critique, which displaces representation (BWP 154).

56 In his paper "In the Name: How Not To Keep Silent" (trans. Jeffrey L. Kosky in *God, the Gift, and Postmodernism,* eds. John D. Caputo and Michael J. Scanlon [Bloomington: Indiana University Press, 1999], 20–53), Marion began to stake out a "third way," a way between these either/or alternatives, which he described as "de-nomination," which is a kind of non-objectifying description. Its antecedent can be found in the role of "praise" in his *God Without Being* (GWB 114–15/76). These themes are considered in more detail in Chapter 4 below, in the section "How (not) to speak of God."

57 Marion consistently argues that phenomenology is both the "end" of metaphysics and therefore also "beyond" metaphysics, because it steps outside of the paradigm of causality. See Jean-Luc Marion, "The End of the End of Metaphysics," trans. Bettina Bergo, *Epoché* 2 (1994): 1–22; RD 7–13/1–5; MP.

58 LI 669. Husserl suggests that this gradation of fulfillment is due to a temporal structure because "[i]n the dynamic relationship the members of the relation, and the act of recognition which relates them, are disjoined in time" (695).

59 Levinas, *The Theory of Intuition in Husserl's Phenomenology*, 67. The careful distinction at work here reminds one of language in Augustine, and later Bonaventure, regarding the distinction between "comprehending" God (which is impossible) and "touching" God (which is imperative).

60 I am not so sure that it is a problem for God, however. Indeed, I would suggest that God plays the game by these rules – which ultimately he, as Creator, is responsible for. God is not *forced* to appear under finite conditions; but on an incarnational account, he *chooses* to do so, chooses to give himself as such. God's incarnational appearance is precisely a "concession" to the conditions of finite human perception. How could he appear otherwise? (Cf. Kierkegaard's account of the appearance of the "paradox" in *Philosophical Fragments*, 37–48. I will take this up in more detail in Chapter 5.)

61 A similar structure appears in the earlier *God Without Being*, where the finitude of the creature forbids access to the "crossing of Being," thus the "(sinful) 'economy' of the creature" must somehow be overcome by *unconditioned agape* (GWB 108–10). For his discussion of *saturation* at this stage, see GWB, 46.

62 On Husserl's accounting, a "non-finite intuition" is nonsensical: who would experience this? A non-finite being? God? But God does not "experience" anything; he does not "perceive." Thus we ought not look for a non-finite intuition but rather an *intuition of the infinite*, which, as an intuition, remains the experience of a finite subject (and thus conditioned by horizonality), but nevertheless is experienced in such a way that it indicates transcendence/infinity. We will return to these concerns in the next section.

63 See Jean-Luc Marion, "Is the Ontological Argument Ontological?: The Argument According to Anselm and Its Metaphysical Interpretation According to Kant," *Journal of the History of Philosophy* 30 (1992): 201–18.

64 See Marion, "Die Cartesianische Onto-theo-logie," *Zeitschrift für Philosophische Forschung* 38 (1984): 349–80; idem., "Descartes and Onto-Theology," trans. Bettina Bergo, in *Post-Secular Philosophy*, ed. Philip Blond (New York: Routledge, 1998), 67–106.

65 In RD, this is seen in the thematics of the "claim" (*revendication*). The same experience, including the concluding episode of praise, is analyzed by Levinas in relation to Descartes (TI 210–12).

66 These four traits of the saturated phenomenon map onto the Kantian table of categories: "Neither *visable* according to quantity, no bearable according to quality, absolute according to relation – that is, unconditioned by the horizon – the saturated phenomenon finally gives itself as incapable of being looked at according to modality" (SP 118–19/118).

67 That is, Marion maintains the most classical distinction between faith and philosophy, between phenomenology and revealed theology (MP 588). Thus, while phenomenology can locate and point to the saturated phenomenon, in *identifying* such as "God," it must yield to revealed theology, and faith (see MP). For my critique of Marion on this point, see James K. A. Smith, "Liberating Religion From Theology: Marion and Heidegger on the Possibility of a Philosophy of Religion," *International Journal for Philosophy of Religion* 46 (1999): 17–33.

68 And as we will discover in Chapter 4 below, this is analogous to one of the challenges confronted by Augustine: *my own* subjectivity as a depth which cannot be probed, an "essential secret."

69 It is said that in Paris, one is either a Cartesian or a Pascalian. The Cartesian tradition would represent that which instantiates the violence of the concept which demands grasp; the alternative account of concepts which I will sketch would fall within the Pascalian tradition which maintains an irreducibility of, for instance, the order of faith. I will consider the Pascalian impetus in more detail in Chapter 3.

70 And for Derrida? Does not Derrida concede this point also? Does not Levinas? Do they

not both also accept that philosophy is Greek, and thus the Hebrew is necessarily non-philosophy? Must we give the Greeks the game of philosophy and play it by their rules? Could we not have a Hebrew philosophy? Or a Christian philosophy? Could we not think philosophy *otherwise*?

71 This last qualification regarding *language* is significant: it pushes the question of the "Greekness" of philosophy to the conceptual tradition of philosophy, rooted in the Greeks. In other words, Derrida is asking whether one could say something otherwise-than-Greek in the conceptual categories of Greek thought? Can one think something non-Greek *in* Greek? Can one translate Hebrew thought into Greek categories? (Was this not the question faced, not by the first Christian communities, but by the second-century apologists, and those to follow?) This raises a deeper question: could one have concepts and categories which are non-Greek? If Greek categories (concepts) are necessarily objectifying, does that mean that categories *as such* are objectifying? Could one not think the concept of concept otherwise?

72 Recall that in "Violence and Metaphysics," Derrida offers an "essay on the *thought* of Emmanuel Levinas." Do we hear in this echoes of a distinction between thought and concepts, content and form?

73 Derrida here notes that for Levinas, in what at first appears a stunning misreading, the primacy of theoretical thought is complicit with mystical communion, insofar as both deny identity to the other and collapse the separation between the same and other, reducing the difference of the other to the same.

74 Writing, for Levinas, is a system of signs, not expressions since the Other cannot be present with the written sign in the same way. In other words, writing constitutes the structural death of the author. See VM, 101ff. for a discussion of speech, writing, and language in Levinas. As such, Levinas's theory would be "logocentric" in the specific technical sense of the term (i.e. privileging speech as a site of immediacy over writing as a site of fallen secondarity). For a discussion of these themes in Derrida and in relation to Levinas, see my *The Fall of Interpretation*, 116–27.

75 "Critique" in an oblique sense, almost like Levinas's own critique of Husserl: a critique of the letter in the name of the spirit.

76 Would this not be Kant, for whom my obligation to the other is transferred from my own consciousness of subjectivity (*Grundlegung* III)?

77 Recall, however, the fateful assumptions which brought us to this point: (1) philosophy is necessarily Greek; and (2) language is necessarily the language of the Same. Can we not question both of these?

78 Cf. Derrida's critique of the violence of silence in "How to Avoid Speaking: Denials." See also my "How to Avoid Not Speaking: Attestations."

79 Cf. Rudolf Otto, who remarks, in *The Idea of the Holy: An Inquiry into the Non-Rational Factor in the Idea of the Divine and Its Relation to the Rational*, trans. John W. Harvey (Oxford: Oxford University Press, 1950), 2, that a wholly "Wholly Other" could not be thought; instead, we must provide an account of the Wholly Other which "requires a comprehension of a different kind. Yet, though it eludes the conceptual way of understanding, it must be *in some way or other* within our grasp, else absolutely nothing could be said of it." This, and Derrida's remarks, point to what will be the core of my incarnational account of a phenomenological appearance of transcendence in Chapter 5.

80 Cf. on this point, Derrida, "Psyche: Inventions of the Other," in *Reading de Man Reading*, eds. Lindsay Waters and Wlad Godzich (Minneapolis: University of Minnesota Press, 1989), 25–65.

81 Derrida, however, seems to concede that the appearing of the infinitely other to the same, its "lending itself to language," remains a violation and violence – an "original, transcendental violence" from which not even Levinas can escape (VM 125). Following Augustine, I will contest this concession.

82 I return to this question concerning predication below, in Chapter 4, when responding to Derrida's criticism of "praise" (in Marion) as a non-predicative strategy.

83 We must distinguish here between two senses of "immanence" for Husserl: on the one hand, the intending act (*noesis*) is immanent in the stream of *Erlebnisse*, whereas the intend*ed* object is transcendent to the stream of consciousness. On the other hand, he also speaks of a "phenomenological immanence" which includes both *noeses* and *noema* – the entire field of conscious experience. Correlatively, that which is "transcendent" in this second sense would be that which transcends experience altogether, which can never be experienced. For Husserl, "God" would be an example of this second kind of transcendence (Id 116, 133–4).

84 Elsewhere Husserl comments: "Necessarily there always remains a horizon of determinable indeterminateness, no matter how far we go in our experience, no matter how extensive the continua of actual perceptions of the same thing may be through which we have passed. No god can alter that any more than the circumstance that $1 + 2 = 3$, or that any other eidetic truth remains" (Id 95).

85 Recall that Marion's argument is based on the conclusion that "unconditioned and irreducible phenomena would become possible only if a non-finite intuition ensured their donation" (SP 102f).

86 Husserl's 1921 gloss on this passage is of importance here:

> It can be seen universally that no matter what its genus may be, any real being of something transcendent can become perceptually given *to* an Ego only through appearances. To be sure, that need not signify that everything real is itself a physical thing which is itself presented by an adumbration with respect to all that which it is. Human beings, other persons, to be sure, are not themselves given to me as unities of adumbration with respect to their beings as Egos or with respect to their Egoic lives, but they can only exist for me by virtue of . . . their bodies . . . which are adumbrated physical things and by means of which they [are] appresented. (Included by Kersten in Id 95 n.195)

Could the same be said of a transcendent God? What if God were to appear in a body? Would that not mean that God – as transcendent in a manner structurally identical to the consciousness of the other ego – could exist for me "by virtue of [his] body"? It is just this incarnational strategy, I am suggesting, which is unthought by Husserl.

87 Here and following, I am drawing on a Johannine discourse, particularly the first chapter of the Gospel according to John which suggests that no one can "see" God – that God could not appear – apart from this one who appears in the flesh, who pitches his tent in the world and dwells as a being-in-the-world (John 1:14–18). Thus God's appearance is possible only on the condition that God appears as a "worldly god."

88 As in John 1:14, where the appearance of the worldly God issues in our amazement in relation to its "full-ness."

89 That is, God's giving himself as crossed (Gxd), giving himself to be crossed, on the cross, is much more violent and horrifying than Marion's reading would suggest (cf. GWB 102–7).

90 Marion concludes that a "plurality of accounts" (such as in the Gospels) "clearly indicates that a saturated phenomenon is at issue" (SP 117 n.40f). But of course Husserl makes the same point regarding the transcendent object which can never be fully or adequately given, hence inviting and requiring stories to be told *ad infinitum*.

91 Derrida, *Memoirs of the Blind*, 129.

Part Two

RETRIEVAL

Having provided something of a history of the challenge of transcendence in phenomenology, and after the provisional sketch of the way in which an incarnational account of the appearance of transcendence can function as a constructive way of grappling with this challenge, the goal of Part Two is to develop this constructive proposal by drawing on two historical resources: the methodological reflections of the young Heidegger (1919–27) and Augustine's philosophy of language as it relates to questions of transcendence. This section is organized according to a regressive procedure which returns to Augustine after working through Heidegger's appropriation of an Augustinian problematic and solution.

3

HEIDEGGER'S "NEW" PHENOMENOLOGY

For the philosophers are free in their choice of expressions, and are not afraid of offending the ears of the religious when treating of subjects very hard to understand, while we Christians are in solemn duty bound to speak in accordance with a fixed rule, for fear that a looseness of language might give rise to a blasphemous opinion about the realities to which they refer.[1]

Towards a new phenomenology[2] with the young Heidegger

The phenomenologies of Husserl and Heidegger are, we shall see, "worlds" apart. However, we will not appreciate the project of the young Heidegger without recognizing it as nevertheless indebted while at the same time radically critical of Husserl's phenomenology – as still a "phenomenology" but in an entirely "new" sense. In the phenomenology of the young Heidegger, we see a *radicalization* of Husserl which is a *Destruktion* in its most positive sense, taking up and critically repeating Husserl's project, but in a different manner (a conceptual/methodological issue), and upon a different field (a question of phenomenology's topic or *Sache*). As such, we discern even a certain continuity, picking up where Husserl left off, or perhaps saying what Husserl left unsaid. After all, Heidegger confesses, while "Luther and exemplary Aristotle" were companions in his search, and Kierkegaard was an "impulse," it was Husserl who "opened my eyes" (GA 63 5). Appreciating this Husserlian horizon will open up a hermeneutic for reading Heidegger's project, from the first Freiburg period up to *Being and Time*, as a *phenomenology of the natural attitude*;[3] in other words, Heidegger sets out to explicate (*auslegen*) precisely what Husserl bracketed: "the natural attitude." This, of course, is just the project left unattended in *Ideen* I; as Husserl remarks,

we do not set for ourselves now the task of continuing the pure description [of the natural attitude] and raising it to the status of a systematically comprehensive characterization, exhausting the breadths and depths of what can be found as data accepted in the natural attitude . . .. Such a task can and must be fixed – as a scientific task; and it is an extraordinarily important one, even though barely seen up to now.[4] It is not our task here.

For us, who are striving toward the entrance-gate of phenomenology, everything needed along that line has already been done. (Id 52/56)

The natural attitude – and hence any further explication of it – is put out of play, bracketed by the phenomenological *epoché* (Id §§31–2), which, of course, is not to deny its existence, but only to turn our theoretical gaze elsewhere; as Husserl continues, "the single facts, the *facticity* of the natural world taken universally, disappear from our theoretical regard" (Id 60/68).

The project of the young Heidegger, I would suggest, is precisely a concern with facticity, taking up this forgotten project in phenomenology, and thus attempting an explication of the natural attitude, considered so "extraordinarily important" by Husserl. Merleau-Ponty suggests the same in his Preface to *Phenomenology of Perception*, where he remarks that "the whole of *Sein und Zeit* springs from an indication given by Husserl and amounts to no more than an explicit account of the 'natürlicher Weltbegriff' or the 'Lebenswelt' which Husserl, towards the end of his life, identified as the central theme of phenomenology."[5] Thus Heidegger, following a trajectory neglected by Husserl, effects something of a relocation of phenomenology, turning its analysis to a different site: pretheoretical experience. Further, Heidegger also seeks to honor the precognitive nature of this pretheoretical experience, or what he will call *faktische Lebenserfahrung*.[6] As he indicates even into *Being and Time*, the task of the *Daseinanalytik* "is not without difficulties. A need is contained in this task which has made philosophy uneasy for a long time, but philosophy fails again and again in fulfilling the task: *the development of the idea of a 'natural concept of the world' [eines "natürlichen Weltbegriffes"]*"[7]" (SZ 52/47–8). The result of this relocation and revisioning of phenomenology – a redirecting of its "theoretical regard" – is a careful correlational analysis of the natural attitude (especially in SZ I.iii–iv).

However, as Heidegger notes, this is precisely where we run into "difficulties" (SZ 51–2/47–8).[8] Bracketing the natural attitude and dealing only with cognitive perception makes things easy[9] – then we are only dealing with the "sphere of the same," that is, with *theoretical* consciousness, putting that which is incommensurate out of play – viz. the irreducibility of pretheoretical, factical life. By focusing on theoretical consciousness, Husserl's phenomenology traffics entirely within the realm of the conceptually commensurate; cognitive, perceptual, and theoretical consciousness lends itself easily to conceptual determination, whereas pretheoretical experience (facticity) does not fit the categories of conceptual, cognitive thought. Heidegger thus takes up a phenomenological analysis of the natural concept of the world, the world which is the "fund" of pretheoretical experience; but this is not to suggest that Heidegger is saying we should not break with the natural attitude in some way; in other words, there is still a reduction operative in Heidegger's phenomenology. What Heidegger suggests is that the "Being" of the being of the natural attitude (Dasein) needs to be questioned, calling into question Husserl's theoreticization of the pretheoretical sphere. Husserl, on Heidegger's account, effects a "cognitivization" of pretheoretical experience which reduces factical life to that of theoretical consciousness, resulting in a leveling of the dynamics of facticity to mere cognitive perception – a subject "knowing" an object. The challenge *of* phenomenology – that which challenges the very project of phenomenological description – is the world of pretheoretical experience which is otherwise than theoretical and hence cannot be reduced to theoretical conceptuality. It is in this turn to the natural attitude or pretheoretical life (in the sense of *Lebenserfahrung*) that we hit upon the problem of *incommensurability*, viz. the incommensurability of cognitive, theoretical thought and pretheoretical experience. When phenomenology, as a mode of theoretical description, attempts to sketch or describe pretheoretical factical life, phenomenology runs up against a wholly other*wise*,[10] a way of being which cannot be captured by theoretical description or traditional concepts. Sebastian Luft suggests that Husserl himself was not attentive enough to the incommensurability of life in the natural attitude and its theoretical description, even though the thesis concerning the natural attitude is one of the "great themes of Husserl's pheno-menology" whose "dominance can be seen by the fact that it ultimately acquires a late recognition and restoration in the *Crisis*." For "[i]f the natural attitude is, as the name suggests, a title for our everyday life, then speaking about it means we have, in one way or the other, already superseded its boundaries on a methodic level. . . . A description of the natural attitude will therefore *nolens volens* stand outside it, occupy or speak in a different attitude."[11] As Heidegger suggests, what we grope for here is a "grammar" (SZ 39/34) a way of "putting-into-words" the richness of experience which exceeds and transcends theoretical consciousness. There is a radical incommensurability between pretheoretical life – the life lived in the natural attitude – and the "concepts" of phenomenological description, an incommensurability which threatens the very task of a phenomenology of the natural attitude.

This relocation of phenomenology, then, is precisely the challenge of phenomen-ology; that is, it challenges the very possibility of a phenomenology: how will it be possible to give a theoretical description of pretheoretical experience, without thereby reducing the texture of lived experience to the stilled life of conceptual thought? Could there even be a phenomenology of the natural attitude? Here we see why Heidegger's early project demanded such sustained methodological considerations: the very task of his phenomenology depended on finding a *way* to "put into words" the texture of everyday life. Thus the challenge becomes one of "concept-formation" [*Begriffsbildung*] (SZ 39/34 and GA 59): Heidegger's new pheno-menology, with its different site, requires a fundamentally different *conceptuality*, a kind of "concept" (and an *employment* of concepts) which attempts to do justice to the otherness of pretheoretical experience, honoring the incommensurability of conceptual thought and lived experience. This method – or "way-of-putting-into-words" – will come to be described as *formale Anzeige*, the formal indication, which is a way of pointing to factical experience, giving a sketch of its world, without claiming to seize it in a rigid concept. The formal indication is a new concept, a new *use* of concepts which announces, signals, and points to that which exceeds and is other-than conceptual thought, where the gaze of Husserl's transcendental pheno-menology can no longer "see"; indeed, the formal indication, we might suggest, operates "in the blind."[12]

The task of this chapter is to provide a sketch of the young Heidegger's project as an explication of the natural concept of the world, or the facticity of Dasein. In order to do so, it will be necessary in the first section to explore the background or horizon in Husserl's discussion of the world of the "natural attitude" (*Ideen* I), the "natural concept of the world" (*Phenomenological Psychology*), and the relation between the two (in *Zur Phänomenologie der Intersubjektivität, Erster Teil*). Before taking up Heidegger's project *vis-à-vis* Husserl's "worlds," I will also briefly note Husserl's later sketches of the *Lebenswelt* in the *Krisis*, particularly his awareness of the "difficulties" involved in providing a phenomenology of the lifeworld – difficulties grounded in the otherness of that world in relation to science. This will then set the stage for considering Heidegger's critique of the earlier Husserl and the need for a relocation of phenomenology to a different site. This relocation, we will discover in the second section, requires a new conceptuality, the formal indication, the role of which I will consider in Heidegger's early methodological work. And since one of the early testing grounds for this phenomenological method was in Heidegger's analysis of religious experience in early Christian sources such as Paul and Augustine, I will raise the methodological challenge of a "phenomenology of religion" and follow his concrete analyses. Finally, in the concluding section of this chapter, I will offer a critical reading of the role of concepts in the published version of *Being and Time* and the lecture "Phenomenology and Theology," in which the formal indication, infected by neo-Kantian Marburg, begins to play the role of traditional, universal concepts – calling for our own *Destruktion* of *Being and Time*.

Taking Husserl at his word:[13] a phenomenology of the natural attitude

Horizons: Husserl's phenomenological worlds

The world of the natural attitude in Ideen *I*

With regard to Husserl's understanding of the world of the natural attitude, the immediate horizon of Heidegger's project from 1919–27 is limited to the First Book of Husserl's *Ideas*, published in 1913, as well as his 1911 *Logos* essay, "*Philosophie als strenge Wissenschaft*."[14] The most systematic development of the theme is found in the first chapter of Part Two of *Ideen* I, "The Positing Which Belongs to the Natural Attitude and its Exclusion" (Id §§27–32). In order to provide the horizon for Heidegger's critique, in this section I will sketch the main lines of Husserl's exposition.

Echoing Kant, Husserl begins by emphasizing that "Natural cognition begins with experience and remains *within* experience" (Id 7/5). What exactly "natural cognition" is, however, seems to be disregarded immediately, in order to consider "the theoretical attitude which we call the *'natural'* <*theoretical attitude*>" (Id 7/5). This shift, in the first lines of the text, becomes decisive: the natural attitude to be considered is the natural attitude in what we might describe as its theoretical, or at least cognitive, mode. In other words, I would suggest that it is important to recognize a duality of the natural attitude, even in *Ideen* I, which distinguishes between (1) "natural cognition" in the most originary, concrete sense of the natural attitude, and then (2) "sciences of the natural attitude," which are a theoretical mode of the natural attitude and operate on the basis of a certain *naïveté* insofar as they are not attentive to constitution.[15] When Husserl turns to a more systematic consideration of the natural attitude in the next chapter, this first, originary level of the natural attitude has dropped from the scene, such that the exposition is more properly concerned with the world of the natural *theoretical* attitude (both, however, operate on the basis of a *naïveté* regarding constitution). But even "natural cognition," which is not theoretical, is still, for Husserl, natural *cognition*; in other words, for Husserl, the being of everyday life is a subject who cognitively grasps objects.

The way to phenomenology begins in the natural attitude, in which "I am conscious of a world endlessly spread out in space, endlessly becoming and having endlessly become in time. I am conscious of it: that signifies, above all, that intuitively I find it immediately, that I experience it" (Id 48/51). I accept the world simply as it presents itself, as a world of things and animate beings, "human beings, let us say," which are "there" for me in the immediacy of experience.

> In my waking consciousness I find myself in this manner at all times, and without ever being able to alter the fact, in relation to the world which remains one and the same, though changing with respect to the composition of its contents. It is continually "on hand" for me and I myself am a member of it. Moreover, this world is there for me not only as a world of mere things, but also with the same immediacy as a *world of objects with values, a world of goods, a practical world.* (Id 50/53)

These things are given, however, against the background of a "horizon" which makes their presentation possible and in which things become illuminated (Id 49/52). The horizon and objects which appear within it constitute my "surrounding world" or environment (Id 50-1/53-5).

While emphasizing that the natural attitude is "a 'knowing of [the world]' which involves no conceptual thinking" (Id 49/52) – indeed a "givenness . . . *prior to any* '*theory*'" (Id 52/56), nevertheless in the natural theoretical attitude, according to Husserl, the world presents itself primarily as a *thing* to be *perceived*.[16] In other words, from the beginning we see a privileging of a cognitive construal of the natural attitude, such that the way in which I am in the world is primarily as a "conscious" subject (Id 48/51) – "embraced by the one Cartesian expression, *cogito*" (Id 50/54). And while the "world" of the natural attitude is "the *natural* world"[17] – the "world of 'real actuality'" (Id 51/54) – it nevertheless is construed as a world of *objects*.[18] In Husserl's sketch of the natural attitude, which he leaves at this point, 'I' live as a conscious subject encountering objects to be perceived. Any further analysis of this attitude, though "extraordinarily important," is not the task of Husserl's phenomenology (Id 52/56).

In fact, the "meditations" (Id 48/51) on the natural attitude are undertaken only to indicate the attitude which will be "excluded" or "bracketed" by the pheno-menological *epoché* (Id §§31–2). "*Instead of remaining in this attitude,*" Husserl remarks, "*we propose to alter it radically*" (Id 53/57). The positing of the natural attitude, whereby the world is "accepted" as it presents itself, is "put out of play," not in the sense of a denial or negation, but in the sense that "we make 'no use' of it" (Id 54–5/59). The purpose of this bracketing or *phenomenological epoché* is "to discover a new scientific domain" (Id 56/60); that is, this *epoché* discloses a field which will now become the site for phenomenological analysis. As such, Husserl's phenomenology brackets "*the whole natural world*" which is continually 'there for us,' 'on hand,' and which will always remain there according to consciousness as an 'actuality' even if we choose to parenthesize it" (Id 56/61). The *epoché*, Husserl always emphasizes, does not skeptically question the existence of the natural world (Id 56/61); rather, it simply means that the world of the natural attitude will "disappear from our theoretical regard" (Id 60/68; cf. 52/56).

Where, then, is the "theoretical regard" of phenomenology directed? To this new domain or "Object-province", the field of the ego as "pure consciousness" which, as intentional, also includes its "pure 'correlates of consciousness'" (Id 58/64). So then, rather than directing our gaze (cf. French *régard*[19]) toward the world of ordinary, worldly experience, "we shall . . . keep our regard fixed upon the sphere of consciousness" (Id 58–9/65) which now becomes "the field of a science of a novel kind: phenomenology" (Id 59/66). The task of phenomenology is an analysis of the phenomenological ego, comprised of *noema* and *noeses* which are, properly speaking, irreal and therefore do not exceed or transcend theoretical (i.e. phenomenological) description; rather, they are wholly commensurate with it. By effecting the phenomenological *epoché*, Husserl makes things easy, reduces the field to a sphere of sameness without being challenged by the transcendence of the world of the natural attitude and thereby bracketing that which exceeds experience. In other words, as Levinas and Marion have argued (see Chapter 2), it would seem that what appears (the phenomenon) is always already playing the game by the rule of the cognitive, constituting ego.

The natural concept of the world in Phenomenological Psychology *(1925)*

It is important to recall here that our consideration of Husserl's exposition of the natural attitude has been undertaken in order to sketch the horizon for Heidegger's project as a phenomenology of the natural attitude. One of the indications for this is found in *Being and Time* (noted above) where Heidegger suggests that the task of the analysis of Dasein is "the working out of the idea of a 'natural concept of the world [*eines "natürlichen Weltbegriffes"*]'" (SZ 52). However, the *natürlichen Weltbegriff* is not discussed in the early section of *Ideen* I, whose focus is rather the *natürlichen Einstellung*, the natural attitude.[20] Why, then, would we suggest that the task Heidegger has set for himself would be linked to Husserl's discussion of the natural attitude?

As we will consider in a moment, Husserl discusses the "natural concept of the world" most thematically in his 1925 lectures *Phenomenological Psychology* (§§10–11). However, the link between the "natural attitude" and the "natural concept of the world" is established much earlier, in 1910/11 lectures on the "Basic Problems of Phenomenology," the first chapter of which is devoted to "*Die natürliche Einstellung und der 'natürliche Weltbegriff*'."[21] There he indicates their relation, calling for "philosophical interest in the higher dignity of a complete and general description of the so-called *natural concept of the world*, that of the natural attitude."[22] The natural concept of the world is the concept included in the natural attitude which is "the pervasive attitude which pertains distinctively to the natural concept of the world."[23] Thus the "natural concept of the world" is the way in which the world is understood or constituted in the natural attitude.

In the lectures on *Phenomenological Psychology*, Husserl returns to this prescientific experiential world in order to trace the origins of scientific concepts such as "nature" and "mind"[24] – concepts which do not exist beforehand but "are formed only within a theoretical interest" (Ps 55/40). In this way, the world of pretheoretical experience is taken to be the "origin" and "substratum" of theoretical articulation; we are returning from scientific concepts such as "nature" and "mind" *back to* "the world which precedes all sciences and their theoretical intentions, as a world of pre-scientific intuition, indeed as a world of actual living which includes world-experiencing and world-theorizing life" (Ps 56/41).[25] "It is taken for granted," then, "that we are remaining in the natural attitude" (ibid.) where we accept the world as it gives itself, as existing actuality.

Husserl recognizes that there is a sense in which "our opinions which stem from our theoretical or practical activities clothe our experience over, or clothe its sense with new layers of sense" such that what passes for simple experience of the world, upon closer inspection shows itself to be sedimented with "previous mental activities;"[26] thus, "it is questionable whether an actually pre-theoretical world can ever be found in pure experience,[27] free from sense-sediments of previous thinking" (Ps 56/41). However, even most of these sediments, Husserl argues, can be traced to actual, originary experience. Having noted this sedimentation, then, we may still retain a fundamental distinction between pretheoretical and theoretical experience; that is, the contrast between

[1] what gives itself to us in each case as immediately perceived, as passively experienced, as existing bodily, which we grasp by merely looking at it itself, and [2] as its opposite, the thinking which we exercise upon it and the thoughts which are formed concerning these things, thoughts which may very well cling to them afterwards and present themselves in subsequent experience as belonging to the experienced thing itself. (Ps 57/42)

The world of originary experience ([1]) is always there for us and, despite changes in itself and our apprehensions, is always "one and the same world." It is the "raw material" for later reflection, the origin of all sciences of the world, "the final substrata of all thought and of all other ideal formations which grow out of mental activity" (Ps 58/43). Any assertions or predicative determinations concerning this world or objects drawn from it are "theoretical formations, existing in the realm of the irreal," though they concern this pretheoretical world. Here, we seem very close to just what the young Heidegger was pursuing.

The radicality of this return to the world of pretheoretical experience seems to be curbed or dulled in two ways, however. First, when Husserl turns to a closer consideration of the experiential (i.e. pretheoretical) world, it becomes a question of *perception*: "In perception, the perceived gives itself as quite immediate and as itself presently existing;" in lived experience things appear "without any contribution from us" (Ps 58/43). This originary experience, then, is characterized by a fundamental passivity, though there is a sense in which (passive) perception can be more attentive, implying a certain kind of "activity." In this mode of "actively accomplishing perception," "we direct our attention to such and such objects of our perceptual field, grasp them and progressively take cognizance of them." However, this is to be distinguished from "all naming, predicating, theorizing activity, as well as any other activity which would burden the experiential object with any novel sense" – that is, activities where the perceiving ego *would* contribute something (Ps 59/43). But while Husserl distinguishes pretheoretical and theoretical experience, emphasizing the integrity of the experiential world, he nevertheless always tends to reduce this experience to one of perception, which still seems to betray a privileging of theoretical consciousness.

The second way in which the radicality of the turn to pretheoretical experience is deflected is in Husserl's search for essences; that is, the so-called return to pretheoretical experience is only a means to disclosing the apriori structures of the experiential world by means of "intuitive universalization" (or imaginative variation).[28] For if the sciences find their origin in the experiential world, then their distinctions must be grounded by tracing them back to this world (Ps 64/47); that is, "every particular scientific province must lead us back to a province in the original experiential world." If this world has a certain universal apriori structure and forms (e.g. space, time), "then an all-inclusive science which refers to this all-inclusive world structure . . . would have to grow up" (Ps 64/48). Thus, "we must ask what can be asserted of the world quite universally in its total consideration, purely as a world of simple experience, whenever and wherever we consider experience as experience of a world;" that is, what are the formal structures of the experiential world? To achieve this description, we must refer back to intuition, which requires an immersion in experience of this world; *look* at it intently; and then determine what carries the weight of universality within our experience. This will require bringing "empty horizons to intuition" either by means of further experience or imaginative variation. We then "lift out just that universal feature which . . . will presumably remain for every arbitrary transformation of experience into possible experiences." This process will yield universal properties which are common to all inner-worldly realities without exception (Ps 66–8/49–50).[29] For instance, no matter what variations we imagine, if it is to be a "world," it must be structured by space, time, the law of causality, etc.; for example, the world can never be non-spatial. It is just the task of a science of the natural concept of the world to disclose these essential, a priori structures.

Far from being a consideration of the particular or singular events of pre-theoretical experience, Husserl's phenomenology quickly makes its way back to the comfortable apriori world of the *Eidos*, seeking, in fact, to put out of play the facticity and singularity which characterizes pretheoretical life. This, then, is just what Husserl means by a "natural concept of the world": "the invariant essence of the already given world of every possible experienceable world" (Ps 70/52). Thus the natural concept of the world is an essential world, the essential structures of the experiential world disclosed by ideation.[30]

Critique: Heidegger's factical world

Relocating phenomenology: explicating the natural attitude

While being ultimately ontological in its aims, on its way to this end – and as part of its very method of explication[31] – Heidegger's *Sein und Zeit* seeks to raise the question of being by unpacking Dasein's preunderstanding of being which it always already possesses. In other words, the very question of being proceeds from a prior, "average, everyday understanding of being" as its presupposition; thus, rather than seeking to eliminate all presuppositions as Husserl, Heidegger's task is an explication of those presuppositions in order to raise the question of being (SZ §2). Heidegger understands this to be an "elucidation" (SZ 6/4) of an "understanding" (*Verständnis*) which is more primordial or elemental than "knowing": "We do not *know* [*wissen*] what 'being' means. But already when we ask, 'What is being?' we stand in an understanding [*Verständnis*] of the 'is' without being able to determine conceptually what the 'is' means" (SZ 5/4). This understanding, then, is more primordial than theoretical or cognitive knowing; it is a kind of "knowing" which "cannot be fixed conceptually" (*ohne dass wir begrifflich fixieren könnten*) precisely because it is *pre*thematic, which is precisely why its phenomenological elucidation (*Auslegung*) is so difficult. This difficulty – the difficulty of philosophy, raising the question of the very *possibility* of philosophy – I am arguing, is traced to the incommensurability of conceptual determination (*begrifflich fixieren*) with pretheoretical "life."

And is not this difficult task precisely that described later as "the development of the idea of a 'natural concept of the world'" (SZ 52/48)? It seems to be the case; thus we find Heidegger's project in *Sein und Zeit* to be an elucidation of that which Husserl put out of play – the being of the Being of Dasein as a being-in-the-world, prior to any theoretical articulation of subject and object. The "one basic issue" which distinguishes Husserl and Heidegger, István Fehér remarks, is

> the delimitation of the specific field of research of phenomenological philosophy itself, in other words, the self-concretization of phenomeno-logical philosophy out of its initial principle or maxim. The basic issue is whether and how phenomenology gets access to and comes to delimit its

own field of research, [and] whether the procedure thereby employed is phenomenologically coherent or not.[32]

At stake, then, is the very "field" of phenomenology and a "method" which correlates with that field. As Heidegger learned from Aristotle, the method must fit the topic.[33]

This core project of the *Daseinanalytik* is the result of a trajectory established much earlier in Heidegger's work, dating back to key breakthroughs in his first tenure at Freiburg from 1919 to 1923. Indeed, the rigorous methodological reflections which were the focus of the young Heidegger are largely submerged in what Kisiel describes as the "final draft" of *Sein und Zeit*.[34] Thus we can better appreciate Heidegger's critique and revisioning of phenomenology in the earlier lecture courses and extant publications in which he effects a relocation of phenomenology. Here he grapples with the question of how it will be possible to conceptually describe "factical life experience" (*faktische Lebenserfahrung*), a mode of being-in-the-world which is radically incommensurate with theoretical description. Heidegger's answer to the question is found in the methodological strategy of "formal indication" (*formale Anzeige*), first sketched in his "breakthrough"[35] semester of 1919 in which he develops his own unique answer to the question, "What is philosophy?" This relocation of philosophy and this new determination of its *Sache* are then the conditions which require a re-thinking of the concept.

In the 1919 course on "The Idea of Philosophy and the Problem of Worldviews" (GA 56), Heidegger engages the neo-Kantianism of his day (and his former teachers) via an inquiry into the nature of philosophy as science, seeking to answer Husserl's call to philosophy as "strict science" in a more radical sense.[36] While both neo-Kantianism and phenomenology seek to disclose the nature of philosophy as science, even as originary science (*Urwissenschaft*, GA 56/57 13–17), Heidegger seeks to demonstrate that they diverge inasmuch as they have radically different starting points (*Ausgangsspünkte*). Heidegger effects a fundamental difference between philosophy and the other sciences by defining it as a *pre*-theoretical originary science – *Urwissenschaft als vor-theoretische Wissenschaft* (GA 56/57 95).[37] And that, he argues, is phenomenology. So what are we to make of this proposal for a "pre-theoretical originary science?" Is this a science which is itself pretheoretical? Or is it a science *of* the pretheoretical? The genitive, we will discover, is somewhat ambiguous.

The question is opened by a displacement of the phenomenological gaze from theoretical consciousness (Husserl's focus) to what Heidegger variously describes as *Leben* (in his more Diltheyen moments), *Faktizität*, and most fully, *faktische Lebenserfahrung*. In factical experience, we do not find the encounter between a subject and an object – which is a derivative experience found in theoretical consciousness. Rather, factical experience is characterized by a certain immediacy such that the subject is not yet rigidly distinguished from the object, but rather finds itself imbedded in its world, its environment (GA 56 73–5). "I" am imbedded in "life," and any distillation of "I" or the "world" as distinct components is always already a derivative mode of being-in-the-world. Now, it is certainly possible for pretheoretical life itself to become impacted and shaped by theoretical consciousness, such that theoretical constructs become "sedimented" in everyday experience (as Husserl later recognized in the *Krisis*).[38] Thus one of the tasks of Heidegger's new phenomenology will be a *Destruktion* which (as much as is possible) takes us back to a non-theoretized experience – back, that is, to "the things themselves." What he is trying to do is restore the *autonomy* and *primacy* of pretheoretical, factical life in relation to theoretical, cognitive consciousness. It is a matter of liberating facticity from the strictures of a cognitivization and exploring it as it is, *on its own terms*.

But here we are confronted with the methodological problem: how will it be possible to philosophically (i.e. theoretically) consider pretheoretical, factical experience "on its own terms" with the tools of conceptual description? In other words, is a philosophy of factical life at all possible? Indeed this raises the question of philosophy itself: can factical, pretheoretical life be apprehended by the theoretical attitude? Can we have a "concept" of "life"? Would this not be imposing something foreign upon facticity, requiring it to speak in terms other than its own, forcing it to play a role it did not choose?[39] This is why the question of "philosophical concept formation" is not an ancillary question, but an issue at the heart of philosophy, for it is a question about the possibility of philosophy itself (GA 59 §1).

The problem with Husserl's phenomenology, as Heidegger (rightly) sees it, is that Husserl "objectifies" and "theoretizes" pretheoretical experience, reducing factical experience to a form of perception, and failing to appreciate both the primacy and uniqueness of a preperceptual being-in-the-world (GA 56 91). The challenge, then, is to develop a phenomenological method which does not engage in such objectification or theoretization of factical life. For theoretical description tends to treat life as an "object," stilling its flux and leveling its dynamism by conceiving it *in terms of* cognitive determination. But for Heidegger, the topic of phenomenology – "life" or the "experienceable as such" (GA 56 115) – is not, properly speaking, an "object." To consider it as such is already a fundamental violation of its being, which is otherwise than theoretical. Thus the question, as Kisiel summarizes it, is:

> How is the nonobjectifiable subject matter of phenomenology to be even approached without already theoretically inflicting an objectification upon it? How are we to go along with life reflectively without deliving it? For reflection itself already exercises an analytically dissective and dissolving effect upon the life stream, acting as a theoretical intrusion which interrupts the life stream and cuts it off.[40]

It would seem that the relocating of phenomenology's topic to the site of factical life would also signal the death of philosophy – its limit and impossibility (to recall Derrida, philosophy's other [non-philosophy] is both its death and wellspring).

Let us recall our project and concern here by understanding Heidegger's methodological challenge in terms I have employed previously: the difficulty for a phenomenological analysis of factical life lies in the fact that *faktische Lebenserfahrung* (as pretheoretical) is incommensurate with the strictures of theoretical concepts which are employed to define and determine its "essence." While the concept traffics on the high road of universality, factical experience is lowly and singular; while the concept is abstract and schematic, "life" is concrete, rich, and dynamic; while the concept is detached and aloof, factical life is engaged and involved; while the concept is a product of *theoria*, experience is a matter of *praxis*.[41] In other words, factical life is otherwise than theoretical and therefore resists and exceeds conceptualization – and to objectify it is to submit it to the conditions of theoretical thought, thereby violating its autonomy. Here it is important to appreciate the way in which the young Heidegger's concerns in fact *anticipate* (influence?) Levinas's own critique of phenomenology: by subjecting the other (the incommensurate) to "a third term" (TI 42), the concept violates its alterity, forcing it to appear in terms of the constituting ego, rather than on its own terms. The tool of philosophy – the concept – is in fact a weapon of domination.

Or as the young Heidegger describes in the context of the early Jaspers review, the phenomenon can be subsumed under philosophy's "technique":

> When objects are approached by way of a specifically oriented mode of apprehension, and when this mode of apprehension is, whether explicitly or not, understood and used as a technique, i.e., basically as a means of defining these objects that is not, however, restricted to them, it might turn out that these objects become lost for good by being forced to conform to a particular type of apprehension that is alien to them. (JPW 8–9)

This then constitutes the heart of his critique of Jaspers, who objectifies "life" and treats it as "a thing-like object" (JPW 9) based on submerged preconceptions and the technique employed. Behind Jasper's method is an assumption that "life" is something which can be grasped in its totality; as a result, "[e]very attempt to understand life is forced to turn the surge and flux of the aforementioned process into a static concept and thereby *destroy* the essence of life, i.e., the restlessness and movement . . . that characterize life's actualization of its ownmost qualities" (JPW 16). In particular, Jaspers's "technique" imposes an assumption upon factic life which is in fact foreign to it, viz. that the subject–object split is primordial (JPW 17–19) – which for Heidegger is a perfect example of the way in which philosophy imposes theoretical constructions upon factical lived experience, conceptualizing that which is preconceptual.

But if the tools of philosophy are concepts, and concepts violate the otherness of factical lived experience, would that not mean that a philosophy of factical life is *impossible*? The problem can even take on syllogistic form:

P$_1$ Philosophy employs concepts to describe and define its topic.
P$_2$ Concepts violate the nontheoretical character of factical life.[42]
C   Therefore, there cannot be a philosophy of factical life.

Heidegger, however, challenges the argument and takes on the problem by questioning whether we must employ "concepts" in a philosophy of factical life. Or rather, must we employ traditional, objectifying concepts which reduce factical life to a leveled cognition, or could there be a "new" concept, a *different* kind of non-objectifying concept which could be employed? Since philosophy must remain in some sense reflective (requiring a reduction), Heidegger does not as much challenge P_1 as he does P_2: that concepts are inherently objectifying. At stake in the answer to this question is, on his account, the very possibility of philosophy. And as he goes on to show (and as I have been arguing), this is primarily a problem of *language* – a matter of finding a non-objectifying language.

A logic of the heart and a critique of the primacy of theoretical consciousness

And so we hit upon the heart of Heidegger's critique of Husserl: like the dominant tradition in philosophy, phenomenology remains implicated in a privileging of theoretical consciousness which construes human being-in-the-world in terms of cognitive models, such that "everyday" experience is painted with a theoretical brush, denying the richness thereof. In Husserl's phenomenology, Heidegger contends, the self's being-in-the-world is always already taken to be a modality of (cognitive) knowledge (*Wissen, Erkenntnis*), especially perception, as considered above in *Ideen* I and *Phenomenological Psychology*. "The phenomenon of being-in has for the most part been represented exclusively by a single exemplar – knowing the world (Welt*erkennen*)" (SZ 59/55). As a result of this primacy of theoretical consciousness, "knowing has been given this priority," reducing factical being-in-the-world to mere cognition – and thereby reducing the self to a "subject" and the world to an "object." Heidegger's project, in contrast, is to explicate a more originary way of being-in-the-world, to elucidate an understanding which is *pre*cognitive, *pre*theoretical, and *pre*thematic. This he describes as "understanding" (*Verstehen*) – which in fact *founds* "knowing" or cognition; in other words, Husserl provided a phenomenological analysis of a *derivative* way of being-in-the-world, viz. perception, which is itself grounded in understanding (*Verstehen*, SZ §31), as "being-in-the-world" (SZ 61/57). "Knowing," he concludes, "is a mode of Da-sein which is founded in being-in-the-world. Thus, being-in-the-world, as a fundamental constitution, requires a prior interpretation" (SZ 62/58).

It is here that we hit upon one of the Augustinian motifs in the work of the young Heidegger, noted as such in the lecture course of summer semester 1925 (GA 20). Engaged in an exposition of Husserl's account of intentionality,[43] Heidegger criticizes his mentor for construing the intentional relation as primarily *cognitive* and thus understanding Dasein's relation to its world primarily as one of *knowing* (GA 20 160). But this privileging of the cognitive is nothing new: "The priority which has always been granted to cognitive comportment from ancient times is at the same time associated with the peculiar tendency to define the being of the world in which Dasein is primarily in terms of how it shows itself for a cognitive comportment" (GA 20 163). In this way, the relation between Dasein and its world is reduced to the relation between a subject and an object – "a relation between two entities which are on hand [*vorhanden*]" (GA 20 160). But this, according to Heidegger, is to construe as primordial that which is in fact derivative. It is not the case that in "knowing" Dasein first establishes a relation to the world, nor is such a relation "first 'produced' by a cognitive performance" (GA 20 162). Rather, "knowing" in the cognitive sense is possible only because Dasein is always already involved with a world, related to it more primordially. Instead of founding, cognitive knowing is founded in a non-cognitive, pretheoretical mode of being in the world. As such, "[k]nowing is nothing but a mode of being-in-the-world; specifically, it is *not even a primary* but *a founded way of being-in-the-world*, a way which is always possible only on the basis of a non-cognitive comportment" (GA 20 164). This non-cognitive relation to the world, labeled *Verstehen* in SZ, is the condition of possibility for (cognitive) "knowing" (*erkennen*). What Husserl's phenomenology provides, he suggests, is a close analysis of cognitive perception which, as far as it goes, Heidegger does not question. But what Husserl failed to appreciate was the *being* of Dasein – that Dasein's being-in-the-world is primarily a matter of the heart.

This is why Heidegger suggests that his own disclosure of the primordiality of Dasein's non-cognitive relation to the world is also not really anything new: it is simply "the ontological fundament for what Augustine and above all Pascal already noted" (GA 20 165) – a "logic of the heart" (PIA 369). Attentive to a more primordial mode of being-in-the-world, "[t]hey called that which actually knows not knowing but *love and hate*" (GA 20 165). In other words, for Augustine, intentionality is not primarily cognitive, but rather erotic, or at least *affective*.[44] The "world" is constituted not by cognitive perception, but as that which is "loved" – either rightly (*caritas*) or wrongly (*cupiditas*), for we must not forget that there is a "right order of love" (DC 1.27.28).[45] Invoking an Augustine of existential lineage,[46] in SZ Heidegger includes Scheler along with Augustine and Pascal in his development of the analysis of *Befindlichkeit*, which involves a disclosure more primordial than knowing. Indeed, "the possibilities of disclosure belonging to cognition fall far short of the primordial disclosure of moods" (SZ 134/127) since "mood as a primordial kind of being of Dasein [is that] in which it is disclosed to itself *before* all cognition and willing and *beyond* their scope of disclosure" (SZ 136/128).

Heidegger's account is by his own confession a repetition of an Augustinian theme, one also taken up in Pascal. Dasein's heart, Pascal would tell us, has reasons of which reason knows nothing.[47] Following the lead of Jansenius, author of (the heretical) *Augustinus*, Pascal points to an irreducible (even paradoxical) heart-knowledge which cannot be reduced to the registers of reason since it is a kind of "knowing" which is *felt* rather than deduced.[48] "We know the truth not only by means of reason," he argues, "but also by means of the heart. It is through the heart that we know the first principles, and reason which has no part in this knowledge vainly tries to contest them."[49] And in the same way that Heidegger argues that *Verstehen* founds *Erkenntnis*, so Pascal argues that those "first principles" which we know by heart are the condition of possibility for that which we know by reason, for "it is on this knowledge by means of the heart and instinct that reason has to rely, and must base all its argument."[50] As a result, reason is characterized by a certain "powerlessness" which "ought to be used only to humble reason."

The same Augustinian insight is repeated, as Heidegger suggests, in Scheler, particularly the seminal essay "Ordo Amoris." There, Scheler locates the "being" of the self in the heart – the *ordo amoris* ("order of love") which indicates the values-complex of the individual. And it is in this logic of the heart that the self is unveiled, for "[*w*]*hoever has the* ordo amoris *of a man has the man himself*. . . . He sees before him the constantly simple and basic lines of his heart running beneath all his empirical many-sidedness and complexity. And heart deserves to be called the core of man as a spiritual being much more than knowing and willing do."[51] This "value structure" – the *ordo amoris* – constitutes the preunderstanding of the self which shapes its "environment" and so constitutes its world in a most primordial sense. And so before "knowing" the world, Dasein has already *affectively* constituted the world as an object of love (or hate): "The goods along the route of a man's life, the practical things, the resistances to willing and acting against which he sets his will, are from the very first always inspected and 'sighted,' as it were, by the particular selective mechanism of his *ordo amoris*."[52] This is what Heidegger will later describe as Dasein's preunderstanding and the prior (affective) interpretation of the world.

What makes Heidegger's task so difficult is that by committing himself to an elucidation of the pretheoretical, non-cognitive mode of being-in-the-world of Dasein, his phenomenology is really attempting to disclose a paradoxical logic of the heart – to describe theoretically how Dasein pretheoretically discloses its world (GA 20 162). It is this "prior interpretation" (SZ 62/58) of being-in-the-world that Heidegger takes up in SZ I.3, providing what we might describe as a correlational analysis of the natural attitude – a being in the world which is more primordial than cognitive perception. Here, "the nearest kind of association [*Umgang*] is not mere perceptual cognition [contra Husserl], but rather, a handling, a using, a taking care of things which has its own kind of 'knowledge'" (SZ 67/63). The intentionality of perception, privileged in Husserl's phenomenology, is founded in care (*Besorgen*), a more originary meaning of the world whereby the world is not constituted as a collection of objects to be perceived, but as things (*pragmata*) to be used within an environment (SZ 68/64). Indeed, for a thing to be perceived as an "object," there must be a certain breakdown within one's environment; that is, what phenomenology has taken as the exemplary relation to the world is in a certain sense abnormal: "When we just look at things 'theoretically,' we lack an understanding of handiness" (SZ 69/65).

This question of the theoretical attitude is significant, I think, since what is at stake here is the possibility of philosophy – which *is* theoretical in a certain sense; that is, philosophical descriptions must be somewhat reflective. But there is also a sense in which I would say that the theoretical attitude is in a way *un*natural, a modification of and abstraction from everyday naïve experience. Or as Kovacs puts it, "the theoretical attitude is not the rule but the exception in living."[53] Thus, when Heidegger traces the genealogy[54] of the theoretical attitude, we find that "science" or theory is a derivative mode of being-in-the-world (SZ 357/327): "circumspect taking care of things at hand changes over into the investigation of things objectively present found in the world." The "change-over" from the natural to the theoretical attitude is not a move from praxis to theory (since science itself is a praxis), but rather a changing of the horizon upon which one projects beings, such that the tool in circumspection is now thematized as an "object" with properties to be analyzed (SZ 361–3/330–2). A change of attitude is effected by transforming the "understanding of being" which functions as the horizon against which things appear; thus the object "shows itself differently" when that horizon is modified. The world is opened or "released" in a new way. However, this is only possible as a transformation of a previous understanding of being, a modification of being-in-the-world (SZ 364/332–3).

It is important for us to appreciate here the derivative character of the theoretical attitude – which, Heidegger contends, is precisely that which Husserl, for the most part, was concerned. More generally, by privileging cognitive perception as primordial, we might suggest that Husserl effected a certain theoreticization of the intentional relation. While a phenomenological analysis of theoretical consciousness and cognitive perception is certainly possible (as in Husserl), it fails to sketch the being of "life" in its fullness, insofar as the "reduction" reduces the field to only perceptual consciousness. In this way, phenomenological description is concerned only with the "same," with a field which is completely commensurate with theor-etical description. Husserl's bracketing of the natural attitude effects what the young Levinas (following the early Heidegger) described as a "neutralization" of life:

> But by virtue of the primacy of theory, Husserl does not wonder how this "neutralization" of our life, which nevertheless is still an act of our life, has its foundation in life. . . . Consequently, despite the revolutionary character of the phenomenological reduction, the revolution which it accomplishes is, in Husserl's philosophy, possible only to the extent that the natural attitude is [construed as] theoretical.[55]

Phenomenology, so long as it is concerned only with a theoreticized experience, a cognitive consciousness, is not challenged by anything other than itself, by anything different. It is only when phenomenology seeks to elucidate the excessiveness and irreducibility of pretheoretical "life" that it is confronted by the problem of the incommensurability between pretheoretical experience and theoretical description. Since that is precisely the project taken up by the young Heidegger, we must move on to consider how such a phenomenology will be possible. For have we not run up against the limits of phenomenology, even philosophy? Could there be a philosophical description of precognitive experience? What could be *said*?

Finding words for facticity: formal indication as a "grammar"

"Words are lacking": the demand for new "concepts"

The elusiveness of facticity

It is the relocation of phenomenology and taking up the task of an elucidation of factical life (heir of the natural attitude) that brings Heidegger to the fundamental problem of concept formation. In the summer of 1920 he devoted an entire lecture course to the problem, where he suggests that the issue of concept formation (*Begriffsbildung*) lies at the very heart of phenomenology as a question of method and the possibility of "access" to pretheoretical "life."[56] The following summer, at the beginning of his course *Einleitung in die Phänomenologie der Religion*, he again takes up the issue of concept formation as central to the problematics of phenomenology *vis-à-vis* factical lived experience (GA 60 §§1–4). As Jean Greisch comments, "The questions of method, which have an effect on the philosophy of religion, primarily take up the question of the status of phenomenology itself, and even the status of philosophy itself in the sense of *an appropriate conceptuality*."[57]

When phenomenology moves to consider and explicate pretheoretical or factical life, it is met by a dynamics and flux which both exceeds and resists theoretical articulation. Philosophy, as necessarily *reflective* rather than *immediate*, is faced with the challenge of expressing subjectivity without becoming "objective" (in the Kierkegaardian sense[58]) – which was precisely the problem with "traditional" concepts and Husserl's phenomenology. Based on a logical prejudice, theoretical concepts treat the world as a collection of objects present-at-hand and therefore function predicatively (SZ §33). As is generally the case (particularly in SZ), when Heidegger wants to demonstrate that such objectification characterizes Husserl's phenomenology, he shows the way it is operative in Descartes. Considering the way in which "the tradition passed over the question of the worldhood of the world" (GA 20 171), he considers the example of Descartes: "In what way is the being of the world defined here? – from a very precise kind of knowledge of objects, the mathematical. The being of the world is nothing other than the *objectivity of the apprehension of nature through calculative measurement*" (GA 20 181). As such, the world is subjected to a particular theoretical prejudice (here mathematical) rather than being disclosed *from itself*, from the ground up. The world is created in the image of theoretical thought. "It is thus in Descartes," he concludes, "that we see most clearly and simply that a whole chain of presuppositions deviates from the true phenomenon of the world" (GA 20 184). The world remains "*deprived of its worldhood,* since the primary exhibition of the authentic reality of the world should be referred to the original task of an analysis of reality itself, which would first have to disregard every specifically theoretical objectification" (GA 20 184).

This critique of the objectifying character of theory hits home for Heidegger, however. For is not Heidegger nevertheless engaged in philosophical discourse? Is not Heidegger's own philosophy (whether it be the "hermeneutics of facticity" or "fundamental ontology") subject to the same criticisms he leveled against the Western philosophical tradition? Is not the analysis of Dasein an objectifying discourse inasmuch as it employs theoretical concepts? Heidegger poses these questions to himself: "But how shall the worldhood of the world be positively determined? *How can something be said* about the structure of worldhood so that we first of all disregard all theory and particularly this extreme objectification?" (GA 20 185, emphasis added). Would not the very articulation of worldhood already compromise its pretheoretical character, insofar as it would be formulated with the use of concepts? Notice the very formulation of the question: it is not a matter of *what* can be said, but *how* it can be said. In response to these questions, Heidegger contends that not all concepts (or *employment* of concepts) are objectifying: there is a distinction between theoretical assertions which objectify nature as present (*Aufzeigen*), and quasi-theoretical assertions which merely "indicate" (*anzeigen*). In other words, Heidegger points to a kind of third way between objectification and immediacy (an immediacy which would constitute a "philosophical silence"[59]).

So "if phenomenology as the hermeneutics of facticity is *neither* the immediacy of life *nor* scientific concept formation, what is it?"[60] When we take up a phenomenology of the natural attitude, Heidegger says, we find that "not only most of the words are lacking but above all the 'grammar'" (SZ 39/34). Since philosophy tends to traffic in objectifying concepts which are unsuited and do violence to factical life, the phenomenologist of facticity finds his or her previous set of conceptual tools unhelpful, even harmful. It is this challenge which forces Heidegger to employ an awkward and "inelegant" mode of expression that contributes to "the complexity of our concept-formation" (SZ 39/34). The challenge for a phenomenology of factical life is to find the words – indeed, a "grammar" – which will do justice to the fullness of lived experience, a way of describing and giving an account of pretheoretical life without stilling its flux and reducing its dynamics to static theoretical concepts. It becomes, in short, a question of how one speaks. *Comment ne pas parler?* How will it be possible to "put into words" that which exceeds language? How will a phenomenology of the natural attitude (factical life) avoid the theoreticization which accompanied Husserl's project?

The ethics of Begriffsbildung

As Heidegger concludes, then, the relocation of philosophy as a phenomenology of facticity calls for an entirely new conceptuality – one that is not a concept at all, a concept which avoids grasping. But why is this such a critical question for Heidegger? Why this attentiveness to method? Because, in essence, I would suggest, there is an *ethics* of method. Heidegger is answering a kind of methodological imperative which resonates with the call of justice. For the question he is really grappling with is: how can one do justice to the incommensurability of factical lived experience? The radically new categories of factical life experience collapse the "traditional system of categories" and call for a retooling of theory itself (GA 60 54). This requires, however, that one reject the presupposition that description is always theorizing, as well as the assumption that verbal expression always constitutes a generalization or objectification (GA 56/57 111–12). Thus Heidegger rejects any notion that language is inherently a violation of transcendence or unable to grant non-violent "access" to the incommensurable. He does recognize that, coupled with a certain attitude or *Bestimmung*, theoretical concepts do function in an objectifying manner. That, however, is the product of the attunement and not the concepts *per se*. In other words, if concepts are treated or interpreted as delivering the world "as it is," present-at-hand, then the accompanying theoretical description will necessarily be objectifying. But if philosophy discards both the presupposition that experience can be made present-at-hand, *and* rejects the assumption that description is inherently objectifying, then it is possible to have a science of pretheoretical experience. And such a philosophy will avoid the pitfalls of neo-Kantian theoretical primacy by interpreting concepts as formal indications.

In a recent essay, John van Buren suggests that it is precisely in the methodological notion of formal indication that we find an indication of ethics in the early Heidegger.[61] The methodological strategy of formal indication is the product of a concern for "humility before the mystery" of the *mysterium tremendum* of the mystical tradition,[62] behind which operates "the profoundly ethical significance of a stress on . . . alterity."[63] As I have tried to sketch here, this is particularly the case if by "ethics" we mean *respect* for alterity and otherness. Heidegger's project seems to be grappling with the question of justice: namely, how can we do justice to the incommensurability of factical life experience? How can we describe factical life in such a way that honors its excessiveness? While Heidegger's concern is not specifically the alterity and transcendence of the ethical other (Levinas) or God (Marion), I do want to suggest that the strategy of formal indication grapples with an analogous challenge of incommensurability and can be helpfully adopted as a strategy for *speaking* of those other particular instances of transcendence. What I mean to point out is this: what we find in Heidegger is *not* a Levinasian ethics of the widow, orphan, and the stranger – since as John Caputo has remarked,

> If one asks, from a Levinasian perspective, what has become of the biblical call of the "widow, the orphan, and the stranger" in Heidegger's later writings, the answer is that it was never there, that it was omitted from the earliest Freiburg period on, that it was excised from his hermeneutics of the factical life of the New Testament right from the start, in favor of the machismo of Christian soldiering.[64]

However, what we *do* find in the young Heidegger's methodological considerations is an *answer* to the Levinasian critique of theory and conceptualization. Levinas considers conceptual thought, and phenomenology in particular, to be inherently violent insofar as it undoes the transcendence and alterity of that which is "known" (see Chapter 2 above). "This mode of depriving the known being of its alterity," Levinas argues, "can be accomplished only if it is aimed at through a third term," that is, "a concept" (TI 42). Thus the "object" is co-opted by the knowing ego, deprived of its transcendence (or incommensurability) and forced to appear within the sphere of the same under the rules of appearance established by the ego (TI 44). Captured by the concept, the object "is somehow betrayed, surrenders, is given in the horizon in which it loses itself and appears, lays itself open to grasp, becomes a concept. To know amounts to grasping being out of nothing or reducing it to nothing, removing from it its alterity" (ibid.).

But is this not precisely Heidegger's concern regarding the traditional interpretation of concepts, which treats things and experience as something that can be seized by the concept and made objectively present (*Vorhandenheit*)? Is it not precisely the violence of the traditional concept which motivated the production of *formale Anzeige* as a non-objectifying and non-violating mode of description? As Heidegger formulates the thematics of formal indication, he suggests that it establishes a relation which nevertheless maintains the object in its otherness – a relation from which the terms are absolved, perhaps even a "relation without relation," as a relation in which the "knowing being remains separated from the known being."[65] It is the phenomenon or object which determines the interpretation; in other words, the interpreter is constrained by the *Sache* which confronts and challenges description. This is why the indication is *formal*: it maintains its object at a distance, in suspense as it were: "the formal indication is a defense [*Abwehr*], a safeguard, so that what is indicated is kept free from any particular relation" (GA 60 64). It is, in fact, the formality of the indication that allows philosophy to be surprised by alterity, inasmuch as the formal indication is not predetermined.[66] Rather than forcing the phenomenon to play a role it did not choose in a theatrics of present-at-hand categories, formal indication maintains and *respects* the alterity and incommensurability of the phenomenon. Attentive to the violence of conceptual thought, Heidegger produces a philosophical methodology which revolves around doing justice to that incommensurability.

A factical grammar: the logic of formal indications

The relocation of phenomenology therefore demands new "concepts" – a new *use* of descriptive language. The question of "use" is crucial here: while Heidegger does seek different language and words to describe factical life, they are nevertheless words and therefore could still become static concepts; that is to say, it is not the case that some words are objectifying while others are not. What is important is the *way* in which language is used and the way in which one comports oneself to the world via language. It is not only a question of concept-formation but also concept-employment and concept-interpretation.[67] As Heidegger suggests in *The Fundamental Concepts of Metaphysics*, concepts require interpretation; that is, the *way* in which concepts are perceived is the result of a construal. Essentially, what Heidegger was suggesting in "The Idea of Philosophy" (GA 56) was that a pretheoretical science was considered impossible because of a misinterpretation of the nature of concepts. The problem was not with concepts *per se*, but rather with their interpretation. Thus, in the later 1929/30 course, he outlines two fundamental misinterpretations of concepts, the first of which is a misinterpretation which considers philosophical problems as something that can be made present-at-hand by philosophical concepts.[68] The reason for this, Heidegger suggests, is because

> ordinary understanding examines everything it finds expressed philo-
> sophically *as though it were something present at hand* and, especially since it
> seems to be essential, takes it from the outset on the same level as the things
> it pursues everyday. It does not reflect upon the fact and cannot even

understand that *what philosophy deals with only discloses itself at all within and from out of a transformation of human Dasein.* (GA 29/30 292)

It is a question of relation and how one comports oneself to the *Sache* of description. Because philosophy is radical questioning, and because "a questioning never allows what is questioned to become something present at hand," an interpretation of concepts as formal indications maintains the subject matter (factical experience) as other and transcendent, questioned and putting into question. "All philosophical concepts," Heidegger concludes, "are *formally indicative*, and only if they are taken in this way do they provide the genuine possibility of comprehending something" (GA 29/30 293–4). They open up experience by pointing, indicating, in the sense that "the meaning-content of these concepts does not directly intend or express what they refer to, but only gives an indication, a pointer to the fact that anyone who seeks to understand is called upon by this conceptual context to undertake a transformation of themselves into their Dasein" (GA 29/30 297). Heidegger makes a careful distinction here between "scientific" concepts which treat matters as present-at-hand, and "philosophical" concepts which are formally indicative (cf. GA 29/30 294). On his account, the problem arises when this formally indicative character is forgotten and treats philosophical concepts like scientific concepts (GA 29/30 297).

That is why, more than just words, a phenomenology of factical experience demands a "grammar": rules for the use of language which will honor the richness of experience. Such a non-objectifying "concept" attempts to describe pretheoretical experience, but in such a way that it honors or "respects" the dynamics and excess of "life" which cannot be stilled or grasped by theoretical concepts (i.e. traditional concepts, concepts understood scientifically). This is why the Husserlian notion of "fulfillment" becomes, for Heidegger, a matter of "enactment," or what he describes as the *Vollzugsinn*, the "enactment-sense" in which the meaning of the concept is only fulfilled when the "listener" is directed to experience the thing itself. Thus the grammar and language of SZ is characterized by a certain "obliqueness,"[69] a way of speaking which points to phenomena but at the same time deflects one to the experience itself.[70]

The secret of facticity

It seems to me that we can understand Heidegger's methodological development by considering his challenge in terms of the thematics of a "secret." Dasein's factical experience, as radically *mine*, and thus singular and private, constitutes what Kierkegaard would describe as an "essential secret." In fact, one of the anticipations of Heidegger's "formal indication" is found in Kierkegaard's strategy of "indirect communication." How are the two related? Both,[71] I am arguing, are strategies of obliquely "indicating" a secret which cannot be told, a secret which is incommensurate with the public traffic of language.

Recall the main contours of Kierkegaard's notion of indirect communication: the most developed discussion of indirect communication in the pseudonymous corpus arises in the *Postscript* to Climacus's *Philosophical Fragments*. As such, I think it is important to suggest that a consideration of the methodological question in the *Postscript* must start within the project of the *Fragments*, viz. the exploration of the possibility of a historical moment having eternal significance. On Climacus's accounting, the genius and novelty of Christianity (unnamed in the *Fragments*) is its thought of time – that history is essential to the "happening" of truth. And if the moment (*Augenblick*) of truth, so to speak, is to have decisive historical significance – that is, if it is to be more than the Socratic "occasion" whereby time is forgotten – then the learner must lack the condition for the truth; that is, he must be in untruth. The learner or follower must not be in possession of the condition, otherwise learning is simply Socratic recollection and the moment is only an occasion and has no significance. Instead, it is necessary that the god[72] himself appear in history and provide the condition for the learner. This is because in order to provide the condition, the teacher must be the god; but in order for him to put the learner in possession of it, he must be human. The object of faith, then, is not an ahistorical teaching but rather a historical teacher; as such, the teacher cannot be discarded as in the Socratic. But inasmuch as faith does not consist in mere historical knowledge but rather eternal concern with the historical existence of the teacher, it is possible for the contemporary of the teacher nevertheless to be a non-contemporary because the god cannot be known immediately. Thus, one does not become a contemporary by virtue of historical proximity but rather by faith; as such, later followers enter into the same relation as contemporaries.

At this juncture, the question arises: what, then, is the advantage of being a contemporary follower? None, concludes Climacus, with respect to one's relation to the god. However, while the contemporary follower does not have an advantage, the primal community of followers nevertheless has significance inasmuch as they provide the original attestation to the appearance of the god.

> Just as the historical becomes the occasion for the contemporary to become
> a follower – by receiving the condition, please note, from the god himself
> (for otherwise we speak Socratically) – so the report of the contemporaries
> becomes the occasion for everyone coming later to become a follower – by
> receiving the condition, please note, from the god himself.[73]

It is not the case that the contemporaries received the condition from the god and that later generations now receive the condition from the contemporaries; if that were the case, then the later generations would come to believe not in the god but in the contemporary. Instead, the god provides the condition both for the contemporaries and the later followers, but for the contemporary, the historical appearance of the god is the occasion for faith, whereas for the later follower, it is the "report" of the contemporaries which functions as the occasion. Thus it is imperative, even though "the single individual's relation to the god [is] unthinkable," that the contemporaries bear witness to the appearance of the god.

Further, inasmuch as faith is an eternal concern with the historical, the contemporary's report "must be in regard to something historical." What is this historical something, Climacus asks?

> The historical that can be an object only for faith and cannot be communicated by one person to another – that is, one person can communicate it to another, but, please note, not in such a way that the other believes it; whereas, if he communicates it in the form of faith, he does his very best to prevent the other from adopting it directly.[74]

The historical,[75] then, is something that cannot be communicated, and yet can be communicated: it cannot be communicated directly, laid open to the loupe of "the historiographer's scrupulous accuracy." It can be communicated in a certain way, however, communicated in such a way that avoids (direct) communication (*Comment ne pas communiquer?*): "in the form of faith." The historical details of the communiqué are not important, though history is essential; the "heart of the matter is the historical fact that the god has been in human form." Thus,

> [e]ven if the contemporary generation had not left anything behind except these words: "We have believed that in such and such a year the god appeared in the humble form of a servant, lived and taught among us, and then died" – this is more than enough. The contemporary generation would have done what is needful, for this little announcement, this world-historical nota bene, is enough to become an occasion for someone who comes later.[76]

The historical report of the contemporary (the occasion) must then be appropriated by faith (the condition) provided by the god.

There is, though, a certain necessity constraining the contemporary community: it is necessary ("needful") that they leave some report of the god's appearance in order that the occasion may be provided for someone who comes later. It is necessary that the contemporary communicate a certain minimal historical content; but it is also necessary that this be communicated in a certain way, viz. in a manner that will prevent the other from adopting it directly. The contemporary then is faced with the dilemma of how to speak: how to communicate in such a way that the report functions only as an occasion which establishes a direct relationship between the follower and the god, and only an indirect relationship to the proclaimer of good news. The believer must pass the report on "in such a way that no one can accept it directly or immediately."[77] This is accomplished, Climacus contends, when the reporter makes the announcement "in the form of faith": rather than making historiographical pronouncements, the believer communicates his or her faith in the historical appearance of the god. This, he continues, "actually is not a communication at all . . . but merely an occasion. Thus, if I say that this and this occurred, I speak historically; but if I say, 'I believe and have believed that this happened,' . . . I have in the very same moment done everything to prevent anyone else from making up his mind in immediate continuity with me and to decline all partnership."[78] But at the same time, I have communicated historical content, even though it remains a content that is only for faith. Thus, it is by means of the report of the contemporary believer that the later follower is provided with the occasion to believe, by virtue of the condition provided by the god.[79]

The contemporary follower or apostle is faced with a double-bind, between kataphatic objectification and apophatic silence. *Comment ne pas communiquer? Comment ne pas prêcher l'Evangile?* How (not) to spread the good news? On the one hand, the historical fact of the god's appearance cannot be communicated directly lest God be defrauded and the later follower come to believe in the contemporary and not the god. On the other hand, it is necessary that the contemporary leave a report of the god's appearance, for this functions as the occasion for later generations. The contemporary's responsibility, therefore, constrains him to communicate in a certain way – a manner that is actually not a communication at all.

It is in the *Postscript* to this imaginative project that this form of communication is labeled "indirect" and the logic of it unpacked. An essential part of the logic of indirect communication is a more originary logic of the secret and the secret of subjectivity. It will be recalled from the *Fragments* that indirect communication was necessary in order to preserve the direct relationship between God and the believer and maintain the indirectness of the contemporary's relation to the later follower. This is due to the fact that the single individual's relation to God is utterly private: "unthinkable"[80] and therefore inexpressible. It is this "inwardness" of the God-relationship which, as subjective, signals the double bind which calls for a distinct "form of communication": "he simultaneously wants to keep his thinking in the inwardness of his subjective existence and yet wants to communicate himself."[81] Because "ordinary communication" between persons "is entirely immediate," to communicate one's faith in the god's appearance directly "is a fraud toward God" inasmuch as it robs God of the direct relationship and infringes on the singularity of the individual God-relationship.[82] Thus the double bind requires a certain "art," a poetic means of communication which preserves inwardness and avoids "the meddling busyness of a third person."[83]

Indirect communication is that form which discloses that "a person's God-relationship is a secret" and yet at the same time maintains the secret as a secret, without betrayal. This is the secret of indirect communication. Ordinary, direct communication has no secrets: it is an inherently public and therefore leveling enterprise which compromises the individuality of the God-relationship in the name of "objectivity"; that is why direct communication of religious truth is "downright irreligiousness."[84] It is only indirect communication which maintains this essential secret: that the God-relationship is essentially secret. The absolute relationship with the absolute is a site of deep interiority which Climacus terms an "essential secret." An accidental secret admits of the possibility of disclosure, such as the secrets between an attorney and client. The secret is accidental inasmuch as it "can be understood directly as soon as it is made public." The essential secret, on the other hand, can never be disclosed – it is structurally concealed and can never be made present-at-hand. Here we would include the God-relationship insofar as "[e]very-thing subjective, which on account of its dialectical inwardness evades the direct form of expression, is an essential secret."[85]

Because the radical privacy and deep interiority of the individual's relationship to God constitutes an essential secret, and because such a secret must nevertheless be communicated in some way (based on the evangelistic imperative), Climacus must then produce an alternative form of communication – a non-objectifying language or poetics which indicates a secret without betraying a secret. This is because the God-relationship exceeds the grasp of objective conceptual categories whose reach cannot probe the depths of subjectivity. Silence, however, is not an option inasmuch as the believer's testimony is the occasion for faith in others and the believer is responsible to give this report. Thus Climacus finds himself between the Scylla of kataphatics (objective thought, positivist theology) and the Charybdis of apophatics (negative theology), between the system and silence. And the way he navigates the strait is by means of a non-objectifying form of communication which signals and indicates this interiority in such a way as to deny a direct relationship which would compromise its privacy and singularity. There can be no direct expression of inwardness,[86] but there can be *some* expression of such a relation. The secret – which is also a bit of an art – is to point to the secret without disclosing it to the public eye, to point others to the possibility of a private relation with God in such a way as to not infringe on its singularity.

For Heidegger, not only the God-relation, but facticity itself is characterized by this radical singularity which is incommensurate with its articulation in language. Life is too "concrete" (JPW) to be captured by its description; for instance, how can the "*experienced* antinomies" referred to by Jaspers "really be 'rationally formulated' and thought of as 'contradictions' without further ado? Do they not thereby lose their genuine sense?" (JPW 22). But on the other hand, if we could not somehow speak of this experience, would we not be doomed to silence? Between these unacceptable alternatives, Heidegger outlines formal indication as a means of sketching or pointing to factical lived experience in a non-reductive manner, pointing to the secret without divulging the secret. Since the "I am" of experience is radically concrete, the "am" of *existence* must be understood in a formally indicative manner (JPW 25). But the "formality" of this discourse, far from essentializing or reducing experience to the abstract, actually serves to preserve the fullness of lived experience in itself, by maintaining a respectful distance and simply pointing. But that pointing (*intentio*), if it is to become meaningful, must be fulfilled, and such a fulfillment must be effected *in experience*. Thus Heidegger concludes that "the basic experience of having-myself is not available to one without further ado [i.e., it cannot be made present-at-hand], nor is it a kind of experience that is aimed at the 'I' in such general terms. Rather, if one is to be capable at all of experiencing the specific sense of the 'am' and appropriating it in a genuine manner, the enactment of one's experience must have its origin in the full concreteness of the 'I'" (JPW 27). My facticity is a secret, but one that I can obliquely indicate – for *your* sake. Not in order to disclose the secret, but to direct you to appropriate your own self, to come to know the secret which cannot be shared because of its radical singularity. This is why Derrida suggests the notion of "obliqueness"[87] when pressed to tell his "secret," to explain himself. The oblique strategy, which indicates both a pointing and a deflection, is a disclosure without full disclosure, an expression without divulgence, a speaking without seizing. So the oblique strategy of formal indication is a non-objectifying employment of concepts which enables one to point to the incommensurable.

Formale Anzeigen *as conceptual "icons"*

To draw one more analogy, the formal indication could also be described as a conceptual *icon*, following Jean-Luc Marion's description, while at the same time answering his critique of phenomenology; that is, in Heidegger's development of the formal indication as a new kind of "concept," we find a response to Marion's (and Levinas's) critique regarding the leveling of transcendence in phenomenological description.[88] For Marion, the idol is a matter of *constitution*; in other words, no object or sign is inherently idolatrous, rather, it is constituted as such by a subject which intends the object as either that which will absorb its aim/gaze (the idol), or that which will deflect the gaze beyond itself to that which it refers (the icon).[89] It is a question of modality: "The idol and the icon determine two *manners* of being for beings, not two classes of beings" (GWB 8, emphasis added). What, then, is the difference between the idol and icon? The *way* in which they "signal" (as *signa*) that to which they refer. "The idol and the icon," Marion argues, "are distinguishable only inasmuch as they signal in different ways, that is, inasmuch as each makes use of visibility in its own way" (GWB 9).

The way in which they signal, however, is dependent not upon the object, but the way in which they are constituted by the "gaze" of the subject (GWB 10). In the idol, the worshipper's gaze is satisfied by the idol itself, finds its end in the idol, and fails to be referred beyond it. Thus the gaze settles for immanence and finitude, and it is this operation of the gaze which constitutes the idol. "The gaze makes the idol, not the idol the gaze" (GWB 10). That is why it is not a matter of "fabrication," for idols and icons are both fabricated. The object is constituted as an idol only by the worshipper's gaze:

> For the fabricated thing becomes an idol, that of a god, only from the moment when the gaze has decided to fall on it, has made of it the privileged fixed point of its own consideration; and that the fabricated thing exhausts the gaze presupposes that this thing is itself exhausted in the gazeable. The decisive moment in the erection of an idol stems not from its fabrication, but from its investment as gazeable, as that which will fill a gaze. (GWB 10)

The idol is constituted as idol insofar as it no longer refers to a transcendence, but has become an immanence or presence which satisfies the gaze of the worshipping subject. And this is its fundamental difference from the *icon*, whose sole function is to point beyond itself, to refer the gaze through and beyond it to a transcendence which cannot be made present. The icon's purpose is to (ap)present that which cannot be made present, that which is absent; or, the icon is a visible indicator of the *in*visible[90] in which the gaze is to "overshoot and transpierce itself" (GWB 11) whereas "the idol allows no invisible" (GWB 13).

While we might speak of perceptual idols (graven images), Marion particularly singles out the *concept* as an instance of an idol which becomes an end in itself in which the theoretical gaze is satisfied and settled, thus reducing its referent to that encompassed by the concept. "The concept," he suggests, "consigns to a sign what at first the mind grasps with it (*concipere, capere*)" (GWB 16). As such, the object is reduced to the measure of the subject's grasp. This is particularly true with respect to a "concept" of God which, "when it knows the divine in its hold, and hence names 'God,' defines it. It defines it, and therefore also measures it to the dimension of its hold" (GWB 29). In the "concept," the infinite is grasped by the finite, the transcendent encompassed as immanent. But Marion also notes that the concept does not *necessarily* function idolatrously. As with any object, it is a matter of constitution, and so we have open the possibility of an *iconic concept*: "the icon can also proceed conceptually, provided at least that the concept renounce comprehending the incomprehensible, to attempt to conceive it, hence also to receive it, in its own excessiveness" (GWB 22-3). But note that the responsibility lies with the constituting subject to constitute the concept as such, to ensure that the concept respects the incommensurability of its referent. It is a matter of the gaze.

It seems to me that in the formal indication we find that the "concept" does just this: attempts to "renounce comprehending the incomprehensible, to attempt to conceive it, hence also to receive it, in its own excessiveness." The traditional (Husserlian) concept is an "idol," both Marion and Heidegger would contend, because it collapses the difference or *distance* between that which is otherwise than theoretical and thereby reduces it to the mode of conceptual thought. In contrast, the conceptual "icon" – the formal indication – *respects* this distance:

> it is not a question of *using* a concept to determine an essence [*pace* Husserl] but of using it to determine an intention – that of the invisible advancing into the visible and inscribing itself therein by the very reference it imposes from this visible to the invisible. The hermeneutic of the icon meant: the visible becomes the visibility of the invisible only if it receives its intention, in short, if it refers, as to intention, to the invisible; . . . Visible and invisible grow together and as such: their absolute distinction implies the radical commerce of their transferences.[91]

Heidegger's formal indication is developed with just such a concern in mind: the radical difference, the absolute distance, between dynamic pretheoretical life in the "natural attitude" and the static world of theoretical description.

In this sense, the formal indication functions as an "icon"[92] which signals and points across this distance to "sketch" the contours of factical life. Lived experience, which exceeds philosophical description, is nevertheless indicated and becomes a fresh impetus for philosophical reflection; in other words, the theoretically invisible – that which is otherwise than sight – "advances into the visible" and "inscribes itself therein," but in such a way that it is not rendered visible, but "imposes" in it a reference to its invisibility, its excess. Factical lived experience (*faktische Lebenser-fahrung*) thus inscribes itself into philosophy, disturbs and disrupts philosophical reflection, "giving" that which was unthought in philosophy. The formal indication is a way of grappling with factical life's disruption of philosophical conceptuality – a disruption aimed at a renewal of philosophy via the concrete experience of Greek ethical life and the lived experience of the New Testament.[93] In this early methodological work, then, the formal indication marks a certain boundary – a philosophical limit through which philosophy is challenged by factical life. In particular, I am interested in the way in which *religion* functions as a kind of limit-case for Heidegger's retooling of phenomenology. As such, in the next section we will consider just what a "phenomenology *of* religion" would look like for the young Heidegger.

Religious experience, the religious phenomenon, and a phenomenology of religion

"The field of religion," Jean-Luc Marion suggests, "could simply be defined as what philosophy excludes or, in the best case, subjugates" (SP 79/103). But this state of affairs, of course, puts the "philosophy of religion" (if there were such a thing) face-to-face with an impossibility, viz. the task of constituting and objectifying that which can neither be constituted nor objectified. This impossibility places the "philosophy of religion" in a double-bind – the bind we have encountered consistently in this study – in which "it would then find itself confronted with a disastrous alternative: either it would be a question of phenomena that are objectively definable but lose their religious specificity, or it would be a question of phenomena that are specifically religious but cannot be described objectively" (SP 79/103). The religious phenomenon, then, is an impossible phenomenon, thus making a phenomenology of religion an impossibility.

Despite its impossibility, however, the phenomenology of religion has developed quite an illustrious history, from its origins in the work of Otto and Scheler, through its developments by Van der Leeuw and Eliade, to its revisioning in the work of Ricoeur and Westphal.[94] In fact, with the gradual establishment of "religious studies" as a field of investigation distinct from theology – and the correlative establishment of departments of religion at secular or state institutions – phenomenology has been the methodology of choice in, at least, North American research.[95] The very *possibility* of religious studies as a discipline is generally traced to movements in Germany in the first part of the twentieth century – and in particular to the work of Rudolf Otto.[96] And in the same year that Marion sketched the impossibility of a phenomenology of religion, Louis Dupré was proclaiming a time of revival: "For various reasons," he remarked, "the time appears ripe for a reconsideration of the phenomenology of religion."[97] What is required in this reconsideration is precisely a rethinking of the very possibility of a phenomenology of religion.

Given this history of the phenomenology of religion and its impact on the field of religious studies, why is it that Marion thinks it to be impossible? His answer, of course, is that the "religious phenomenon" is impossible: "A phenomenon that is religious in the strict sense – belonging to the domain of a 'philosophy of religion' distinct from the sociology, the history, and the psychology of religion – would have to render visible what nevertheless could not be objectivized. The religious phenomenon thus amounts to an impossible phenomenon" (SP 103/79). But what *is* the religious phenomenon? What differentiates the *religious* phenomenon (is there only one?) from other phenomena? And what would that tell us about the phenomenology of religion and its im/possibility? What will become evident as these questions are explored is that Marion's religious phenomenon is utterly singular, without rival, the phenomenon above all phenomena. As I will attempt to argue, Marion's "religious phenomenon" is collapsed into a *theological* phenomenon; correlatively, his (albeit impossible) phenomenology of religion slides toward a very possible, and very particular, theology. The result is both a *reduction* of religion to theology, and also a *particularization* of religion as Catholic or at least Christian – which, of course, is also a kind of reduction, a reduction which reduces the size of the kingdom and bars the entrance to any who are different. Part of my project will be to locate the *ethical* issues behind these apparently benign discussions of method, suggesting that behind Marion's understanding of the phenomenology of religion lies a certain kind of *in*justice.

But what if we were to delineate religious phenomena *differently*, in the plural? My goal is to argue that just such a space for difference is opened in the work of the young Heidegger, particularly in his lecture "Phenomenology and Theology" (1927) and the earlier lectures from 1919–23. Raising the question of the relation between sciences in the 1927 lecture, Heidegger carefully distinguishes the ontological "field" of phenomenology, the regional "field" of a phenomenology of religion, and the "field" or *Sache* of theology – a helpful corrective to Marion's philosophy/phenomenology of religion which collapses these fields. Heidegger wants to recover or liberate (*relever*?) religion, as a pretheoretical mode of existence, *from* its theoretical sedimentation as a "science of God" in theology. The phenomenology of religion, as a *Religionswissenschaft* distinct from theology, brackets committed participation in a faith community and analyzes the intentions or meanings of a religious community or tradition. As such, it stands in contrast to theology, which investigates religious existence *from within* the commitments of the community; but it also stands in contrast to a traditional philosophy of religion (if there is one) which generally becomes linked to a particular theism.[98] Heidegger's phenomenology of religion does not consider its "field" to be God but rather the experience and constructions of meaning within religious communities, opening space for a more pluralist field with space for difference. Thus, Heidegger's attention to the distinctions between phenomenology and theology in fact opens the space for a distinct science of religion or "religious studies" (*Religionswissenschaft*) – which would be precisely a phenomenology of religion distinct from both phenomenology (as ontology) and theology. This is a space for the study of religion for which Marion provides no account. Further, and perhaps more importantly, this distinction between theology and religion opens the space for an understanding of religion or religious experience as a pretheoretical mode of being-in-the-world, rather than a "theologized" body of dogma. In other words, religion is a matter of the heart, whereas theology is a matter of cognition. While this does not exclude the latter, we ought not reduce religion to a theology.

Parisian scholastics: the God of phenomenology and the colonization of religion

The horizon for Marion's consideration of the religious phenomenon is his notion of the "saturated phenomenon" (treated in detail above, Chapter 2, pp. 32–41). The religious phenomenon is an impossible phenomenon, for Marion, not because it fails to measure up to the "criteria of phenomenality," but because it *overwhelms* those conditions – it exceeds them, bedazzles them, *saturates* them with a donation which far exceeds the intention. However, let us recall that this impossibility can be overcome; "by faith" (and participation in the Eucharist), the saturated phenomenon will be recognized as "God," the "being-given par excellence" who "gives himself and allows to be given more than any other being-given" (MP 588). This is why, on Marion's accounting, phenomenology offers a relief (*relève*) from metaphysics: in metaphysics (as defined by Suarez and accepted by Husserl), God plays the role of the *causa sui*, the origin or giv*er*. In Marion's radical phenomenology, however, God appears not as donor, but as the being-giv*en*. As such, the "God" of phenomenology differs in very important ways from the god of metaphysics.

It is now at this juncture that Marion's conception of a phenomenology of religion makes its appearance. We must distinguish, he suggests, two types of saturated phenomena: (1) "pure historical events" and (2) "the phenomena of revelation" (SP 126–7/121). Further, phenomena of revelation (in a strictly phenomenological sense of "an appearance that is purely of itself and starting from itself, which does not subject its possibility to any preliminary determination") occur in three domains: the aesthetic spectacle (idol), the beloved face (icon), and finally, in *theophany*. "And it is here" – in the domain of theophanic revelation – "that the question of the possibility of a phenomenology of religion would be posed in terms that are not new . . . but simple" (SP 127/121–2). The object or topic (*Sache*) – the "field" – of a phenomenology of religion is thus linked to a (particular) theophanic revelation: "The being-given par excellence in fact bears the characteristics of a *very precise* type of manifestation – that of the saturated phenomenon or, more precisely, of the saturated phenomenon typical of revelation" (MP 590). The possibility or impossibility of a phenomenology of religion depends upon the possibility of locating this very precise and particular saturated phenomenon as its field.

The impossibility, or at least difficulty, of a phenomenology of religion is directly linked to phenomenology's incapability of *recognizing* the saturated phenomenon. All that phenomenology can do is *locate* its possibility, prepare the way for its advent, crying in the wilderness in order to clear the space for its appearance, going before (*pre*) to prepare an avenue (*ambulacrum*) for its Triumphal Entry. To *recognize* the saturated phenomenon as the religious phenomenon requires something more.

> The intuitive realization of that being-given requires, *more than* phenomenological analysis, the real experience of its donation, which falls to revealed theology. Between phenomenology and theology, the border passes between revelation as possibility and revelation as historicity. There could be no danger of confusion between these two domains. (MP 590, emphasis added)

While phenomenology can signal the possibility of the appearance of the face, "it cannot and must not understand that face as a face of charity; when the being-given turns to charity . . . , phenomenology yields to revealed theology" (MP 590–1).[99] Or as he concludes his discussion of the saturated phenomenon, "In every case, *recognizing* the saturated phenomenon comes down to thinking seriously *aliquid quo majus cogitari nequit*[100] – seriously, which means as a final possibility of phenomenology" (SP 127–8/122).

What, then, is the role and field of a phenomenology of religion? According to Marion, the *field* or topic of such a phenomenology is the saturated phenomenon, which can only be approached as a possibility; thus its *role* is merely propaedeutic[101] – clearing the space for its appearance, signaling its possibility, then yielding to "revealed theology" which is able to *recognize* and *name* the saturated phenomenon. The object of the phenomenology of religion is precisely the "'God' of phenomenology," more traditionally identified (following Pascal) as the "God of the philosophers" (who are now – after metaphysics – phenomenologists[102]). "Of course," he concedes, "even if it is decidedly opposed to the metaphysical figure of a *causa sui* 'God,' the figure of 'God' in phenomenology that we have just outlined nevertheless still concerns the 'God of the philosophers and the scholars' and in no way the 'God of Abraham, of Isaac, and of Jacob.' But one could again object that *the figure of 'God' in phenomenology is hardly distinguished from this latter*," precisely because the saturated phenomenon is a revealed phenomenon (MP 589–90, emphasis added). The topic of a phenomenology of religion is precisely this theophany; what distinguishes it from theology is simply its mode of knowledge or perception. In other words, for Marion, a phenomenology of religion and a positive theology are concerned with the same object or field; what distinguishes them is an experience of mere possibility (phenomenology) which must be supplemented by a "real experience" of this donation as historical and actual (theology). The "God" of phenomenology is simply the God of "reason – here, philosophy in its phenomenological bearing" (MP 587).

This construal of the relation is a typically Parisian gesture, not of the deconstructive variety but within a very scholastic tradition. Indeed, we have a similar framework developed by another professor from the University of Paris, who suggested just such a distinction a number of years ago:

Even as regards those truths about God which human reason can investigate, it was necessary that man be taught by a divine revelation . . . It was therefore necessary that, besides the philosophical sciences investigated by reason, there should be a sacred science by way of revelation.[103]

Thus, we must carefully distinguish ("there could be no danger of confusion between these domains") theology "included in sacred doctrine" (i.e. revealed theology) and "that theology which is a part of philosophy" (i.e. the God of phenomenology). Just as grace perfects or completes nature (a dangerous supplement?), so also does revealed theology actualize what is only a possibility in phenomenology. Phenomenology, which locates the possibility of the saturated phenomenon, is a kind of "preamble" to revealed theology, which names and recognizes the saturated phenomenon as the God of Abraham, Isaac, Jacob, and Jesus of Nazareth.[104]

Thus for Marion, as for Aquinas, the phenomenology of religion remains tied to the God of Abraham, Isaac, and Jacob as its horizon; the phenomenology of religion simply "prepares the way" (*preambula*) for faith (*fidei*). Marion's religious phenomenon is in the end collapsed into a very particular *theological* phenomenon; correlatively, his (albeit im/possible) phenomenology of religion slides toward a very possible, and very particular, theology. The result of this rather insidious movement is two-fold: first, this conception of a phenomenology of religion *reduces* religion to theology; that is, it effects a leveling of the plurivocity of (global) religious experience and forces it into a rather theistic, or at least theophanic, mold. Religion, for Marion, turns out to be very narrowly defined and, in a sense, reduced to its theological sedimentation. Second, and as a result of this, Marion *particularizes* religion and the religious phenomenon as quite Christian – at best, monotheistic, and at worst, downright Catholic. (After all, once one pushes beyond the limits of phenomenology, the saturated phenomenon will be *recognized* as the God of Abraham, Isaac, and Jacob – even God on the cross.) This *particularization* is yet another kind of *reduction*: a reduction which reduces the size of the kingdom, which keeps the walls close to Rome and makes it impossible for any who are different to enter. First, one has to make it past the bishop, "the theologian par excellence."[105]

What I want to suggest is that behind this question of methodology and the construction of the "field" of a phenomenology of religion lies an *ethical* question – a matter of doing justice to the other, to the other's religion and the religion of the Other. By reducing the religious phenomenon to the theological phenomenon, Marion at the same time reduces the field of a phenomenology of religion, thus leaving little space for difference. The phenomenology of religion then becomes little more than a "natural" or "rational" theology, which claims universality but in the end turns out to be a kind of theological colonialism; in the name of a "phenomenology of religion" all *different* religious phenomena are subjected to the imperialism of a covert theology. Once again, in the name of redemption and deliverance (*relève*), different religious phenomena are visited by the violence of a colonization of the field, carried out by phenomenologists of religion in the name of the God of phenomenology.

Liberating the phenomenology of religion: indications in Heidegger

The young Heidegger was intent on another kind of *relève*, a relief from scholasticism and deliverance from its static interpretative structures which leveled and colonized religious, and particularly mystical, experience. As Hugo Ott notes, "Not the least of the effects of Scholasticism, according to Heidegger, was that it endangered the immediacy of religious life, that it lost sight of religion in pursuing theology and dogma."[106] Turning to Luther and Schleiermacher (particularly the second of his *Speeches*), Heidegger sought to recover *religion* – in a particular, determinate form[107] – from its theoretical sedimentation in both scholastic theology and (neo-Kantian) "philosophy of religion"; this recovery would amount to a kind of liberation, a releasing of religion from these oppressive metaphysical and objectifying structures in order to retrieve its pretheoretical or existential immediacy, its facticity. As such, his phenomenology of religion falls within the larger project of a radicalization of phenomenology's method and topic, in order to "make factical life speak for itself on the basis of its very own factical possibilities" (PIA 246/367).

This more radical phenomenological *method* required a certain kind of liberation, a loosening up of restrictive and even oppressive conceptual frameworks which denied the immediacy of factical experience. "Thus," he suggests, "the phenomenological hermeneutic of facticity sees itself as called upon to loosen up the handed-down and dominating interpretedness in its hidden motives, unexpressed tendencies, and ways of interpreting; and to push forward by way of a *dismantling return* [*im abbauenden Rückgang*] towards the primordial motive sources of explication" (PIA 249/371). This loosening up is more specifically a "phenomenological destruction" (*Destruktion*), a dismantling of these sedimented structures with the goal of liberation – a project motivated by Luther and "Reformation theology" (PIA 250/372). And as a correlate to this method, the *topic* or "field" of phenomenology must also be revisioned; once philosophy has made this shift to a radical phenomenology (which for Heidegger, also means a commitment to atheism[108]), "then it has decisively chosen factical life in its facticity and has made this an object for itself"; that is to say, the topic of this radical phenomenology is "the ways in which factical life temporalizes itself and *speaks* with itself in such temporalizing" (PIA 246/367–8). What we see in this radicalization of phenomenology is Heidegger's critique of both Husserl and the Marburg School, both of which accorded a primacy to theoretical experience. In contrast, the young Heidegger seeks to relocate phenomenology's topic in pretheoretical or factical experience; as we have already seen, due to this shift in topic, the character of phenomenology itself is revisioned as a "pretheoretical originary science [*vortheoretische Urwissenschaft*]" (GA 56/57 95–117) – a hermeneutics of facticity which attempts to describe the meaning and intentions of pretheoretical existence.

What, then, would this return to facticity by means of *Destruktion* mean for a phenomenology of religion? And how would it differ from Marion's proposal? As Gadamer suggests, Heidegger here asks whether "God" could ever be the topic of research: "Can one speak about God like one speaks about an object? Is that not precisely the temptation[109] of metaphysics to lead us into arguments about the existence and characteristics of God as if we were arguing about an object of science?"[110] In other words, would the topic of a phenomenology of religion be "God" (as in Marion), or something other, something different – perhaps even a plurality of topics?

As the methodological suggestions in the 1922 "Aristotle-Introduction" indicate, a phenomenology of religion which explores "the facticity of the human being" will be concerned not with God as a religious phenomenon, but rather the *meaning* of faith, i.e. "the ways in which factical life temporalizes itself and *speaks* itself" – the intentions of the faithful community (PIA 246/393, 368), whatever that community may be (despite the fact that Heidegger's analyses were restricted to Protestantism). A phenomenology of religion is not restricted to a phenomenon of revelation (*whose* revelation?), let alone theophany (of whom? for whom?); rather, its field is the meaning of a community of faith. And for the young Heidegger, any other (more metaphysical) suggestion borders on the absurd; indeed, he questions "whether the very idea of a philosophy of religion [*Religionsphilosophie*] (especially if it makes no reference to the facticity of the human being) is pure nonsense" (PIA 246/393). As he suggested in winter semester 1920/21, what is currently practiced under the rubric of a "philosophy of religion" is grounded in a neo-Kantian *philosophy*, which reduces experience to only a theoretical manifestation; therefore, as a neo-Kantian philosophy of religion, it reduces *religion* to either a "religious a priori" (Troeltsch) or a kind of rational theology (Kant). Even something like Otto's emphasis on the "non-rational" element in religion necessarily operates against the horizon of this rationalization of religion (GA 60 75–8).[111] But as Heidegger suggests, this imposes something foreign upon religious experience and fails to allow facticity to "speak for itself." As suggested above, this "imposing of something foreign" amounts to a kind of imperialism or colonization of religious experience by a particular theological/ theophanic/theistic tradition (viz. for Heidegger, scholasticism). The project of a radical phenomenological destruction is to emancipate factical religious experience from the (Scholastic) categories of conceptual thought – a delivery (*relève*) from theology.

For Heidegger, and in contrast to Marion, "God" is not a field or topic of research; "God" could never be a *Gegenstand* – even for theology.[112] As he delineates several years later in 1927, theology is not what its etymological indicators would suggest (a science of God): "God is in no way the object of investigation in theology" (PT 25/ 15). Rather, the *positum* or *Gegenstand* of theology as a positive science is *faith*, or "believing comportment itself" (PT 21/11–12). As a science of faith, theology is also a kind of intentional analysis which reflects on meaning within the believing community *from within* the believing community. Thus theology might be defined as "faith's conceptual interpretation of itself": it arises out of faith, reflects upon faith, for the sake of cultivating faithfulness (PT 22/12).[113] We can further clarify the task of theology, Heidegger continues, by a kind of *via negativa* "showing what theology is *not*." It is not a speculative knowledge of God, since it cannot be in any way a science of God. It must also be distinguished, he adds, from a "philosophy of religion . . . , in short, a *Religionswissenschaft*" (PT 25/15). Theology and a philosophy or phenomenology of religion[114] are distinct, even "heterogeneous" sciences (PT 26/16) – distinguished not simply by mode of knowledge as in a scholastic (or Marionesque) nature/grace distinction, but by a difference of *fields* or topics, as well as a difference in *attitude*. Indeed, the burden of Heidegger's lecture is to demonstrate that the tension between faith and philosophy is not due to a competition over a common field or topic – it is not a question of competing worldviews (PT 13/5); rather, it is a distinction between an ontic, or positive science (theology), and an ontological field of research (phenomenology). Theology's field is particular and concrete: one's faith community; in addition, theology functions *within* faith and makes no *epoché*. A phenomenology of religion, on the other hand, is able to range across religions and communities (though Heidegger himself does not do this, staying pretty close to home); thus, the phenomenologist of religion is not necessarily destined to discover only the "God of phenomenology" (Yahweh in disguise); instead, the phenomenologist is able to explore and describe the factical experience of any believing community.

Although undeveloped in this 1927 lecture, Heidegger nevertheless provides *indications* for the development of a phenomenology of religion which, when read retroactively with the 1920/21 lectures, provides a portrait of a phenomenology of religion which is distinct from both a traditional "philosophy of religion" which is, for Heidegger, either *ein purer Widersinn* or just a covert theology (*à la* Marion); but it is also distinct from theology which is a positive science *of* faith, in both senses of that pregnant genitive: as a science which has faith as its object, and a science motivated by participation in the community of faith. Theology, then, would always be particular and concrete – the theology of this particular believing community. A phenomenology of religion, however, brackets such participation and is able to range across religious communities.[115]

We find here a marked difference between Marion and Heidegger's phenomenologies of religion. While both assert that, in a sense, a phenomenology of religion is without faith or puts any commitments out of play, the results of their reductions (*epoché*) are quite different: for Marion, though the phenomenology of religion is without faith, it nevertheless remains tethered to the God of faith; the "God of phenomenology" is, of course, behind the veil, the God of Abraham, Isaac, Jacob, and Pope John Paul II. Marion's reduction, then, is also a particularization which reduces the size of the field and restricts both entry and appearance. What one will encounter in the phenomenology of religion is the saturated phenomenon, which is a kind of theophany – a mediated appearance, but one nevertheless dispatched by Yahweh. The result is that religion itself is reduced and particularized – or, more aptly, colonized in the name of a Christian imperialism (or, as Rahner suggested, Buddhists are really just anonymous Christians). Marion's *piety* leaves no room for difference and will not permit any other gods to appear; indeed, one may be concerned that this pious phenomenology of religion is not beyond crusading to eliminate such paganism.

In contrast, we can locate indications which suggest that Heidegger's reduction is at the same time an *opening* for difference; in constructing the field of a phenomenology of religion, we find the young Heidegger (in contrast to his later escapades) to be something of a Las Casas bent upon liberating religion from such colonization (viz. scholasticism) and providing space for plurality and alterity – though I would also suggest that his mission fell short of a radical liberation of religion from theology, since he retains a focus on Christian religion.[116] But a phenomenology of religion developed from these indications in Heidegger would radically differ from the theistic imperialism of "philosophy of religion" in both Marion and contemporary analytic practice. Thus, in these methodological discussions as well, we locate a certain "ethics of method" – an attempt to construct a field and develop a methodology which is able to do justice to the plurality and facticity of religious experience. In doing so, Heidegger effects a certain recovery or delivery (*relève*), retrieving factical religious experience from its sedimentation in theology and liberating it from the oppressive and restrictive structures of theoretical concepts. The return to facticity as a topic, and the development of phenomenological *Destruktion* as a method, generates a phenomenology of religion as a distinct discipline which is not tethered to a particular theism, but rather, in its paganism, is able to range across religious communities and at the same time do justice to the religious experience *of* the other.

The return of the concept: Destrukt*ing* Being and Time

In the earlier stages of Heidegger's methodological reflections – which are largely submerged in *Sein und Zeit* but surface occasionally – the formal indication is a way of grappling with the impetus that factical life imposes upon philosophy. As an *iconic* conceptuality, the formal indication respects the excessiveness of factical life and attempts to provide an account of it which does not grasp it in a (traditional) concept but obliquely "points" to its contours. Here, it is factical life which imposes itself upon and challenges "philosophy"; but by the time of *Being and Time*, we will find that it is now philosophy which is imposing itself on factical life. That is, the formal indication undergoes a radical shift during its tenure in neo-Kantian Marburg such that it begins to take on the characteristics of a (Kantian) "idol." We can detect this in two ways in the later stages of "early" Heidegger.

"Phenomenology and Theology": philosophy as "corrective"

This transformation of the formal indication can be seen very clearly in the lecture, "Phenomenology and Theology," delivered shortly after the publication of *Being and Time*, in both Tübingen and Marburg (1927). Within a very neo-Kantian project of demarcating the regions of the sciences, Heidegger here considers the relationship between philosophy, theology, and faith. Harking back to earlier methodological reflections, Heidegger again emphasizes the incommensurability between theology's "object" – lived, faithful experience – and its "scientific" task of conceptual determination.

As a science theology must be able to demonstrate and to form concepts which are appropriate to that which it has undertaken to interpret. But is it not the case that that which is to be interpreted in theological concepts is precisely that which is disclosed only through, for, and in faith? Is not that which is supposed to be grasped conceptually something essentially inconceivable [*Unbegreifliche*], and something whose content is not to be fathomed, and whose legitimacy is not to be founded by purely rational means? (PT 62/17)

The challenge for theology, then, is to find "appropriate conceptual interpretation," which will require "pushing these concepts to their very limits" (ibid.); otherwise, we are left with only silence – the inconceivability would remain "mute." All of this only repeats what had been Heidegger's concern for the last decade and our concern throughout this study: the way in which theoretical thought must grapple to articulate its "other," viz. pretheoretical lived experience. And it is precisely this experience which disrupts "science," including philosophy. In particular, for Heidegger, it was a return to the factical world of the New Testament and Luther's theology of the cross which effected this disruption and issued this challenge to philosophy, calling for a "reform" of philosophy and demanding a new "concept": *die formale Anzeige*.

But now, in 1927, it is no longer factical experience which challenges philosophy; instead, we now find philosophy functioning as a "corrective" to theology. The guardian of "ontology,"[117] the task of philosophy is to "point out" (*anzeigen*) the ontological conditions for determinate, "ontic" meanings (PT 64/19). For example, Heidegger offers, the ontic, theological concept of "sin" is grounded in and determined by the ontological concept of "guilt" (PT 65/19).[118] Thus philosophy, or what is now equated with "ontology," functions "*as a corrective to the ontic, and in particular pre-Christian, meanings of basic theological concepts*" by formally indicating "the ontological character of *the* region of Being" to which such ontic concepts refer (PT 64–5/19).

While it was originally (Luther's) theology pointing to the limits of philosophy, within the neo-Kantian project of late Marburg it is philosophy which lays down the rules for theology. In the final draft of *Sein und Zeit* and the accompanying lecture, "Phenomenology and Theology," formal indication has been co-opted into transcendental philosophy. Originally intended as a "new" concept integral to a "new" phenomenology, the formal indication has now undergone a Kantian conversion, has repented of its concern with singularity and facticity, and now takes up the arduous task of explicating the apriori structures which determine and condition human experience. The "concept" has once again become a concept; the *icon* has become an *idol*.

The Kantian turn and the return of the concept in SZ

The final draft of *Sein und Zeit* – the "Kantian" draft which is published as a torso[119] – already represents a certain forgetting of factical life – and consequently, a failure to do justice to the incommensurate, which is precisely why Marion is right in his reading of *Sein und Zeit* and *History of the Concept of Time* (GA 20). But that is because, by 1925, it's already too late. Factical lived experience is no longer returned to in order to confront philosophy with its other; rather, philosophy looks to factical, everyday experience as its handmaiden on the way to ontology. While *Being and Time* gives us a powerful "phenomenology of the natural attitude," we must remember, Heidegger reminds us (SZ §§3, 9, 45), that all of these analyses are only "preliminary" to a fundamental ontology. The task is to now disclose the "characteristics" or "primordial structures" – the *existentialia* (SZ 44/42; 54–5/50–1) – which universally characterize Dasein as being-in-the-world. The structures that are disclosed – disposition, understanding, (discourse,) and fallenness – are taken to be apriori and "primordial" characteristics of Dasein, without respect to culture or history. Therefore, the "concepts" which disclose these apriori structures fall within the Kantian legacy of the traditional concept with universal pretensions.

But is not this turn to Kant also a return to Husserl? Has not the young Heidegger's "phenomenology of the natural attitude" now become the handmaiden of a "transcendental" (albeit Kantian) phenomenology? Is this not precisely to repeat Husserl, viz. that we are concerned with the natural attitude only on the way to transcendental philosophy and the realm of essences? And is not this transcendental penchant in *Being and Time* at odds with the project which serves as its original impetus, viz. a phenomenology of facticity or the natural attitude? Would we not be justified, then, in reading the young Heidegger against himself, to effect a *Destrucktion* of SZ in the name of the younger Heidegger's "new" phenomenology?

Notes

1 Augustine, *De civitate dei*, 10.23, cited as the motto for Heidegger's lecture course of 1920, *Phänomenologie der Anschauung und des Ausdrucks: Theorie der philosophischen Begriffsbildung* (GA 59).

2 By referring to Heidegger's "new phenomenology," I mean to allude to what Janicaud describes as *la nouvelle phénoménologie* in the work of Levinas, Marion, and Henry.

3 Earlier, Hubert Dreyfus and John Haugeland suggested a similar heuristic, in "Husserl and Heidegger: Philosophy's Last Stand," in *Heidegger and Modern Philosophy*, ed. Michael Murray (New Haven: Yale University Press, 1978), 222–38. While my reading has received an impetus from their interpretation, I would suggest that Dreyfus and Haugeland's analysis is lacking in two ways: (1) they fail to problematize the relation between the "natural attitude" of *Ideen* I and the "natural concept of the world" which Heidegger refers to in SZ, 52; (2) they too quickly equate Husserl's natural attitude with Heidegger's "everydayness." This should not be considered a rejection of their thesis, but only an attempt to follow it up with more careful analyses.

4 In Husserl's own marginal comments in a copy of *Ideen* dating from *c.* 1929 (post *Sein und Zeit*), at this point he notes "Heidegger says the opposite." This must refer only to the final clause: that the task "has been barely seen up to now." As we will see below, Heidegger considered this to be a "task which has made philosophy uneasy for a long time" (SZ 52/48).

5 Merleau-Ponty, *Phenomenology of Perception*, trans. Colin Smith (New York: Humanities Press, 1962), vii–viii.

6 By referring to "pretheoretical experience," neither I nor Heidegger mean to suggest some kind of "pure," uninterpreted experience; rather, it refers to a more fundamental, *non-cognitive* mode of being-in-the-world which is not representational, but rather what we might describe as "affective." The Pascalian insight that "the heart has reasons of which reason knows nothing" captures the notion well (and indeed, Pascal was an influence on the young Heidegger, as discussed below). My thanks to Amos Yong for pushing me to articulate these matters more clearly.

7 The issue of continuity and connection between Husserl's notions of the "natural attitude" (*die natürliche Einstellung*) and the "natural concept of the world" (*der natürliche Weltbegriff*) will be considered below.

8 Difficulties which, we will see below, Husserl himself came to appreciate (see *Krisis* IIIA). See also John Scanlon, "Husserl's *Ideas* and the Natural Concept of the World," in *Edmund Husserl and the Phenomenological Tradition*, ed. Robert Sokolowski (Washington: Catholic University of America Press, 1988), 223.

9 This judgment regarding the "easiness" of a phenomenology concerned with only theoretical consciousness is Heidegger's own charge. This is reflective of a general preference, in Heidegger, for the difficult – symptomatic of both his Jansenist influences (Pascal was an important figure for Heidegger in this period, as was Luther) and what John Caputo describes as his militaristic *Kampsphilosophie* which valorizes "struggle" and "difficulty." (This is developed in John D. Caputo, *Demythologizing Heidegger* [Bloomington, IN: Indiana University Press, 1993].) As an anonymous reader for the journal *Symposium* pointed out, Husserl might respond that it is Heidegger who has skirted the difficulties of phenomenology by a flight to unverifiable descriptions of phenomena such as death, anxiety, and guilt. But Heidegger would respond that it is just such phenomena which are most difficult, since they are incommensurate with theoretical description. We might suggest that Heidegger is pursuing here what Anthony Steinbock describes as "limit phenomenology" (see Steinbock's discussion of these themes in his review of *Alter: Revue de phénoménologie* in *Husserl Studies* 16 [1999]: 65–75). My thanks to the reader for pushing me to clarify these matters.

10 Not a "wholly other" in the sense of Levinas's "Other" or Marion's "God," but rather an incommensurable. However, as I have suggested elsewhere (and recalling my "formalization" of this problem above in Chapter 2), the problem of alterity encountered by Levinas and Marion is *formally* analogous to Heidegger's methodological problem: all of them are attempting to provide an account of how one can speak of that which is incommensurate with the order of conceptual and theoretical thought. For a first suggestion in this regard, see my "Alterity, Transcendence, and the Violence of the Concept," *International Philosophical Quarterly* 38 (1998): 369–81.

11 See Luft, "Husserl's Phenomenological Discovering of the Natural Attitude," *Continental Philosophy Review* 31 (1998): 153–4. It is just these matters, I am suggesting, that were the central focus of the young Heidegger's methodological considerations.

12 Cf. Jacques Derrida, *Memoirs of the Blind*, 52–3, on that which is structurally invisible, wholly otherwise than the sight of *theoria*, cannot be 'seen' as a phenomenon, a "transcendentality" incommensurate with seeing (drawing on Merleau-Ponty). Recall also my discussion of phenomenology's "faith" in apperception above.

13 "We want to take Husserl as his word." This was Heidegger's marginal comment in his copy of *Philosophie als strenge Wissenschaft*, responding to Husserl's maxim, "To the things themselves!" Reported by Thomas Sheehan to Hans-Georg Gadamer and recounted in Gadamer, *Heidegger's Ways*, trans. John Stanley (Albany: SUNY Press, 1994), 171.

14 Heidegger, of course, was deeply affected by the earlier *Logical Investigations*, particularly the development of categorial intuition in the Sixth Investigation. However, with regards to the question of the world of pretheoretical experience, the *Logical Investigations* do not play a significant role for Heidegger's project.

15 John Scanlon also suggests that "we can discern essentially different attitudes within the overall natural attitude": the first would be the concrete experience of the interested, involved participant (what I have linked to "natural cognition"); the second is a disinterested, theoretical attitude. Scanlon points to *Ideen* II for the further development of this distinction. See Scanlon, "Husserl's *Ideas* and the Natural Concept of the World," 229–31. Notice, however, that already the more primordial mode is described as *cognition*.

16 This privileging of perception is seen already at Id 7/5: "the 'natural' experience that is presentive of something *originarily* is *perception*."

17 That is, the objects of the natural world of real actuality, as opposed to the irreal world of, e.g. pure numbers, which I am "in" only in the "arithmetical attitude" (Id 51/54). The natural world, however, is *always* there for me "as long as I go on living naturally."

18 As John Scanlon perceptively asks at this point, "What has happened to the friend reaching out to shake my hand?" [cf. Id 48/51]. Scanlon, "Husserl's *Ideas*," 228.

19 At stake here is a whole thematics of the "gaze," of theoretical "regard" (Rück*sicht*), and the matter of "seeing" (criticized by Foucault's "archaeology of the medical gaze [*régard*]" in *Birth of the Clinic*). By effecting the phenomenological reduction, Husserl's phenomenology reduces its "world" to what phenomenology can see. What Heidegger is interested in, I would suggest, is how one gives an account of what cannot be seen so clearly, what lies beyond sight, where the theoretical gaze/regard can no longer penetrate. Here one would proceed not by sight, but by a certain faith, entrusting oneself to the wholly-other-than-phenomenological-sight, viz. factical life. One could then read Derrida's *Memoirs of the Blind* as a critique of the phenomenological gaze, pointing out that its "blind spots," which are structurally invisible, can never appear as phenomena. See esp. *Memoirs*, 51–4.

20 The phrase "natural concept of the world" is in quotation marks in SZ; thus, it seems clear that Heidegger has a specific source in mind, though no reference is given, nor is one provided in the GA edition. At issue here is just what the reference would be. My suggestion is that, though Heidegger refers to the *natürlichen Welt*begriffes, he seems to be aiming much more at the *natürlichen Einstellung* of *Ideen* I. He does tell us that he had access to Husserl's unpublished materials (SZ, Int. II, n.5 and I.i, n.2); however, given the fact that he would already be in Marburg, it seems unlikely that Heidegger would be familiar with the 1925 lectures.

21 In *Husserliana*, Bd. XIII: *Zur Phänomenologie der Intersubjektivität, Erster Teil: 1905–1920*, Hg. Iso Kern (The Hague: Martinus Nijhoff, 1972), Nr. 6, Aus den Vorlesungen "Grundprobleme der Phänomenologie," Wintersemester 1910/11, 111–54.

22 Ibid., 125, emphasis original (translation mine). See also Husserl, *Analysen zur passiven Synthesis. Aus Vorlesungs- und Forschungsmanuskripten 1918–1926, Hua.* XI, Hg. M. Fleischer (The Hague: Nijhoff, 1966), 344.

23 Scanlon, "Husserl's *Ideas* and the Natural Concept of the World," 218.

24 The task of this lecture course is the development of a phenomenological psychology, hence Husserl emphasizes the role of the "mental" and is most interested in provided something of a genealogy for the psychological concept of "mind."

25 Anthony Steinbock, in *Home and Beyond*, describes this as Husserl's "regressive" procedure, as opposed to the "progressive" procedure of the later *Krisis*.

26 Cf. Husserl's analyses in Part II of *Krisis* which consider just such a theoreticization of experience after Galileo.

27 Cf. here his earlier engagement with Avenarius's critique of "pure experience" in *Hua.* XIII, 1910/11, Nr. 6, §10, 131ff.

28 The method is unpacked in *Phenomenological Psychology*, §§8–9. Below, we will see that Heidegger's formal indication, once filtered through a transcendental turn in Marburg, begins to effect the same operation, whereas in its earlier moments, the strategy of formal indication would only disclose what we might describe, following Foucault, as "historical aprioris."

29 Ibid., 66–8/49–50.
30 Space does not permit me to here consider a third important question: having considered the role of the natural attitude in *Ideen* I, and the natural concept of the world in *Phenomenological Psychology*, it would then be necessary to consider their relation to and continuity with the *Lebenswelt* of the later *Krisis*. My project does not here permit that consideration, since neither the *Krisis* text, nor Husserl's later work generally, exerted an influence on Heidegger's early work, which is my focus. However, we might ask whether the later Husserl and the early Heidegger were not concerned with similar problems. Indeed, Husserl's later "return" to pretheoretical life is much more attentive to just the kinds of problems Heidegger was concerned with, particularly the radical incommensurability between theoretical description and pretheoretical experience. Thus he asks, "How are we to do justice systematically – that is, with appropriate scientific discipline – to the all-encompassing, so paradoxically demanding, manner of being of the life-world?" What this calls for, Husserl concludes, is a "new science." A new phenomenology? I hope to return to this matter in another context.
31 The method being that of a "hermeneutical circle," elucidating the presuppositions of Dasein (SZ §63). As Heidegger emphasizes, however, this is not a vicious circle because it is not a matter of deduction, but rather elucidation (*auslegen*).
32 István M. Fehér, "Phenomenology, Hermeneutics, *Lebensphilosophie*: Heidegger's Confrontation with Husserl, Dilthey, and Jaspers," in *Reading Heidegger From The Start: Essays in His Earliest Thought*, eds. Theodore Kisiel and John van Buren (Albany: SUNY Press, 1994), 84.
33 *Nichomachean Ethics*, I.iii. For Heidegger's analysis, see GA 61.
34 As I will argue below, the traces of the early Freiburg period which can be glimpsed in SZ are largely overwhelmed by a neo-Kantian transcendental turn which characterized Heidegger's Marburg and post-Marburg lectures (1924–27).
35 As described by Theodore Kisiel, "Heidegger (1920–21) on Becoming a Christian: A Conceptual Picture Show," in *Reading Heidegger From The Start*, 177.
36 A line of inquiry also taken up in *Basic Problems of Phenomenology* (GA 24), §§1–3.
37 For a close analysis of this notion, see George Kovacs, "Philosophy as Primordial Science in Heidegger's Courses of 1919," in *Reading Heidegger From The Start*, 91–107.
38 Elsewhere I have argued that this "theoretization" is particularly found in religious communities which "theologize" religious experience. See James K. A. Smith, "Liberating Religion From Theology: Marion and Heidegger on the Possibility of a Phenomenology of Religion," *International Journal for Philosophy of Religion* 46 (1999): 17–33, and "Scandalizing Theology: A Pentecostal Response to Noll's *Scandal*," *PNEUMA: Journal of the Society for Pentecostal Studies* 19 (1997): 225–38. The same theme, I would suggest, is found throughout Kierkegaard, and is alluded to by Heidegger in GA 59, 21.
39 See GA 59, 23: "Man sieht heute nun mehr oder minder klar, dass die bisherige Erforschung der Erlegnisgestalten entweder sehr roh oder durch das Vorwalten der theoretischen Einstellung und ungeprüfter Voraussetzungen schief war; allenthalben befriedigen solche Versuche philosophisch nicht mehr. Sofern aber Philosophie – also jeder ins Werk zu setzende Versuch, diesem Ungenügen abzuhelfen – irgendwie rationale *Erkenntnis* sein soll, erhebt sich für sie die Frage, ob überhaupt eine Betrachtung des Erlebens möglich ist, die es nicht sofort and notwendig theoretisch verunstaltet. Diesen Einwand hat die Philosophie selbst gegen sich erheben müssen."
40 Kisiel, *Genesis*, 48.
41 This is also why Heidegger finds an impetus for these methodological reflections in Aristotle's *Ethics*, which is very attentive to the inadequacy of conceptual determination in matters of practical life. (My thanks to Jack Caputo for his formulation of these matters.)
42 One enthymeme is at work, what I think is an *ethical* assumption: "Reducing factical life to theoretical or cognitive terms is wrong."

43 Heidegger is not calling into question intentionality as such, but the cognitivization of intentionality in Husserl's phenomenology.

44 The same is suggested by Patrick Gorevan in describing that which is common to Heidegger and Scheler: "both thinkers sought to thematise the problem of philosophy from an integrally human viewpoint. In their rejection of Husserl's transcendental phenomenology, both opt, instead, for an *affective* route to human existence in the world, avoiding the emphasis on intellectual intentionality which they found in Husserl." Patrick Gorevan, "Heidegger and Scheler: A Dialogue," *Journal of the British Society for Phenomenology* 24 (1993): 279.

45 I will take up a detailed analysis of *love* as the primordial intentional relation in Augustine in Chapter 4 below.

46 As opposed to the metaphysical, substantialist Augustine we inherit from Descartes. For a helpful study of this relation, see Stephen Menn, *Descartes and Augustine* (Cambridge: Cambridge University Press, 1998). Heidegger appropriates an Augustine mediated not by Descartes, but Pascal and the Jansenist tradition.

47 As per the Pascalian dictum, Augustinian in inspiration: "The heart has its reasons which reason itself does not know." Blaise Pascal, *Pensées and Other Writings*, trans. Honor Levi (Oxford: Oxford University Press, 1995), 158.

48 Ibid., 36 [fragment 142].

49 Ibid., 35 [fragment 142]. He goes on to show that this is why skepticism ("Pyrrhonism") is ineffectual. Much that we know we know not by reason, whereas the arguments of the skeptics can only call into question that which we have deduced in the order of reason.

50 Ibid., 36 [fragment 142].

51 Max Scheler, "Ordo Amoris," in *Selected Philosophical Essays*, trans. David Lachterman (Evanston: Northwestern University Press, 1973), 100. For a helpful discussion of Scheler's "*logique du coeur*," see James J. McCartney, *Unborn Persons: Pope John Paul II and the Abortion Debate* (New York: Peter Lang, 1987), 26–30 (Scheler was a formative influence for Karol Wojtyla).

52 Scheler, "Ordo Amoris," 101.

53 Kovacs, "Philosophy as Primordial Science," 99.

54 As Heidegger notes, he is not concerned with the ontic, historical development of the sciences, but rather "the *ontological genesis* of the theoretical mode of behavior" (SZ 357/ 327). What this aims at is "an *existential concept of science.*" For an earlier consideration of the "genesis of the theoretical," see GA 56/57, 84–97.

55 Emmanuel Levinas, *The Theory of Intuition in Husserl's Phenomenology*, 2nd ed., trans. André Orianne (Evanston, IL: Northwestern University Press, 1995), 157.

56 GA 59, 3–4. (All translations from GA 56/57, 59, and 60 are my own; English translations employed for other volumes are noted in the list of abbreviations.) See also p. 25: "Sofern aber Philosophie – also jeder ins Werk zu setzende Versuch, diesem Ungenügen abzuhelfen – irgendwie rationale *Erkenntnis* sein soll, erhebt sich für sie die Frage, ob überhaupt eine Betrachtung des Erlebens möglich ist, die es nicht sofort und notwendig theoretisch verunstaltet."

57 Jean Greisch, "Bulletin de philosophie herméneutique: Heidegger, Schleiermacher, Ricoeur, Gadamer, Misch, Abel," *Revue des sciences philosophiques et théologiques* 80 (1996): 640, emphasis added, trans. mine. See also his masterful analysis of GA 58 in Greisch, "La 'tapisserie de la vie.' Le phénomène de la vie et ses interprétations dans les *Grundprobleme der Phänomenologie (1919/20)* de Martin Heidegger," in *Heidegger 1919–1929: De l'herméneutique de la facticité à la métaphysique du Dasein*, ed. Jean-François Courtine (Paris: Vrin, 1996), 131–52.

58 The Kierkegaardian horizon of this challenge is succinctly summarized in Merold Westphal, "Heidegger's 'Theologische' Jugendschriften," *Research in Phenomenology* 2 (1997): 250–1. It is only because philosophy as phenomenology retains some form of reduction

that the challenge presents itself; that is, philosophy remains characterized by a certain kind of universality, otherwise it would simply be prereflective subjectivity. But it is not: prereflective subjectivity is its *topic* (or "object" in a weak sense) and so phenomenology must effect a certain "break" from such absorption in the world. But the trick is to do so without leveling the pretheoretical character of factical life and "essentializing" experience.

59 I want to adumbrate here what I believe is an analogy in Augustine (explored in Chapter 4 below). Both, I am arguing, indicate a "third way" (*pace* Dionysius) between predicative, kataphatic discourse on the one hand, and silence (apophasis) on the other – a third way between violence and silence, pointing to a non-violent (i.e. non-objectifying) speaking. But here, with respect to Heidegger, the literal antithesis to theoretical objectification would be simply the immediacy of factical life. But insofar as such immediacy is non-reflective, it would constitute a certain "reflective silence."

60 Westphal, "Heidegger's *'Theologische' Jugendschriften*," 251.

61 John van Buren, "The Ethics of *Formal Anzeige* in Heidegger," *American Catholic Philosophical Quarterly* 69 (1995): 157–70; see also idem, *The Young Heidegger*, ch. 15.

62 In an illuminating analysis of Husserl's correspondence, Rudolf Schmitz-Perrin has suggested that the same mystical concern served as the impetus for the development of Husserl's phenomenology. Thus (much to Dominique Janicaud's chagrin) we find at the very origins of phenomenology a fundamentally religious project. See Rudolf Schmitz-Perrin, "La phénoménologie et ses marges religieuses: la correspondance d'Edmund Husserl," *Studies in Religion/Sciences religieuses* 25 (1996): 481–8.

63 van Buren, *The Young Heidegger*, 319. What is at work here, van Buren notes, is the Lutheran contrast between the hybris of a *theologia gloriae* and the humility of *theologia crucis*.

64 John D. Caputo, *Demythologizing Heidegger* (Bloomington: Indiana University Press, 1993), 74.

65 See TI, 48, 80, and *passim*. For Heidegger's discussion of formal indication as a relation, see GA 29/30, 292–3.

66 For a helpful discussion of this point, see Dahlstrom, "Heidegger's Method," 782–4.

67 A relevant analysis in this regard is SZ §§31–3. See also the careful analysis of Ryan Streeter, "Heidegger's Formal Indication: A Question of Method in *Being and Time*," *Man and World* 30 (1997), esp. §3, where he considers the "employment" of the assertion.

68 The second misinterpretation, which is not of concern here, is the false interconnection of philosophical concepts.

69 Cf. a similar strategy and thematic in Jacques Derrida, "Passions: 'An Oblique Offering,'" trans. David Wood in Derrida, *Sauf le nom*, ed. Thomas Dutoit (Stanford: Stanford University Press, 1995), 3–31, which I will consider below.

70 In terms of SZ, its author's relation to his readers must be one of "leaping ahead" (*vorausspringen*) rather than "leaping in" (*einspringen*) [SZ 122/114–15]. The formal indication is a use of concepts which attempts to avoid the sedimentation that becomes characteristic of predicative assertions (SZ §33).

71 To which I will add a third instance in Chapter 4: Augustine's strategy of "confession."

72 With regards to the almost pagan appellation "the god" used throughout the *Fragments*, Climacus explains in the *Postscript* that the pamphlet "took its point of departure in paganism" in order to signal something beyond paganism: "The pamphlet, in order to obtain a breathing space, did not say that what was imaginatively constructed is Christianity, lest it immediately be swept into historical, historical-dogmatic, introductory, and ecclesiastical issues about what actually is Christianity and what is not" (*Concluding Unscientific Postscript to Philosophical Fragments*, Kierkegaard's Writings XII, ed. and trans. Howard V. Hong and Edna H. Hong [Princeton: Princeton University Press, 1992], 361–2). The *Fragments*, then, represent a formalization of Christianity effected by a certain *epoché*, while the *Postscript* presents the issue in its historical and theological garb.

73 Søren Kierkegaard, *Philosophical Fragments/Johannes Climacus*, Kierkegaard's Writings VII, ed. and trans. Howard V. Hong and Edna H. Hong (Princeton: Princeton University Press, 1985), 100.

74 *Postscript*, 103.

75 The notion of the "historical" is developed as a "core phenomenon" in Heidegger's analysis in GA 60, 37–9.

76 *Fragments*, 104.

77 Ibid., 104.

78 Ibid., 102.

79 Ibid., 104.

80 Ibid., 101.

81 *Postscript*, 73.

82 For Kierkegaard, the problematics of the singularity of the subjective God-relationship is two-sided: on the one hand, the faith of the "evangelist" is a secret which cannot be expressed; on the other side of the indirect communication, the subjectivity of the "recipient" must also be respected. The strategy of indirect communication attempts to preserve the subjectivity – keep the secret – of both the speaker *and* hearer.

83 Ibid., 77. On indirect communication as an art and poetics, see 74, 76, 77, 78, 79.

84 Ibid., 76.

85 Ibid., 79–80.

86 Ibid., 236.

87 Derrida himself catalogues his use of the term "oblique" in *On the Name*, 138 n.7.

88 In Chapter 2, I considered Marion's critique of SZ and what he described as even the "early" work of 1925 (GA 20). But if Marion would proceed to the young Heidegger's earliest period (1919–23, pre-Marburg), he would find quite a different formulation of matters, one which is in fact very close to his own concerns. On why his critique *does* apply to SZ and Heidegger's Marburg tenure, see below.

89 In Chapter 4 below, I will unpack Augustine's account of idolatry, which is completely consistent with the phenomenological account offered by Marion.

90 Or even what Marion describes as the "invisable" – more than that which cannot be seen, that which cannot be aimed at (GWB 13).

91 GWB, 23, emphasis added. Note here two motifs which I have emphasized above: (1) a concern with the *use* of concepts; and (2) the heuristics of visibility and invisibility. Here it must be noted that I am effecting a certain "formalization" of Marion's concern and discourse; for him, the concern is with the way in which the conceptual idol "measures the divine according to the scope of a gaze that freezes" (p. 24). I have formalized this to be a more general concern with the way in which that which is incommensurate and exceeds conceptual thought (e.g. *Lebenserfahrung*) is reduced to the conceptual gaze.

92 This understanding of the icon survives in a computer age, where an "icon" is no longer found only in churches but on my computer's "desktop." It is the image (*eikon*) which is not an end in itself, but rather opens up beyond itself when double-clicked. In other words, the icon functions as an indicator to that which is beyond itself; if it does not refer to this other (e.g. software application) it no longer functions as an icon. It is simply a picture, without reference. My thanks to Tim Shanahan for suggesting this contemporary image.

93 For a discussion, see John D. Caputo, *Demythologizing Heidegger* (Bloomington: Indiana University Press, 1993), 39–59.

94 These three pairs represent three movements or "styles" within the phenomenology of religion. In a useful schema, Sumner Twiss and Walter Conser describe the first as *essential* phenomenology of religion, the second movement as *historical-typological* phenomenology of religion, and the third as *existential-hermeneutical* phenomenology of religion. To a certain extent, they are borrowing Max Scheler's own distinction between

what he described as "*concrete* phenomenology of religious objects" and "all types of eidological or *essential* phenomenology of religion." Scheler, *On the Eternal in Man*, trans. Bernard Noble (New York: Harper & Row, 1960), 159–60. For a helpful elucidation of this schema, see Twiss and Conser, "Introduction," to *Experience of the Sacred: Readings in the Phenomenology of Religion*, eds. Sumner B. Twiss and Walter H. Conser, Jr. (Hanover, NH: Brown University Press, 1992), 1–74.

95 For a recounting of this story, see Walter Capps, *Religious Studies: The Making of a Discipline* (Minneapolis: Fortress Press, 1995), and George A. James, "Phenomenology and the Study of Religion: The Archaeology of an Approach," *Journal of Religion* 65 (1985): 311–35.

96 Rudolf Otto, *The Idea of the Holy: An Inquiry into the Non-rational Factor in the Idea of the Divine and its Relation to the Rational*, trans. John W. Harvey (Oxford: Oxford University Press, 1950). Even Husserl himself described the book as a "first beginning for a phenomenology of religion" and a book that "had a strong effect on me as hardly no other book in years." The seminal work of Ernst Troeltsch should also be noted as a direction in research which opened the space for non-theological investigation of religious reality.

97 Louis Dupré, "Phenomenology of Religion: Limits and Possibilities," *American Catholic Philosophical Quarterly* 66 (1992): 177. Dupré justifiably chides the discipline for its lack of methodological rigor in this regard, noting that "those who practiced the phenomenological description most successfully – particularly Van der Leeuw and Eliade – totally sidestepped the ontological problems in an area where those problems were most pressing. Their comparative analyses of religious phenomena are unquestionably inspired by Husserl's phenomenological description, but they seldom surpass the empirical level of an anthropological typology and rarely attain the philosophical justification Husserl required."

98 This is especially the case in the renaissance of philosophy of religion in Anglo-American circles. For my critique of theism in the name of Christian philosophy, see "The Art of Christian Atheism: Faith and Philosophy in Early Heidegger," *Faith and Philosophy* 14 (1997): 71–81. I should note that Marion is also critical of "theism" as idolatrous (GWB 57).

99 Thus Marion considers his work on charity to be distinctly theological. See Jean-Luc Marion, *Prolégomènes à la charité* (Paris: La Différence, 1986). As Graham Ward suggests, "here philosophical discourse ends . . . In fact, after *God Without Being*, Marion seems to have made his philosophical projects and his theological projects distinct." See Ward, "Introducing Jean-Luc Marion," *New Blackfriars* 76 (1995): 322–3.

100 Alluding to Anselm's formula. For a discussion, see Jean-Luc Marion, "Is the Ontological Argument Ontological? The Argument According to Anselm and Its Metaphysical Interpretation According to Kant," *Journal of the History of Philosophy* 30 (1992): 201–18, esp. 208. In light of our present discussion, it is important to recall that the very condition of Anselm's "speculation" is faith (p. 207).

101 Janicaud makes a similar observation, on the basis of different texts, suggesting that as for the scholastics, Wolff, and even neo-Thomism, philosophy (metaphysics, now phenomenology), for Marion, plays the role of a "propaedeutic" to theology. See Janicaud, *Le tournant théologique*, 40–1.

102 For Marion, "when it is a matter of thinking the possibility, and especially the radical possibility, of the impossible itself, *phenomenology alone is suitable*" (MP 590, emphasis added). So, just as he earlier suggested that God prefers Neoplatonism to Thomism, he now seems to suggest that God has a special place in his heart for phenomenology.

103 Aquinas, *Summa Theologiae*, Ia.1.2.

104 For a further analogy, see Aquinas, *Expositio super librum Boethii* De Trinitate, qu. 2, esp. art. 3.

105 See GWB, 152ff. In the context of "Metaphysics and Theology," this relates to Marion's assertion that the *recognition* of the saturated phenomenon requires "the real experience of its donation," which happens, of course, in the Mass (MP 590).

106 Hugo Ott, "Biographical Bases for Heidegger's 'Mentality of Disunity,'" in *The Heidegger Case: On Philosophy and Politics*, eds. Tom Rockmore and Joseph Margolis (Philadelphia: Temple University Press, 1992), 105. See also Ott, *Martin Heidegger: A Political Life*, trans. Allan Blunden (New York: Basic Books, 1993), 113–14.

107 This is an important qualification. What I am arguing is that the analyses of the early Heidegger retrieve Christian *religion* from its theologization in scholasticism (of any sort). This is a first, laudable move. However, I do not mean to say that these analyses disclose a universal "essence" of religion (though one gets the sense that that is what Heidegger thinks, at times). Rather, I am suggesting that, by retrieving religion from its theological sedimentation, space is opened to consider religious experience – in whatever determinate form – on its own terms, not in terms of a cognitive theology. But in this case, there will be a plurality: there is no "phenomenology of religion," only phenomenolog*ies* of religion*s*.

108 As he asserts, "if philosophy has decided radically and clearly on its own (without regard for any bustling-about with respect to world-views) to make factical life speak for itself on the basis of its very own factical possibilities; i.e. if philosophy is *fundamentally atheistic* and if it understands this about itself" (PIA 246/367). For my criticisms of this requirement, see my "Art of Christian Atheism," referred to above. What remains to be determined, however, is whether by this "methodological atheism" Heidegger simply means a phenomenological bracketing or *epoché*. If that is the case, then I think "atheism" is a poorly chosen word, since atheism is quite committed to its belief that God does not *exist*; that is, atheism remains within the pale of the "natural attitude" and the question of existence. The *epoché*, however, makes no judgments about existence.

109 Or as Kierkegaard suggests, theology is not only tempted by metaphysics, it eventually becomes a seducer of metaphysics, attempting to lure him [*sic*] into her den: "Theology sits all rouged and powdered in the window and courts its favor, offers its charms to philosophy" and "is willing to sell itself off at a low price." See Kierkegaard, *Fear and Trembling/Repetition*, eds. and trans. Howard V. Hong and Edna H. Hong (Princeton: Princeton University Press, 1983), 32, 48. I would suggest that Kierkegaard, like Heidegger (indeed, inspiring Heidegger), is also attempting to *recover* religion *from* theology. I think that in the end, both think that theology signals the death of factical religious experience. At the end of a 1964 letter to a colloquium at Drew University, Heidegger suggests (echoing Overbeck) that the positive task of theology "includes the question whether theology can still be a science – because presumably it should not be a science at all" (PT 46/30).

110 Hans-Georg Gadamer, "The Religious Dimension," in *Heidegger's Ways*, trans. John W. Stanley (Albany: SUNY Press, 1994), 175.

111 That is to say, Otto, despite many hasty readings, is by no means an irrationalist. Indeed, in his Foreword to the first English edition of *Das Heilige*, Otto instructed his future readers: "And I feel that no one ought to concern himself with 'Numen ineffabile' who has not already devoted assiduous and serious study to the 'Ratio aeterna'" (*The Idea of the Holy*, xxi). Otto also suggests that it is precisely the *rational* component which signals the superiority of a particular religion: "Rather we count this the very mark and criterion of a religion's high rank and superior value – that it should have no lack of *conceptions* about God; that it should admit knowledge . . . of the transcendent in terms of conceptual thought" (p. 1). The rest of the book is simply a "check," a counter-balance to a trend which would reduce religion to just its rational component.

112 My focus here is Heidegger's consideration of these matters in the early work, particularly "Phenomenology and Theology." One should consult Merold Westphal's

forthcoming work for the relationship of this critique to the later critique of "onto-theology" – a relation which Westphal understands as basically one of continuity.

113 For Heidegger, the notion of an "academic" theology distinct from an "ecclesial" or "confessional" theology would also be *ein purer Widersinn*. For him, theology is always a science which reflects *upon* the believing community, *from within* the believing community, *for the sake of* the believing community. As he suggests, the distinction between systematic, historical, and practical theology (*pace* Schleiermacher) must be seen as necessary correlates, not options (pp. 13–15).

114 As indicated in the 1920/21 lectures, Heidegger uses the term "philosophy of religion" (*Religionsphilosophie*) only insofar as it is a current phrase which is taken to name a certain task and region; in the end, he thinks a "philosophy of religion" in this rationalist/theistic sense is "pure nonsense'" and ought to be abandoned for a phenomenology of religion. However, in making this transition, he will sometimes use the term *Religionsphilosophie* to name what he would obviously consider to be a phenomenology of religion. At times, he indicates this translation; for example, when discussing the relationship between a phenomenology of religion and other disciplines which consider religion (such as the history of religions), Heidegger remarks that "the history of religion can provide materials for the philosophy (phenomenology) of religion [*daß die Religionsgeschichte Material für die Philosophie (Phänomenologie) der Religion liefern kann*]" (GA 60 76–7).

115 As Heidegger helpfully emphasizes, however, the phenomenologist of religion is in a sense dependent upon others, particularly theologians, biblical scholars, and historians of religion, to provide the data or material for intentional analysis; that is, the phenomenologist will best be able to phenomenologically describe the *meanings* of the religious community when its intentions and expressions are reflected upon by the theologian within the community (GA 60 76–8). Thus, if one were to engage in a "phenomenological explication of concrete religious phenomena" in early Christianity, what better source could there be than the testimony and witness of a member of the community such as Paul? (This is the motivation behind Part Two of the *Einleitung*.) So also today, if one were to make a phenomenological analysis of the "believing comportment" of, for example, early Pentecostal religion in North America, the most important sources for the phenomenologist would be the testimony of those from *within* the community, rather than the "reports" (*Gerede!*) of sociologists of religion.

116 However, with that said, I would still argue that Heidegger does provide an important critique of the theologization of religious experience which accompanied modernism in both Protestantism and Catholicism. He retrieves the primacy of religious experience as non-cognitive, a matter of the heart.

117 We must appreciate the radical shift that occurred in a space of six years regarding the project of "ontology": in 1923 (GA 63), "ontology" means a "hermeneutics of facticity," a grappling with the singularities and excesses of factical lived experience; by 1926/27, "ontology" is precisely "fundamental ontology," explicating the apriori structures of experience and pointing to the "*ontological* determinants . . . which are pre-Christian and which can thus be grasped purely rationally." For a discussion of this shift, see Daniel Dahlstrom, "How Does Phenomenology Become Fundamental Ontology?," in *Proceedings of the Thirtieth Annual Heidegger Conference*, ed. Robert C. Scharff (University of New Hampshire, 1996), 95–122.

118 This is also a familiar qualifier or disclaimer in SZ, where Heidegger constantly empha-sizes that the analyses of phenomena such as "fallenness" or "care" are not religious or theological, but rather explications of "ontological structures" which precede and condi-tion such "ontic" determinations. See e.g. SZ 179–80/167–8. For my critique of Heidegger's "story" on this, see James K. A. Smith, *The Fall of Interpretation: Philosophical Foundations for a Creational Hermeneutic* (Downers Grove, IL: InterVarsity Press, 2000), ch. 3.

119 For a discussion, see Kisiel, 408–51.

4

PRAISE AND CONFESSION

How (not) to speak in Augustine

We are involved in heaven knows what kind of battle of words.

(DC 1.6.6)

Lost for words?: The challenge of speaking for Augustine

One must be impressed by the almost paradoxical fact that, undergirding the verbosity of the Augustinian corpus, there is a deep and persistent concern regarding the insufficiency of language. We find Augustine the theologian lamenting the impossibility of the theologian's task: "Have I said anything, solemnly uttered anything that is worthy of God? On the contrary, all I feel I have done is to wish to say something; but if I have said anything, it is not what I wished to say" (DC 1.6.6). But we also hear the same concern from Augustine the preacher and pastor: "Stretch your minds, please," he implores his congregation, "help my poverty of language" (Sermon 119.3). Thus this "battle of words" (DC 1.6.6) does not attend only theological or philosophical discourse, but even the non-theoretical discourse of the preacher. For both, it is difficult to "find the words" which could properly or adequately express their referent. While for Heidegger the challenge of speaking arose when considering the possibility of theoretical discourse, for Augustine the challenge confronts even factical life in a sense, insofar as the preacher (*predicator*) – who is no Hegelian system-builder – also must engage in a battle to "find the words" which properly express or communicate their referent. Note again that it is a matter of *how* one speaks, a matter of speaking properly. And as Derrida observes, "The 'how' always conceals a 'why,' and the 'it is necessary' (*'il faut'*) bears the multiple meanings of 'should,' 'ought,' and 'must'" (HAS 85). The imperative to speak "well," to speak "properly," is at root an *ethical* imperative, even a categorical imperative. Far from a "counsel of prudence" in which it is in my best interest to follow its rule, this methodological imperative is a command which issues from the referent, a demand by the phenomenon for respect. And so we are challenged to do justice with words.

What is the source or origin of this inability of language and insufficiency of words, particularly for Augustine? It is located, I would suggest, in what might be described as a formal problematic of *incommensurability*,[1] crystallized in two instances of "transcendence." First, there is an incommensurability between "signs" – most often "words" – and "things"; most simply, words are *not* things (DM 10.31–3); things are otherwise than lingual and thus characterized by a certain excess *vis-à-vis* language. As we will see below, this lack of identity is unbridgeable and cannot be collapsed, and so the word can never present the thing – cannot grasp or comprehend the thing; it can only function as a "pointer."[2] And here the paradigmatic example is *God*: whatever I say about God is inadequate, Augustine says, because no words are worthy of God's infinity: "It is not easy, after all, to find any name that will really fit such transcendent majesty" (DC 1.5.5; cf. 1.6.6, C 1.4.4). This is what we might refer to as an objective or *exterior* transcendence – the transcendence of a thing or object outside of and beyond myself. The metaphor employed here is usually one of "height."

There is also second kind of incommensurability: it is what we could, perhaps oddly, describe as a subjective or *interior* transcendence:[3] the transcendence of the self. For Augustine, I cannot comprehend myself; I transcend my own comprehension. "I find my own self hard to grasp," he says (C 10.16.25) because of the very *infinity* of *memoria*. Here the metaphor is one of "depth," delving into the caverns of the mind, plunging into the abyss of consciousness. And it is because of this inner transcendence of the self – the incommensurability of my thoughts and the possibility of their articulation – that Augustine is faced with the challenge of how (not) to speak of his own experience. Formally, this interior transcendence is confronted by the same challenge as cases of exterior transcendence, viz. the problem of "putting into words" that which resists conceptualization, even language. I will refer to the first challenge linked to exteriority as a problem of *conceptualization*, and to the second challenge linked to interiority as a matter of *expression*.

But if words in particular, and language in general, are unable to comprehend and express their referent – if it is "inexpressible" – then should we not be silent? "This battle of words," Augustine remarked, "should be avoided by keeping silent, rather than resolved by the use of speech" (DC 1.6.6). But then should not Augustine have remained silent? If no words could be found which were worthy of God, should not Augustine have been lost for words? And if so, why and how could he say *so much*?

The injunction of silence, however, is not Augustine's final thought on the matter; indeed, upon the heels of the passage just quoted, he adds a most significant, "And yet . . .." Given the impossibility of finding words which could adequately describe that which exceeds them (e.g. God), it would seem that silence is the only "just" response. "*And yet*," Augustine carefully notes, "while nothing really worthy of God can be said about him, he has accepted the homage of human voices, and has wished us to rejoice in praising [*laude*] him with our words" (DC 1.6.6). My task in Part Three is to consider Augustine's method in the employment of language as a kind of "third way" (*pace* Dionysius[4]) between the violence of kataphatics and the silence of apophatics (characteristics of both a negative *theo*logy and a negative *anthropo*logy). This third way is an *incarnational* account of language which grapples with the methodological question of how (not) to speak of that which exceeds conceptualization and expression. In particular, in the first part of this chapter I will take up what I have described as the problem of "conceptualization": how (not) to speak of that which is (objectively) transcendent, particularly God. For Augustine, neither the theological positivism of kataphatics, nor the silence of apophatics, does justice to the transcendence of God. Rather, his strategy in response to this challenge of conceptualization is to opt for employing language in the mode of "praise," or what I will describe as his "laudatory strategy." After sketching the formal contours of the problematics of conceptualization in Augustine's account of language, I will briefly sketch his development of the notion of "reference." This is in fact located in his discussion of sin and the distinction between "use" (*uti*) and "enjoyment" (*frui*); from this we learn that the world – and words – are intended to function as "pointers," referring to that which lies beyond. In this sense, all the world is (or *ought* to be) an "icon," and so too are (*should be*) words. This will then form the basis for Augustine's account of language as "incarnational" (best seen in his sermons), which in turn sets the stage for "praise" as a means of speaking about God.

If "praise" is a methodological strategy developed in response to the challenge of *conceptualization*, then "confession" is a correlate strategy taken up in response to the challenge of *expression*. In the second part of this chapter, I will consider the way in which "confession" is a linguistic strategy of *expression*[5] which attempts to grapple with the im/possibility of speaking of oneself – a question of how (not) to speak. In order to do so, I will first sketch the conditions which demand such a strategy (viz. the "depth" or interiority of the Augustinian self, which I will refer to as the "secret" of the self) and the ensuing challenge for communication, given the incommensurability of language and self-expression. This will be followed by an analysis of the strategy of "confession," considering the project of the *Confessions* and the way in which this shapes the constitution and employment of language as an incarnational medium which allows one to indirectly "indicate" the secret of the self, without disclosing the secret to the generalizing mechanisms of the "public." In short, in confession, one does (not) tell the secret.

Between predication and silence: how (not) to speak of God

Words and things: the incommensurability of signa and res

As transcendent, God is wholly other – the very paradigm of alterity. And as such, we are faced with the challenge of how it will be possible to speak of that which is wholly other, which is otherwise than language and conceptual thought. Indeed, the *Confessions* open with just such a problem, first in terms of knowledge, which leads to the matter of language: how can I know God to praise him? And then, how can we praise (*laudare*) God adequately with human words (C 1.1.1, 1.4.4)? But while Augustine opens with attention to the *in*adequacy of language, nevertheless, he tells us, there is a God-given impetus or desire to praise the Creator: "these humans, due part of your creation as they are, still do long to praise you. You arouse us so that praising you may bring us joy, because you have made us and drawn us to yourself, and our heart is unquiet until it rests in you" (C 1.1.1 Boulding). Thus the self is confronted by a double-bind – confronted with both the impetus to and impossibility of praising God.[6] In attempting to describe God in 1.4.4, Augustine ends with the same tension: "But in these words what have I said, my God, my life, my holy sweetness? What has anyone achieved in words when he speaks about you? Yet woe to those who are silent about you because though loquacious with verbosity, they

116

have nothing to say." Here we find Augustine torn between kataphatics and apophatics, between a positivist theology which could claim to capture the essence of God in concepts, and a negative theology which, in face of the difficulty, remains silent. Augustine, however, is looking for a third way: "Have mercy so that I may find words," he prays (C 1.5.5).

But for Augustine, the alterity of God is, in a sense, a limit case of the general problem of the incommensurability between words and signs (*verba, signa*) and things (*rei*). In order to sketch this broader incommensurability, I will take up a brief exposition of Augustine's account of language in *De magistro* and *De doctrina christiana*.

Words, signs, and things: indications in Augustine

At the initiation of the early dialogue *De magistro*, Augustine states that the goal of speaking[7] is either to "teach" or to "learn" (DM 1.1). In fact, he goes on to suggest, we might reduce all speaking to *teaching*, for even the asking of a question in order to learn is in fact a kind of teaching: teaching the other what it is that I want to know (ibid.). This coincides with Augustine's brief account of language in *Confessions* I, where signs are an external means of expressing an internal desire or thought (C 1.6.10; 1.8.13). Teaching here must be taken in its broadest sense of *communicating*, and not restricted to a narrow pedagogical notion.

Adeodatus is not satisfied that this accounts for all speaking, for what about singing in private? What would we mean to "teach" here? Augustine's reply is two-fold: (1) if I am singing "for the lyrics," as it were, then they can serve as a *reminder*, as occasions for *recollection*[8] – as, for instance, when I sing a psalm in order to reflect upon the Scriptures and remind myself of the blessings of God; and (2) if we sing not to be reminded but for aesthetic pleasure, it is the melody and not the words which is pleasing. Singing in this instance would be distinguished from speaking. In both scenarios, the equation of speaking with teaching is maintained.

To this Adeodatus offers one other counter-example: *prayer*. In prayer, do we teach (the omniscient) God something? In Augustine's reply, we find an important distinction between an *interior* language (praying "in closed chambers" – in the "inner recesses of the mind") which remains closed off from the sensibility of *exterior* language or *signs*, which is characteristic of "speaking." "Anyone who speaks gives an external sign of his will by means of an articulated sound" (DM 1.2). In other words, speaking is always exterior, implicated in the use of signs. Therefore, really there is "no need for speaking when we pray" (DM 1.2), for to God the abyss of human consciousness lies open (C 10.1.2). But why, then, does Christ teach the disciples to pray with specific words?, Adeodatus asks. The intention of that instruc-tion, Augustine argues, is not to teach words, but rather the *things themselves* "by means of the words" (DM 1.2). This raises the question, pursued in the remainder of the dialogue, concerning the relationship between words and the experience of the things themselves.

In Book I of *De doctrina christiana*, Augustine provides a schematic analysis of the relationship between "signs" and "things," since "all teaching is either about things or signs": *things*, strictly speaking, "are those that are not mentioned in order to

117

signify something," but rather are ends in themselves (DC 1.2.2).[9] *Signs*, then, are those things "which are used in order to signify something else. Thus every sign is also a thing, because if it is not a thing at all then it is simply nothing. But not every single thing is also a sign" (DC 1.2.2).[10]

Words, then, are signs[11] (DM 2.3); but, Augustine asks, "can a sign be a sign if it doesn't signify any*thing*?" Does the word "nothing" signify some*thing*, and if not, can it be a sign? Here Augustine quickly gets to the matter of the relationship between *signum* (*verbum*) and *res*: quoting a line of verse from Virgil, he requests of Adeodatus to indicate the *res* which each *verbum* signifies. He is first held up by "nothing," then the preposition "from," at which point Augustine complains that Adeodatus is merely explaining words by means of words: "you have explained signs by means of signs . . . I would like you to *show* me the very things of which these words are the signs, if you can" (DM 2.4). Adeodatus's reply is pointed: first, we are in discussion, so the medium is precisely words; second, Augustine is also asking about things by means of words (DM 3.5). If he is going to require Adeodatus to point out the things without the use of signs, he requires the same of Augustine, viz. that he raise the question without using signs.

If we ask what the word "wall" signifies, however, could not Adeodatus simply point with his finger toward the wall behind him? Would this not answer the question without using words? It would be non-verbal, but it would remain a sign; that is, words are only one kind of sign; gestures are another. People who are deaf, for instance, teach not by speaking but by gesturing, including non-corporeal things (DM 3.5). Therefore, to answer the question "what does 'wall' signify?" with a gesture is still to indicate the thing to which a (verbal) sign refers by means of a (non-verbal) sign. Augustine wants to know whether it is possible to exhibit the thing *without signifying* (DM 3.6). Adeodatus initially thinks that this is impossible: "I see nothing . . . that can be shown without signs" (ibid.). However, what if one should ask what "walking" signifies, and another were simply to get up and pace the floor? "Wouldn't you be using the thing itself to teach me, rather than using words or any other signs?" Would this not be teaching by means of the thing itself? Yes, Augustine replies, but what if one did not know the *meaning* (definition) of the word (ibid.)? Then the simple demonstration would be insufficient. Thus Adeodatus's initial conclusion seems revalidated: nothing is shown *without* signs (ibid.). However, still seeking the possibility of knowledge without signs (DM 4.7), Augustine introduces a further distinction.

The (in)completion of the sign

Signs can be distinguished in two ways: (1) signs which signify other signs[12] (taken up in DM 4.7–6.18) and (2) signs which indicate things (*rei*) which are not themselves signs. The latter can be further subdivided between (a) those which are self-exhibiting, as "walking" above (DM 10.29–32) and (b) signs which point to things, or what Peter King describes as "instrumentals" (10.33–13.46). Spoken words are not the only signs; we must also include gestures, and written words (DM 4.7–8) –

these make up category (1), signs which signify other signs rather than things. Most important for our concern, however, is his discussion of the second division of signs. Here Augustine considers (a) signs which are self-signifying, like walking above, and (b) signs which function as "instrumentals" or pointers.

At this juncture (the dialogue has become a monologue) Augustine comes to two, apparently contradictory conclusions: (A) "nothing is taught *without* signs" (DM 10.31) because, as the dialogue up to this point has demonstrated, there is no access apart from signs. All speaking (and therefore teaching) is caught up within a system of signification. For instance, should someone ask me what "walking" is, I could simply stand and pace back and forth. But only within a system of signifiers (not necessarily lingual) would the student learn that my activity is walking, and that I am not simply stalling to come up with an answer.[13]

But Augustine later affirms that (B) "nothing is learned *through* signs" (DM 10.33). As he remarks, "When a sign is given to me, it can teach me nothing if it finds me ignorant of the thing of which it is the sign; but if I'm not ignorant, what do I learn through the sign?" (ibid.). The sign is not perceived *as* a sign until the thing which it signifies is known; or in other words, knowledge (experience) of the thing precedes knowledge of the sign (10.34). Thus I learn nothing (new) from the sign (ibid.). Words do not teach; they only "remind us to *look* for things" (11.36), functioning as *pointers*. Augustine uses the example of reading the story in the book of Daniel of the three youths whose *sarabarae* were not burned in the fiery furnace. Here, the word "sarabarae" can teach me nothing, unless I know the thing to which it refers. Should someone point out a visitor for me, and exclaim,

> "'Look: *sarabarae!*' I wouldn't learn the thing I was ignorant of by the words that he has spoken, but by looking at it. This is the way it came to pass that I know and grasp what meaning the name has. When I learned the thing itself, I trusted my eyes, not the words of another – though perhaps I trusted the words to direct my attention." (DM 10.35)

Indeed *sarabarae* is only a sound until it is constituted *as* a sign when that which is signified is known:

> "Before I made this discovery, the word was a mere sound to me; but I learned that it was a sign when I found out of what thing it is the sign – and, as I said, I learned this not by anything that signifies but by its appearance.[14] Therefore, a sign is learned when the thing is known, rather than the thing being learned when the sign is given." (DM 10.33)

This is because the sign is *insufficient*, or *structurally inadequate* – the thing is otherwise than a sign, it is transcendent to the sign, wholly other *vis-à-vis* the sign. The sign and the thing are radically incommensurate. Things are not words or signs; thus, to know a sign is not to know the thing. This means that there is a structural incompleteness to the word, such that it must be accompanied by the experience of the thing itself, and sound is only constituted as a sign when the thing is known:

From words, then, we learn only words – rather, the sound and noise of the words. If things that aren't signs can't be words, then although I have already heard a word, I don't know that it is a word until I know that it signifies. Therefore, the knowledge of words is *made complete* once the things are known. (DM 11.36, emphasis added)

Here we are confronted with something of a restaging of the "Learner's Paradox" in the *Meno*:[15] on the one hand, nothing is learned without signs; on the other hand, nothing is learned by means of signs. I would suggest that Augustine does not necessarily want one of these statements to trump the other; rather, their genius is found in holding them together in paradoxical tension.[16] What we learn from Augustine's analysis is that words, insofar as they are signs, are both *necessary* ("nothing is learned *without* signs") and *insufficient* or *inadequate*, perhaps even ineffectual ("nothing is learned *by means of* signs"). Words cannot present things; when the word is given to me by another, the thing to which it refers is not made present to me.[17] However, the word *does* "point" or "indicate" the thing itself, directs me to experience it for myself.[18] In this sense, we can say both that "we learn nothing *without* signs" (since they point/indicate things) and that "we learn no *thing* with signs" (since the signs themselves are not the thing and require experience of the thing itself). Hence, at times I must *believe* where I cannot *know*; where the sign fails, I learn the thing by faith. The result is not a comprehending knowledge, but belief, the non-knowing of faith: *sans savoir, sans avoir, sans voir*.[19] Here we are taught by the inner Teacher – Christ (11.38).

In a formalized sense, *things* are incommensurate with words or signs – they are wholly otherwise than language and cannot be captured within a concept or sign. However, signs, and specifically words, are able to "point" to things, direct our attention and *refer* us to the thing itself. This movement of reference marks the *completion* of the sign; and yet the word, when constituted as a sign, still retains a kind of *insufficiency* or *structural inadequacy* such that its very constitution is to refer beyond itself. Thus I suggest we refer to this as the *(in)completion* of the sign: the very structure of the sign is to point beyond itself, referring to that which exceeds it. As such, it is incomplete; however, its function is complet*ed* insofar as one is directed to then experience the thing itself – much like Heidegger's account of the fulfillment of the formal indication, not as adequation, but *Vollzugsinn*, the enactment-sense, where the "concept" is only fulfilled in experience. Structurally, the sign *refers* beyond itself, refers to that which transcends it, and therefore the sign can (or at least *should*) never constitute an end in itself. This notion of *reference* is important for Augustine's understanding of language and in the following section, I will take up a closer analysis.

Use, enjoyment, and reference: Augustine's phenomenology of idolatry

Perhaps unexpectedly, it is Augustine's discussion of *sin* which is instructional for understanding his theory of reference. Reference is that structure of the sign which indicates its incompleteness: the sign is only a sign insofar as it is *constituted as* a sign, and thereby understood to refer beyond itself to the thing. Thus words function properly[20] when they point us beyond themselves. In an analogous way, for Augustine, the "world" is to be constituted as a sign – or more particularly, a *sacramentum* – which points beyond itself; that is its proper use and function. In this section, I will sketch Augustine's phenomenological account of sin as a failure of reference and thus fundamentally "idolatry." I will then turn to draw on this in a way which will illuminate his understanding of the proper function of signs.

Intentionality, constitution, and a phenomenology of sin

The inauthentic self[21] is precisely the fallen self, the self alienated from itself by "sin"; but sin, for Augustine, is *intentional* in the sense that it is a "how," not a "what." It is not a question of *substantia*, but rather of the will's *intentio*, the way in which it constitutes its "world." "I inquired what wickedness is," he recalls, "and I did not find a substance but a perversity of will twisted away from the highest substance, you O God, towards inferior things" (C 7.16.22). Things – the world – are not inherently evil or sinful because, as created, they must be good (Gen. 1:31); what is sinful is the self's *relation* to the world, the way in which one directs or comports oneself toward those things.[22] Sin, then, is not a matter of structure or essence, but rather of direction or aim. What Augustine offers is not an ontology but rather a phenomenology of sin.

What is the criterion, then, for determining a sinful relation to the world? What is it that makes the self's *intentio* inauthentic? The authentic self finds its meaning in the enjoyment of God (*frui Deo*); the *in*authentic self, then, finds its ultimate happiness and enjoyment elsewhere, viz. in the world God has created. Here we hit upon a fundamental Augustinian distinction between "enjoyment" (*frui*) and "use" (*uti*), unpacked most systematically in *De doctrina christiana*, Book I. After distinguishing signs and things, Augustine remarks that things can be further distinguished, between those things "which are meant to be enjoyed [*fruendum*]" and others "which are meant to be used [*utendum*]" (DC 1.3.3). Things which are *enjoyed* make us happy, while things *used* "help us on our way to happiness." However, the self plays a pivotal role in the determination or *constitution* of things as enjoyed or used:

> We ourselves, however, both enjoy and use things, and find ourselves in the middle, in a position to *choose* which to do. So if we wish to enjoy things that are meant to be used, we are impeding our own progress, and some-times are also deflected from our course, because we are thereby delayed in obtaining what we should be enjoying, or turned back from it altogether, blocked by our love for inferior things. (DC 1.3.3, emphasis added)

While a certain design inheres in things as the imprint of their Creator, it is fundamentally the human self which constitutes things *as* either things to be used or enjoyed, ultimately by what we choose to *love*, since enjoyment "consists in clinging to something lovingly for its own sake" (DC 1.4.4). Thus, what we enjoy for its own sake, as an end in itself, is loved. However, there is a "right order of love" (DC 1.27.28) which ought to be observed: to enjoy things which ought to be used is to contravene this order.[23] What, then, is to be enjoyed? "The things therefore that are to be enjoyed are the Father and the Son and the Holy Spirit, in fact the Trinity, one supreme thing, and one which is shared in common by all who enjoy it" (DC 1.5.5). To enjoy "the world," then, represents a *misuse* or "abuse" (DC 1.4.4), a substituting of the creature for the Creator (DC 1.12.12).

By describing misuse in this way, Augustine evokes a metaphor which sees enjoying the world as a kind of intentional *idolatry* (cf. Romans 1:18–20). "Let it be clearly understood," Augustine earlier remarked, "that there could have been no error in religion had not the soul worshipped in place of its God either a soul or a body or some phantasm of its own" (VR 10.18). The "world," that which is to be used, is intended to "refer" (DC 1.4.4) or point the soul to that which is to be enjoyed, God. Thus the world is to be constituted as a sign (both *signum* and *sacramentum*[24]) which points to the Creator as the origin of life and meaning for the self. Rather than becoming absorbed in the world and its pleasures (cf. C. 10.27.38–10.36.59), the self is to constitute the world as a sign:

> When something that is loved, after all, is available to you, delight is also bound to accompany it; but if you *pass through this and refer it* to that end where you are to remain permanently, you are really using it, and are said by a figure of speech , and not in the proper sense of the word, to enjoy it. If, however, you cling to it and remain fixed in it, placing in it the end of all your joys, then you can be said really and truly to enjoy it. But this should not be done except with that Divine Trinity. (DC 1.33.37, emphasis added)

The world, then, functioning as a sign, is to be constituted as an *icon* which deflects the intentional aim or "love" of the self to the Creator as that which is to be enjoyed. The fallen or sinful self, by enjoying the world rather than using it, constitutes the world as an *idol* which "absorbs" its love and concern, going against the "right *order* of love."[25] The first, authentic love is *caritas*; the second, idolatrous, inauthentic love is described as both *cupiditas* and *concupiscientia*:

> What I mean by *charity* or love is any urge of the spirit to find joy in God for his own sake, and in oneself and one's neighbor for God's sake; by *cupidity* or greed [is intended] any impulse of the spirit to find joy in oneself and one's neighbor, and in any kind of bodily thing at all, not for God's sake. (DC 3.10.16)

It is "not that the creature is not to be loved," Augustine cautions, "but if that love is related to the Creator it will no longer be covetousness but charity. It is only covetousness when the creature is loved on its own account. In this case it does not help you in your use of it, but corrupts you in your enjoyment of it."[26] To love the world is to plunge into idolatry, enjoying the world rather than using it; in contrast, to use the world as something which points beyond itself to the origin of meaning and the end of happiness, is at the same time to constitute the world as an icon which refers the intentional aim to the Creator.

Idols, icons, and the Incarnation

We see, then, that the world or thing can be constituted as either an "idol," in which the intentional aim (love) is absorbed and the world is enjoyed as an end in itself, substituting for God; or, the world can be constituted as an "icon" which refers beyond itself, pointing to that which is transcendent and inviting one to complete the sign with the experience of the thing itself (God). The conceptual idol represents a kind of semiotic sin, a failure of reference which is a failure to recognize the (in)completion of the sign, but rather treats it as an end in itself. On the other hand, an icon, as a sign, shares the same structure of incompleteness described above; and this structural incompleteness is precisely what marks the structure of reference. It is precisely when the sign (world or word) is taken to be complete in and of itself that we fall into idolatry, since we fail to be referred beyond it. The idol represents the forgetting of transcendence, the reduction to immanence, and the denial of alterity; the icon represents respect for transcendence, the rupture of immanence, and reference to an alterity.

And if things can be so constituted, then *words*, as "things" (DC 1.2.2), can also be constituted and employed as either idols or icons. Words, when constituted as iconic signs, are thus understood as structurally incomplete and therefore referring beyond themselves. Thus they function as "pointers" to transcendence from a sphere of immanence. It is in this sense, then, that Augustine unpacks his *incarnational* understanding of language. His conception of language helps him understand the Incarnation, and the Incarnation is a heuristic for understanding the function of language. "These reflections [on the Incarnation and language] move in two directions," Mark Jordan observes. "On the one hand, they are meant to illuminate the features of human signification by tracing them back to their exemplary cause. On the other hand, Augustine's reflections move towards some analogous description of the knot which is the Incarnation itself."[27] The Incarnation is precisely an immanent sign *of* transcendence – God appearing in the flesh. Thus it is a structure of both presence and absence: present in the flesh, and yet referring beyond, the Incarnation – as the *signum exemplum* – retains the structural incompleteness of the sign which is constitutive of language, for to constitute the God-man as only man is to idolize the body, failing to constitute it as a manifestation of the divine. Divinity, while it cannot be reduced to this body, is nevertheless infleshed in it and thus signaling beyond itself. This is why the God-man is a *mediator* between divinity and humanity, finitude and the Infinite. This is also why, for Augustine, all signs function as mediator*s*: they are precisely that which both appear and at the same time maintain what they refer to in their transcendence. By referring or pointing to what is other than themselves, signs make knowledge of transcendence possible.[28]

Thus, when unpacking the meaning of John 1:1 for his congregation, Augustine the *predicator* draws on an analysis of the operation of language in order to illuminate the Johannine notion of "the Word":

> I'm driving at something about the Word; and perhaps a human word can do something similar. Although it's no match at all, very very different, in no way comparable, still it can suggest to you a certain similarity. Here you are then, here's the word which I now am speaking to you; I had it first in my mind. It went out to you, and didn't go away from me. It began to be in you, because it wasn't in you before. It stayed with me, when it went out to you. So just as my word was presented to your perception, and didn't depart from my mind, so that Word was presented to our perception, and didn't depart from his Father. My word was with me, and went out into the sound of my voice; the Word of God was with the Father, and went out into the flesh. (Sermon 119.7)

Note the multi-leveled consideration of dis/analogy at work here: in order to show the way in which God is manifest in the Incarnation, which itself functions on the basis of analogy or "participation,"[29] Augustine employs the second analogy of language. And just as there is a radical incommensurability between the finite and the Infinite (between God's transcendence and our "perception") – a difference "bridged" in the Incarnation – so it is the same principle which makes the second analogy (with language) possible. Though "the Word" and human words are "very very different, in no way comparable," nevertheless the analogy *is* possible. It is possible to *say something*. The difference is not *so* different that nothing can be said. Thus Augustine's account here would be close to what Anthony Godzieba describes as a classically "dialectical" understanding of the character of God: "transcendent yet immanent, mysterious yet available, absent yet present."[30] Which is also why Augustine's account of how (not) to speak of God is contrary to nominalism (medieval [Ockham], modern [Barth], and postmodern [Marion?]) whose insistence upon God's utter transcendence puts God "beyond reach" and thus "extrinsic to human experience."[31]

Consider the "logic" of incarnation which Augustine unpacks here in Sermon 119: in my speaking to you,[32] a "word"[33] is presented in the sound of the *verbum* I utter. The original thought ("word") as present in my mind is inaccessible to you, *transcendent vis-à-vis* your consciousness; or, in other words, if we could push a different metaphor, the thought was *absent* from you. However, when I express this thought in an articulated sound, the word (thought) becomes *present* to you, though not in its fullness, or not in a manner identical to which it resided "in me." Furthermore, in its *exitus* – its "going out" – it did not depart from me; in being made present to you, it did not become absent from me. "It has reached you," he tells his congregation, "and has not been separated from me. Before I spoke, I had it, and you did not have it; I have spoken, and you have begun to have it, and I have lost nothing. Why, isn't my word marvelous! So what must the Word of God be?" (Sermon 120.3).

But if the logic of incarnation is fundamentally a means of dealing with incommensurability, where is the incommensurability in this analogy? It is found in the relation between the minds of the speaker and listener. In a way not unlike Husserl's account of one's consciousness being essentially inaccessible to another, for Augustine my "thoughts" are absent to the other, just as the other's thoughts are absent from me. The other's thoughts (consciousness) cannot be made present to me, nor can my thoughts be experienced by the other. But this is precisely where Augustine's incarnational account of language indicates the possibility of overcoming this incommensurability without erasing it. For in my words, I am able to bridge this chasm and make "present" (in a weaker sense[34]) my thoughts to another in a way which makes connection possible, but at the same time preserves the difference. It seems to be precisely a "relation without relation" of which Levinas speaks,[35] for the word is able to be *both* present *and* absent, appearing within the sphere of the same without being reduced to the sphere of the same, presented to perception but maintaining its otherness.

It is in this way that language functions like the Incarnation of the God-man: when the "Word became flesh" (John 1:14), the transcendent God descended into the realm of immanence (finitude), but without thereby denying or giving up his transcendence. Here we see a consistent theme of "descent" or even *con*-descent in Augustine's incarnational reflections.[36] God's transcendence is inaccessible to us, but the way in which this is remedied is precisely by God's humiliation and descent to the order of the (fallen) creature. It is God who moves toward finitude, rather than lifting up (as an operation of *Aufhebung*) the finite.[37] David Meconi argues that this is one of the moments where Augustine departs from the Platonism of Plotinus by thinking of "participation" as a *downward* movement, which is also precisely why when commenting on the "books of the Platonists" and the thought of the Incarnation, he emphasizes: "*that* these books do not have" (C 7.9.14). Why is the thought of incarnation absent from Platonism? Because to think its possibility, one would have to reverse the movement of Platonic "participation," imagining a *descent* of the eternal to the temporal, of the intelligible to the temporal.[38] "With this new ability to imagine an underived, immutable essence participating in the imperfect, mutable contingents of this fallen world," Meconi comments, "Augustine is now able to speak of the perfect's participating in the imperfect: that which-is taking part in that which-is-not."[39] Such a downward movement of the divine is able to bridge the chasm between humanity and God in the paradox of Christ – and "no Platonist could ever hold that the Forms actually condescend to participate in this world of mutable particulars, an insight which prepares the way for Augustine's full acceptance of Christ's dual nature."[40] Thus the movement which grapples with the "chasm" or incommensurability is a downward movement on the part of the transcendent, a condescension on the part of the divine to the strictures of finitude: "The food which I was too weak to accept he mingled with flesh, in that 'The Word was made flesh,' so that our infant condition might come to suck milk from your wisdom by which you created all things" (C 7.18.24). The result of this condescension is that we see "divinity become weak by his sharing in our 'coat of skin'" (C 7.18.24), and yet it remains *divinity* that we "see."

It seems to me that this notion of "condescension" or downward participation also marks a fundamental difference between Marion[41] and Augustine: for Marion, in conceptual determinations of God in which God must appear within the horizons of the finite ego, God (the Infinite) is reduced to the concept (the finite) – which is precisely the problem, on his account, since the Infinite God would thus be reduced to the measure of the finite constituting ego, undoing God's transcendence. I am not so sure that this is a "problem" for God, however, and it is precisely Augustine's incarnational account which suggests this. What I am suggesting, following Augustine, is that God plays the game by these rules – which ultimately, as Creator of finitude,[42] he is responsible for. That is to say, God's incarnational appearance is precisely a condescension to the conditions of finite, created perceivers. How could he appear otherwise? The Incarnation signals a connection with transcendence which does not violate or reduce such transcendence, but neither does it leave it in a realm of utter alterity without appearance.

The same incarnational logic is repeated later in *De trinitate*. Attempting to "see him by whom we are made by means of this image which we ourselves are" (*De trinitate* 15.8.14), Augustine concludes that the place to look is within, at our "thoughts," which are "a kind of utterance of the heart" (ibid., 15.10.17). There we encounter a "word that belongs to no language," a word we utter in our hearts which is neither Greek, nor Latin, nor even Hebrew (15.10.19). But when we seek to convey this knowledge possessed in the inner word, we need to employ a sign to do so. And again we find the same incommensurability between the word as "thought" (the inner word) and the word as "sound" (the outer or external word):

> Thus in a certain fashion our word [thought] becomes a bodily sound by assuming that in which it is manifested to the senses of men, just as the Word of God became flesh by assuming that in which it too could be manifested to the senses of men. And just as our word becomes sound without being changed into sound, so the Word of God became flesh, but it is unthinkable that it should have been changed into flesh. It is by assuming it, not by being consumed into it, that both our word becomes sound and that Word became flesh. (*De trinitate* 15.11.20)

That which is not sensible – incommensurate with sensibility – nevertheless is manifested by making itself known *by means of* and *in terms of* the sensible. It is made known, we might say, "according to the mode of the perceiver" – to evoke a Thomistic epistemological principle which strikes me as fundamentally Augustinian in this regard. This account takes up the "battle of words" on two fronts: on the one hand it argues that, in contrast to any representationalism, that which exceeds and precedes the Word cannot be made fully present in the external word; there remains an absence. But on the other hand, there *is* a manifestation, a revelation, a *certain* presence, such that transcendence is able to "show up" in terms that a finite perceiver or sensible perception can understand. When the inner word is uttered inwardly, it is heard "just exactly as it is" (*De trinitate* 15.11.20). But "when it is uttered vocally [externally] or by some bodily sign, it is not uttered just exactly as it is, but *as it can be seen or heard* through the body" (ibid., emphasis added). While in its external utterance there is a degree of dissimulation, this in fact preserves its otherness, just as God's appearing in flesh did not entail the loss of his divinity. So by understanding language as incarnational, we see the possibility of speaking of transcendence.

And the sign, as incarnational, is able to refer to transcendence in a fundamentally *non-violent* manner. For Levinas and Marion, the problem with phenomenological conceptualization is that it reduces the other to the same; it effects a violation of the other, a fundamental *violence*: it reduces transcendence to immanence. By thinking of signs as instances of incarnation, Augustine is able to understand language *not* as essentially violent, but rather as that which grants access to things, but at the same time leaves them in their transcendence. Here we find the analogy with the Incarnation of God in Christ: the God-man, though present in the flesh (sphere of immanence), did not cease to be God (sphere of transcendence). The incarnation of transcendence "in flesh" does not undo its transcendence; the *signum* does not deny the *mysterium*, but rather points to it. This is seen clearly in *De doctrina christiana* 1.12.13:

> How did she [wisdom] come, if not by the Word becoming flesh and dwelling amongst us? It is something like when we talk; in order for what we have in mind to reach the minds of our hearers through their ears of flesh, the word which we have in our thoughts becomes a sound, and is called speech. *And yet* this does *not* mean that our thought is turned into that sound, but while remaining undiminished in itself, it takes on the form of a spoken utterance by which to insert itself into their ears, without bearing the stigma of any change in itself.

The Word, in appearing in flesh, is not reduced to corporeal reality, and yet it is able *to appear*. In the word, the referent is not reduced to the sign, but nevertheless the thing is indicated by the sign. We learn nothing by means of signs; we learn nothing without signs.

How (not) to speak of God: the icon of praise

What would this incarnational account of language entail, then, with respect to speaking of God – transcendence *par excellence*? How does an incarnational account of language do justice to the alterity of God? For as Augustine reminds his congregation, God is the very paradigm of alterity, which resists comprehension and conceptualization:

> But you are quite unable to imagine or think of such a thing. And such ignorance is more religious and devout than any presumption of knowledge. After all, we are talking about God. It says, *and the Word was God* (Jn. 1:1). We are talking about God; so why be surprised if you cannot grasp it? I mean, if you can grasp it, it isn't God. Let us rather make a

devout confession of ignorance, instead of a brash profession of knowledge. Certainly it is great bliss to have a little touch or taste of God with the mind; but to completely grasp him, to comprehend him, is altogether impossible. (Sermon 117.5)

Nevertheless, as he emphasizes, God "has accepted the homage of human voices" (DC 1.6.6). But for Augustine, this "praising him with human words" is an order of discourse which is more *affective* than cognitive. "That in fact is what is meant by calling him God," he remarks. "Not, of course, that with the sound made by these two syllables [*Deus*] any knowledge of him is achieved; but still, all those who know Latin are moved, when this sound reaches their ears, to reflecting upon some most exalted and immortal nature" (DC 1.6.6, trans. modified). The point of speaking is not for the provision of cognitive data, but to move the listener to reflection and experience of the thing itself, viz. an experience of God.[43] Thus in the concluding fourth book of *De doctrina christiana*, wherein Augustine sketches what we might loosely describe as a "Christian rhetoric," he suggests that "through *another kind of eloquence*"[44] we find that "the words they are said with seem to spring spontaneously from the subject matter,[45] rather than to be contributed by the writer, so that you could almost imagine wisdom stepping out from her own house, that is from the breast of the wise man" (DC 4.6.10). The directionality of the relation has shifted – it is the referent determining how one speaks, rather than the speaker's categories imposing themselves upon the object. It is not the speaker's word which comes to grasp Wisdom, but Wisdom which comes to us through the words of the speaker. But one must recall here that this is not characteristic of all speaking, but only of that speaking which employs "another kind of eloquence," another kind of rhetoric. It is the case only when one speaks *well*.

When it is a matter of speaking well of God, we are again confronted by this fundamental challenge: for "what, after all, could be greater than God himself? Does that mean that we cannot learn about him?" (DC 4.19.38). As he indicated earlier (DC 1.6.6), the answer in the face of this challenge is not *silence* but *praise*:

> But when God is being praised [*laudatur*], either in himself or in his works, what a vast prospect of beautiful and glowing language will occur to the speaker, in order to praise as best he can the one whom nobody can praise as befits him, [but whom] nobody fails to praise somehow or other [*qui potest quantum potest laudare, quem nemo conuenienter laudat, nemo quomodocumque non laudat*]! (DC 4.19.38, trans. modified)

Thus it is possible to speak about God, but in the mode of *praise*, as a non-objectifying, non-positivistic mode of conceptualization which does not reduce God to a concept, but rather employs language in such a way that respects God's transcendence and *refers* the listener to experience the thing itself. Praise capitalizes on the (in)completion of the sign, such that the language of the preacher (*predicator!*) functions in a way to direct the listener beyond the words offered to an experience of the thing itself. The words offered by the *predicator* are no longer representations or predications, but rather iconic pointers which deflect the gaze beyond themselves. But nevertheless, the "referent"[46] (in this case God) does "appear," in a sense, in the saying (not in *what* is said but *how* it is said). In this way Augustine provides an account of language – and theological method – which avoids the violence of positivist kataphatics and the silence of apophatics, charting a "third" way which enables one to speak.

What I want to suggest, with (but perhaps beyond) Augustine, is that *praise*[47] constitutes a mode of non-objectifying, non-predicative discourse about that which is transcendent, or at least incommensurate with the order of predication. In other words, it offers a way of speaking of the incommensurable, rather than consigning us to silence. It provides a way to avoid (not) speaking, for in praise we stave off both the violence of predication and the silence of apophatics. This is why I think an Augustinian account is fundamentally *en*abling in the face of both the "rationalizing tendency of modernity and ontotheology" and also the "*no, not, never* of dogmatic postmodern philosophy of religion."[48] However, to assert that "praise" is a non-objectifying mode of speaking is not without challenge; in order to defend it, I will need to situate this claim within the context of Derrida's critique of "praise" and Marion's response – and then attempt to inhabit a space between them.

Praise as predication: Derrida's critique

While I have located the laudatory strategy of "praise" [*laudatio*] in Augustine, it can be found both earlier and later: the notion was brought into contemporary discussions by Jean-Luc Marion's account of *hymnein* in the work of Dionysius, which he suggests constitutes a non-objectifying saying which is no longer "speaking" in a predicative sense – which in fact tends toward "prayer" (*euche*).[49] In *God Without Being*, Marion emphasizes that Dionysius's "naming" of God as first "Good" is not meant to constitute *the* "proper name" of God; rather, "in the apprehension of goodness the dimension is cleared where the very possibility of a categorical statement concerning Gxd ceases to be valid, and where the reversal of de-nomination[50] into praise becomes inevitable" (GWB 76). It is praise which displaces conceptual idols, a praise that "feeds on the impossibility or, better, the impropriety of the category" (ibid.). Praise is otherwise than predication because it does not attempt to capture God in the idol of conceptual determination, but rather functions as an iconic reference. Predication eliminates distance/difference, whereas praise opens that space. "In other terms," Thomas Carlson comments,

> one might say that the difference between praise and predication in Marion marks a distinction – much like Levinas's between the saying and the said – between a pure signifying or endless reference, on the one hand, and a determinate meaning or referent on the other. The naming of God in praise would signify endlessly toward God without securing (predicatively) any final meaning for God.[51]

Therefore, with respect to God, "predication must yield to praise" (GWB 106), for "only then can discourse be reborn" (GWB 107).[52]

But if praise still says something *about* God, though not conceptually or ontotheologically, does it not therefore remain predicative (and therefore violent)? Does not praise continue to *determine* God, even if not conceptually? And does not this determination still constitute a kind of violence, a reduction of God to the determination of the one who praises? These are the questions posed to Marion by Derrida, who argues that "the encomium [praise], although it is not a simple attributive speech, nevertheless preserves an irreducible relationship to the attribution. No doubt, as Urs von Balthasar rightly says, 'Where God and the divine are concerned, the word *hymnein* almost replaces the word "to say."'" Almost, in fact, but not entirely" (HAS 111). Praise "almost" replaces speaking, but insofar as in praise one still qualifies God and thus determines the other, praise remains within the horizon of attribution, even if it has stepped outside of the horizon of conceptual (metaphysical) determination. Insofar as praise still says something *about* the divine, it continues to objectify its referent in the very *naming* (HAS 111).

> For if the encomium or the celebration of God indeed does not have the same rule of predication as every other proposition, even if the "truth" to which it lays claim is the higher truth of a hyperessentiality, it celebrates and names what "is" such as it "is," beyond Being. Even if it is not a predicative affirmation of the current type, the encomium preserves the style and the structure of a predicative affirmation. It says something about someone. [Praise] entails a predicative aim, however foreign it may be to "normal" ontological predication. (HAS 137)

Predication, Derrida argues, has a certain "style" and "structure," both of which are retained in the economy (is it?) of encomium. However, what exactly this "structure" is, Derrida does not specify, except to suggest that every speaking *about* someone is predicative (HAS 137). (We will need to interrogate this thesis in a moment, unpacking the logic of predication or determination.) Given this link between praise and predication (as opposed to their distinction emphasized by Marion), Derrida suggests that only *prayer* proceeds non-predicatively, and thus he distinguishes between prayer and praise (HAS 136 n.16). For while praise still says something *about* someone, "[t]his is not the case of the prayer that apostrophizes, addresses itself to the other and remains, in this pure [!] movement, absolutely pre-predicative" (HAS 137). "Pure" prayer is undetermined because it does not speak *about*, but speaks *to*; rather than predication, it is an address (HAS 110).

But does not the address require an address*ee*? While the missive may be lost in the postal system,[53] does not even the mode of address require, at the very least, an intentional aim? Or to repeat a Husserlian maxim differently: is not every address an address *to*, even if the addressee is indeterminate? While we might say, as Derrida would like, that the addressee is undetermined, is not the mode of address still a form of intentionality? Prayer, then, does not reverse the intentional direction, but rather maintains the priority of the subject; in fact the opposite of prayer would be the "l'interloqué," the claim (RD 198) which alone would signal the decentering of the subject. In Derrida's "pure prayer," we still see a subject addressing the Other (what he does not know), rather than an Other addressing me. Would that not mean that prayer, as praise, also retains the structure of attribution? If so, then the question is whether there can be a mode of determination or attribution which is non-violent and non-objectifying; in other words, we will need to question whether determination *per se* is inherently violent.

Further, we must question whether prayer can be "pure" (HAS 110, 137). Does this not indicate in Derrida a latent desire for purity akin to his desire for a "religion without religion," a form without content, a pure structure? And is that not strictly impossible, from a deconstructive standpoint? Isn't that asking for a little too much, getting a little greedy with one's prayers? Having taken up a critique of this thematics of purity elsewhere, I will not repeat it here.[54] "If prayer were absolutely pure appeal," Carlson comments, "it could 'occur' only once; it would prove singular, unique – to the point of resisting all repetition, which would reduce the singularity of the appeal to the iterability of a name, a common name, or even a concept, transmissible by tradition."[55] And more than this – for could it even be said *once*? Wouldn't its very articulation in language – its being said – betray its singularity, placing it within the traffic of a necessarily public language which is not singular but general? Its expression in language, which is common and public, would always already disrupt the singularity of the prayer, with the result that the only prayer which would be "pure" would be one "unsaid."[56] In any case, if such a pure prayer is impossible, what would this mean for "impure" prayer? Unfortunately, Derrida does not specify just what it would be which would taint prayer. Would an unpure prayer be a prayer which is *determined* in some way, addressed to someone *in particular*? It seems that this is Derrida's intention (HAS 110); but this raises another concern: if "pure" (i.e. purely formal) prayer is impossible (just as a purely formal religion is impossible[57]), then does that mean that all prayer is also predicative and objectifying, insofar as it is determined? If that were the case, then it would seem that indeed there would be no way to speak of transcendence; we would be consigned to silence, for any speaking would always already be a form of predication, and hence objectification, and hence violence. For if even prayer is predicative, what more (or less) could be said?

Praising otherwise than predication: Marion's response

But what are we to make of Derrida's logic here, which makes praise and determined prayer simply another mode of predication and hence violence? Does the first (determination) entail the second (objectification, violence)? The question we must address at this point is whether all "determination" is "predicative." Is all saying "about" a form of predication? What exactly do we (and Derrida) mean by predication? The "style" and "structure" of predication for Derrida seems to be simply "saying something about someone" (HAS 137) such that every description would constitute a determination. But is this the case? And further, is every "determination" necessarily an instance of "objectification"?

Marion takes up the gauntlet thrown down by Derrida in his most recent piece, "In the Name." Here, Marion sets out to demonstrate that praise is not another, subtle form of predication or attribution. Rather, "praise" constitutes a "third way" which steps outside of the binary logic of affirmation (kataphasis) and negation (apophasis), and thus also steps outside of the order of predication.

> The third way is played out beyond the oppositions between affirmation and negation, synthesis and separation, in short, the true and the false. Strictly speaking, if thesis and negation have it in common to speak the truth (and spurn the false), the way which transcends them should also transcend the true and the false. The third way would transgress nothing less than the two truth values, between which the entire logic of metaphysics is carried out. If the third way is no longer about saying the true or the false, if it is precisely a matter of its not saying them, one can no longer claim [as Derrida does] that it means to affirm a predicate of a subject, not even beneath the absurd dissimulation of a negation, nor that it has the least bit of interest in doing so. The third way does not hide an affirmation beneath a negation.[58]

Rather than a procedure of "naming" (*nom*-ing), it is a matter of "de-nominating" God, a mode of speaking "which denies all relevance to predication."[59] It is not a new language, nor a new lexicon, but rather a new "pragmatic" *function* of language which simply "refers" to the "unattainable yet inescapable interlocutor beyond every name and every denegation of names." Constituting a reference without sense, the denomination is left incomplete, without end, so that denomination is a "referring to Him who is no longer touched by nomination."[60] I have tried to locate a similar account of iconic reference in Augustine (see above): for Augustine, the sign is to function as a pointer which refers us beyond itself to that which exceeds it. In "praise," we find a saying which does not grasp or encompass the transcendent, but rather refers to it – determinately, yes, but not definitively (if I could be permitted that distinction). In other words, praise is quasi-predicative and quasi-determinative: it says something about someone, but without prescription or definition. In "praise," I do not claim to grasp God in a concept, but rather to ascribe beauty, majesty, justice to him in words which are insufficient but necessary.

In order to reply to Derrida's criticism, we need to unpack the logics of predication and objectification. What constitutes the "violence" of predication is not mere determination, but rather the *how* of speaking wherein a final meaning is secured and defined – where reference is halted. It seems to me that Levinas's discussion here is paradigmatic: the ethical problem with "theory," or simply "knowledge" in the Western tradition (or at least in modernity[61]), is that it always already designates *comprehension*, such that the relation between knower and known is one of totalization wherein the "object," as objectified, is deprived of its alterity (TI 42). However, "this mode of depriving the known being of its alterity can be accomplished only if it is aimed at through a third term, a neutral term, . . . a concept" (ibid.). As such, knowing, as comprehending, becomes a matter of *grasping*: "To know amounts to grasping being out of nothing or reducing it to nothing, removing from it its alterity" (TI 44). And it is this denial of alterity *in the concept* which produces domination, tyranny, violence (TI 46–7).

But Levinas himself suggests a *different* knowing, a non-objectifying, non-violent "relation" with the other which is nevertheless a contact. For "knowledge" could also designate "a relation with being such that the knowing being lets the unknown being manifest itself while respecting its alterity and without marking it in any way whatever by this cognitive relation" (TI 42). Here we would have a knowledge *which is not comprehension* – the possibility of a knowing which does not attempt to encompass and grasp. And this is precisely the order of "knowing" we find in Augustine's laudatory strategy of praise, which denies any ability to grasp God, but does not deny that we might "touch" him (Sermon 117.3). Thus we find the possibility of a speaking (about God – or any incommensurate) which is a saying of something about someone, but nevertheless is not conceptual, and therefore not objectifying, and therefore not violent. Indeed, must not *Totality and Infinity* itself be an example of just such a speaking?

It would seem, then, that we can subvert Derrida's thesis regarding praise as predication in one of two ways: either (1) by denying that all forms of "saying something about someone" are forms of predication, or (2) by denying that all forms of predication are objectifying and violent. My strategy would be the second: I would agree with Derrida that every "saying something about someone" is predicative *in a sense* and therefore constitutes a "determination" – "formally" or "structurally" we might say. However, not every predication or determination is necessarily an "objectification." And insofar as the violence of the concept is precisely the violence of objectifying that which is transcendent or incommensurate by means of conceptual description, our (ethical/methodological) concern is really with objectification and not predication *per se*. "Violent" or "objectifying" predication is the halting of reference, the security of a meaning, and the adequation of the concept and object. But praise is characterized by *in*completion, reference without end, and a fundamental *in*adequation. The intentional aim is not halted in praise, but only deflected, without consummation or completion. *And yet*, one is able to speak of transcendence, since the transcendent God "has accepted the homage of human voices, and has wished us to rejoice in praising him with our words" (DC 1.6.6). But praise in no wise claims to comprehend such transcendence, which is why Augustine consistently distinguishes between "knowledge" and "comprehension."[62]

In the laudatory strategy of praise, one speaks well of God, with/out determination, such that the one who praises can still ask: "What do I love when I love my God?" (C 10.7.11; cf. 10.6.8). That is why praise does not deny undecidability, but rather recognizes such as the condition of possibility for praise – which is, in the end, an operation of faith.[63]

How (not) to tell a secret: interiority and the strategy of "confession"

In this section, I will argue that "confession" (*confiteri*), like "praise" (*laudare*), is an enabling linguistic strategy adopted in the face of incommensurability. While praise addresses the challenge of speaking of exterior alterity – what I have described as a problem of "conceptualization" – confession is a means of addressing the challenge of speaking about facticity (which is also incommensurate) – what I have described as a challenge of "expression."[64] Both, however, are non-objectifying modes of speaking which enable one to speak of the incommensurable. But while praise is a way of speaking of the Other, confession is a way of speaking of oneself – of a self that eludes itself, that has deep secrets which cannot be brought to the surface; yet one must speak (not to would be a sin). And so the question: *comment ne pas confesser?* How (not) to speak of oneself? How to keep a secret secret when there is an imperative to speak? How (not) to tell a secret?

Interior secrets: on not knowing who we are

For Augustine, the self finds its "meaning" – its identity and definition – in its *relations*, in its "love" as its intentional aim. In other words, the self is defined by what it loves, by what it directs itself toward, what it refers itself to.[65] The meaning of the self is a question precisely because of the fundamental *ambiguity* of the self, the mystery of one's own being. The self is not transparent to itself, cannot be made an "object" for itself.[66] The odyssey of the soul is toward self-knowledge, "to know as I am known" (C 10.1.1), precisely because there are things about myself which I do *not* know, which exceed my grasp, yet are laid open to God – for "to your eyes the abyss of human consciousness is naked" (C 10.2.2). While St. Paul remarks that "no man knows the being of man except the spirit of man which is in him" (1 Cor. 2:11), "yet," Augustine continues, "there is something of the human person which is unknown even to the 'spirit of man which is in him.' But you, Lord, know everything about the human person" (C 10.5.7); in fact, "I nevertheless know something of you which I do not know about myself." Thus, his confession – which is for his own sake, not God's – is a confession of a lack of self-knowledge, a confession of the mystery of his own selfhood: "let me confess what I know of myself. Let me confess too what I do not know of myself. For what I know of myself I know because you grant me light" (ibid.).[67] Indeed, Augustine remarks that he does not know his best friend Alypius either, for which Reason playfully scolds him: "Do you dare to say that your most familiar friend is unknown to you?" "*Seeing that I do not know myself,*" Augustine replies, "how can I be reproached for saying that I do not know him, especially since, I dare say, he does not profess to know himself either" (Sol 1.3.8).[68] As Brian Stock comments, "If we do not know ourselves (that is, if we cannot express what it is about ourselves that we know), then we cannot know others or express anything about them."[69] While in the phenomenological context of Husserl's Fifth Meditation, it is the *other's* mind which is structurally "absent" – an inaccessible "mystery"

134

– for Augustine it is *my own soul* which cannot be made fully present, even to myself. There is, I would suggest, an absence at the core of the self. Thus Augustine's lack of knowledge concerning what is most familiar becomes a central theme in Heidegger's analysis of Dasein: "What is ontically nearest and familiar is ontologically the farthest, unrecognized and constantly overlooked in its ontological significance."[70] The confession, then, is ultimately a question posed to the self: who am I? Who am I, who has become an enigma (C 10.33.50), a question to myself (C 4.4.9)?

The mysteriousness and ambiguity of the self, for Augustine, is grounded in the *depth* of the soul's interiority. In the quest of the soul to answer the question, "Who am I?" – which is always already to ask, "Who is my God?" – Augustine "turns away" from the external world into himself, an inward turn towards reflection on himself (C 10.6.9). The first half of Book X recounts this inward turn, couched in the Neoplatonic metaphor of interior ascent, a journey from the outer world to the secret recesses of the soul. Thus he begins by considering the external world, then moves to the self as body, on to the self as soul, through the stages of vegetative and sentient soul, and finally to memory (C 10.8.12ff.). While portrayed in terms of ascent to a height (*pace* Plotinus), it is in fact more of a *de*scent into an abyss (cf. 10.2.2), penetrating deeper and deeper into the soul until reaching the "caves and caverns of my memory" (C 10.17.26; 10.8.13). Rather than an ascent to mountain heights, Augustine's quest for self-knowledge is construed in terms of a journey to the center of the earth.

It is in these interior caverns that the self becomes even more mysterious; it is as though, by penetrating to the heart of the soul, one were to find at its center a bottomless abyss which could not be sounded. Indeed, as Augustine reflects on the powers of memory, he is struck and overwhelmed by an *infinity*:

> This power of memory is great, very great, my God. It is a vast and infinite profundity [*penetrale amplum et infinitum*]. Who has plumbed its bottom? This power is that of my mind and is a natural endowment, but *I myself cannot grasp the totality of what I am.* Is the mind, then, too restricted to compass itself, so that we have to ask what is that element of itself which it fails to grasp? Surely that cannot be external to itself; it must be within the mind. How then can it fail to grasp it? This question moves me to great astonishment. Amazement grips me. (C 10.8.15, emphasis added)

The self cannot grasp itself, cannot conceptualize itself, but not because it is external or outside of itself; rather, the self eludes itself because of its own depth which opens on to an infinity. The odyssey into the recesses of the soul brings the self face-to-face with its own mystery, with the secret which cannot be made present (except to God, for whom "the abyss of human consciousness" is an open book). It is here that we encounter difficulty: "I at least, Lord, have difficulty as this point, and I find my own self hard to grasp. I have become for myself a soil which is a cause of difficulty and much sweat" (C 10.16.25). Like Heidegger's contours of "facticity," for Augustine also this is, paradoxically, a question of *proximity*: "It is not surprising that whatever is

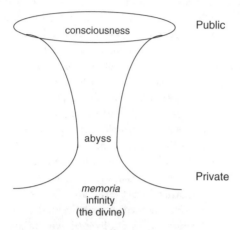

Figure 1 The interior transcendence of the self.

not myself should be remote, but what can be nearer to me than I am to myself?" (C 10.16.25 Boulding[71]). Again, this encounter with memory – with himself – is understood as an encounter with infinity which causes amazement:[72] "Great is the power of memory, an awe-inspiring mystery, my God, a power of profound and infinite multiplicity. And this is mind, this is myself" (C 10.17.26). This mystery or ambiguity of the self, then, is grounded in its interiority, which signals an interior incommensurability – an infinity whose end I never reach (ibid.) (see Figure 1 above). But because of this infinity which precludes definition, we are still left with the question: "What then am I, my God?" (ibid.).

Anticipating an engagement with Derrida's *Speech and Phenomena* below, it will here be important to point out the difference between the Husserlian and Augustinian ego – while still affirming Husserl's claims regarding their continuity (CM 157). As Derrida observes, "lived experience," for Husserl, "does not have to be . . . indicated because it is immediately certain and present to itself" (SP 43). Thus the "certitude of inner existence" does not need to be signified because "it is immediately present to itself" (SP 43). But is this the case of the Augustinian subject, or at least a *certain* Augustinian subject?[73] While Derrida will subvert the self-present Husserlian ego by pointing out the absence at its origin, is not Augustine already attentive to this absence "within" the ego? By emphasizing the infinity, mystery, and enigmatic character of the self, Augustine points to an alternative understanding of the ego as one always already characterized by the presence of absence – an excess which cannot be grasped.

Silence and secrets: interiority and the problem of communication

Language, which for Augustine constitutes the condition for the necessity of inter-pretation, finds its origin in a space construed as a *rift*, an abyss between interiorities.

Signs are required in order to express the soul's desires and intentions, since others "have no means of entering into my soul" (C 1.6.8), which is radically interior and thus inaccessible. The infant, for example, "manifests" her wishes and desires by uttering sounds which function as *external* signs of *interior* desires. Thus it is by means of signs more generally, and language in particular, that the soul's interiority is expressed: "Even at that time I had existence and life, and already at the last stage of my infant speechlessness I was searching out signs by which I made my thoughts known to others" (C 1.6.10). The movement from infancy to childhood is a shift from the use of non-verbal signs to verbal signs, viz. words.[74] This permitted Augustine to better "express the intentions of my heart" and so "communicate the signs of my wishes to those around me" (C 1.8.13).

In this opening narrative of the *Confessions*, Augustine reiterates a fundamental aspect of signs as developed in *De magistro*, viz. the mediating function of signs (and language) as that which expresses an interiority to an other who is exterior. Words (as signs) are *external* manifestations of *internal* thoughts or desires. In *De magistro* this arises in a consideration of prayer: if, as Augustine suggests, the purpose of all speaking is to either teach or remind, then what is it that we teach God when we pray? As Adeodatus concludes, "we certainly speak while we're praying, and yet it isn't right to believe that we teach God or remind him of anything" (DM 1.2). But we are commanded to pray, Augustine replies, "in closed chambers" (Matthew 6:6) –

> a phrase that signifies the inner recesses of the mind – precisely because God does not seek to be taught or reminded by our speaking in order to provide us what we want. Anyone who speaks gives an external sign of his will by means of an articulated sound. . . . There is accordingly no need for speaking when we pray. That is, there is no need for spoken words – except perhaps to speak as priests do, for the sake of signifying what is in their minds: not that God might hear, but that men might do so and by remembering might, with one accord, be raised to God. (DM 1.2; cf. C 10.2.2–10.3.4)

Speaking, and language in general, is an *external* sign of an *interior* desire or intention to those who are *exterior* to the soul, viz. other persons. In the case of God, however, who is able to know our innermost thoughts, language and speech is unnecessary.[75] Thus language is necessitated by the inaccessibility of the self's interiority and must function as a mediator between persons – between "interiorities":[76] "So as I make my confession, they wish to hear about my inner self, where they cannot penetrate with eye or ear or mind" (C 10.3.4). Words indicate, but do not "present," an a-lingual interiority which cannot be fully disclosed in speech, but nevertheless can be expressed or manifested. The secret life of the soul can never be fully present in language, which is why the confession must be taken on *faith* – for "although they wish to [know my inner self] and are ready to believe me, they cannot really have certain knowledge. The love which makes them good people tells them that I am not lying in confessing about myself, and the love in them believes me" (C 10.3.4).[77]

While not present in the strict sense, the self is nevertheless manifested or revealed in confession to the other. In this manner, words are able to indicate that which cannot be said.

Thus in *De doctrina christiana*, Augustine asserts that spoken words (*verba*) are the most characteristic form of "conventional" (as opposed to "natural") signs

> which living creatures give one another in order to show, *as far as they can*, their moods and feelings, or to indicate whatever it may be they have sensed or understood. Nor have we any purpose in signifying, that is in giving a sign, other than to bring out and transfer to someone else's mind what we, the givers of the sign, have in mind ourselves. (DC 2.2.3)

Language is required in order to express that which is interior to the soul by means of something external (*verbum*); thus language makes public the "private" intentions and desires of the self; words are therefore "common property," belonging to a community.[78] Language must span a gulf between interiorities, precisely because the other has "no means of entering into my soul." It is the space between souls which requires the mediation of signs, which in turn requires interpretation.[79]

It is here that we locate the tension which poses a problem for "speaking": if my consciousness (soul) is essentially inaccessible to the other (even to myself, in a sense), it represents an interiority which is radically *singular* – what Kierkegaard described as "subjectivity" and the young Heidegger named "facticity." At the heart of the self – in the depths of this interiority – there is a secret, an "essential secret" which is radically incommensurate with the universality of language. The radical *privacy* of the self is incommensurate with the *public* traffic of language. Thus the Augustinian self finds itself in a position analogous to (Kierkegaard's) Abraham who, because of the singularity of the call he received, could not articulate it in the universality of language – since by virtue of its singularity it is incommensurate with language and cannot be disclosed. As Kierkegaard poses the challenge at the opening of "Problema III":

> The ethical as such is the universal; as the universal it is in turn the disclosed. The single individual, qualified as immediate, sensate, and psychical, is the hidden. Thus his ethical task is to work himself out of his hiddenness and to become disclosed in the universal. Every time he desires to remain in the hidden, he trespasses and is immersed in spiritual trial from which he can emerge only by disclosing himself.[80]

For the "tragic hero," such disclosure is possible because the ethical responsibility, which is universal, is commensurate with language, which is also universal. The call or "pronouncement" which the tragic hero responds to can be articulated in the public, universal medium of language:

> Is this pronouncement *publici juris* [public property] or a *privatissimum* [private matter]? The scene is Greece[81]; an augur's pronouncement is

understandable by all. I think that the single individual not only can understand the contents lexically but is also able to understand that an augur is declaring heaven's decision to the single individual. Thus the augur's pronouncement is intelligible not only to the hero but also to all and does not eventuate in any private relation to the divine.[82]

But because Abraham's call was "a purely private endeavor,"[83] such disclosure is not possible. The singularity of the command to sacrifice his son is precisely incommensurate with the universality of language; the privacy of his obligation is incommensurate with the public traffic of speech. And so Abraham remains silent, because he *cannot* speak. Any attempt to articulate the call would compromise its singularity, reducing it to a mere "spiritual trial," and then he would no longer be Abraham,[84] for "[t]he relief provided by speaking is that it translates me into the universal."[85] Abraham has to keep a secret because, as Caputo remarks, "[a]s soon as language has arrived on the scene the singular has already fled, already slipped out the back door."[86] The incommensurability of the singular call and the universality of language demands silence; the secret cannot be told.

Must the self remain silent, then? Does this incommensurability between the private self and public language mark the impossibility of speaking? What would this mean for the very project of the *Confessions*, which is precisely to communicate something of the secret of the self? If Kierkegaard is right, then the incommensurability between the singular secret and universal language must demand silence, since any "saying" would not be able to say anything about singularity *per se* by virtue of the fact that it would already have become universal in its articulation. And if that is the case, then Augustine, like Abraham, should have remained silent, since nothing can be said – and anything that would be said would always already be a public truth, a secret sacrificed.[87]

But is that the end of the story? Is it the case that, given the singular secret of the self, *nothing* can be said – yet another injunction to silence? If that were the case, could we even have *Fear and Trembling*? Is not the very possibility of *Fear and Trembling*, as a kind of "commentary," already testimony to the fact that something *could* be said about Abraham's singular situation and very private affair? Indeed, Kierkegaard's reading must proceed on the basis of the story's *being told*, being articulated in language. Somebody must have said *something*, otherwise how would Kierkegaard know that Abraham's command issued from God? And so the singularity and privacy of Abraham's relation to God is already interrupted, in two ways: first, by the presence of the angel who *justifies* Abraham: "now I know that you fear God, since you have not withheld your son, your only Son, from me" (Gen. 22:12). Here we have the interpolation of a third who interrupts the absolute privacy of the God-relationship and so also its singularity. Second, the privacy of the relation is interrupted by the narrator (divinely inspired, for Kierkegaard[88]), who discloses all that has happened. However, this third does not seem to undo the singularity of Abraham's position: that the command was given only to him, that it was beyond the universal, that it was not commensurate with ethics. So the third does not necessarily undo the singularity of the call, though it does rupture the privacy of the relationship. But even in that regard, much remains private, so that the presence of the third certainly does not constitute something like "full presence," as though everything were "made public." So while the absolute singularity and interiority of Abraham's anxiety remains inaccessible to others, nevertheless something can be said, staving off silence as the only option. The incommensurability of the secret does not preclude *some* "saying" of it; therefore, we must consider just *how* this could be said.

Abraham's challenge is analogous to the follower in the *Philosophical Fragments* who must bear witness to her encounter with the god. As such, the way to (not) tell a secret is already sketched in the strategy of indirect communication.[89] "A person's God relationship," Climacus tells us, "is a secret."[90] But unlike "accidental secrets" which can be disclosed directly in "ordinary communication" when necessary, the God-relationship (as all subjective truth) cannot be so disclosed because it is incommensurate with language: "Ordinary communication, objective thinking, has no secrets; only doubly reflected subjective thinking has secrets; that is, all its essential content is essentially a secret, because it cannot be communicated *directly*."[91] But note, however, that he does not say that such essential secrets cannot be communicated at all; rather, they cannot be communicated objectively, in ordinary or direct communication. While the secret "evades the direct form of expression," it does not defy expression altogether; in other words, the "essential secret," though incommensurate, does not lead to silence. What is at stake then is *how* it *can* be communicated; and it is here that Kierkegaard develops his account of "*in*direct communication," which is still a form of communication, but one which operates in an oblique mode. And it is precisely indirect communication which is the strategy that enables the follower to bear witness to her God-relationship, to tell the secret without divulging the secret – whereby she has "communicated it under a pledge of secrecy."[92]

Confession: the strategy of the interior self

How (not) to tell a secret? This problematic lies at the very center of the *Confessions*, for "confession,"[93] as the expression of interiority, is the very condition of possibility for the work. If it were not somehow possible to *indicate* the secrets of the soul, the *Confessions* could not have been written. But the question is, *how* is this possible? The answer is not found in particular words, but the *way* in which language is *used*; it is not a matter of a lexicon, but a grammar (cf. SZ 39/34), a style. If disclosure is a making present in the form of a concept – tantamount to divulging the secret – then the challenge for the confessor is to find a non-conceptual, non-objectifying mode of expression which can obliquely indicate the secret without divulging it. And that is a bit of an "art."[94]

This is intimately tied up with the very project of the *Confessions*. Upon reflecting on the task of the *Confessions* in his later *Retractationes*, Augustine himself indicates that the *Confessions* were *written* to excite the mind and affections of others towards God (*Retr.* 2.6). For Augustine, this is a very important question, given the interiority of the self's relation to God: if I am making confession to God, for whom the abyss of human consciousness is an open book (C 10.2.2), then why write them down? My confessions do not instruct or inform God (C 5.1.1–5.2.2; cf. DM 1.1). Then why speak/write? Why should this very private affair, which it already seems superfluous to verbalize, be written for others to read? "Why should I be concerned for human readers to hear my confessions?," he asks (C 10.3.3). And "what profit is there, I ask, when, to human readers, by this book I confess to you who I now am, not what I once was?" (10.3.4). "What edification do they hope to gain by this?" (10.4.5).

For Augustine, there is a two-fold reason: first, I write *for myself*, for self-knowledge – "that is why I speak" (C 10.1.1), that I may know as I am known. In this sense, it is a project of self-formation (10.2.2). This is captured well by Brian Stock in his landmark *Augustine the Reader*, where he employs an almost Foucauldian paradigm of "self-construction" to show that the task of the narrative of the *Confessions* is to construct a self in the telling of the story. According to him, Augustine "sees the person who writes in 397 engaging in a process of self-redefinition rather than setting down a definitive version of the life."[95] Thus Stock suggests that what is involved is "an ethics of interpretation": "his concern was ethical before it was literary, and it was literary only in combination with ethics."[96] And we should understand "ethics" here also in a Foucauldian sense of "care of the self." The second purpose involves writing for others: "Why . . . should I be concerned for human readers to hear my confessions?" Augustine asks (10.3.3). Here, the purpose is to "stir up the hearts" of others (10.3.4), to motivate by example (cf. Book VIII). So "the benefit lies in this":

> I am making this confession not only before you with a secret exaltation and fear and with a secret grief touched by hope, but also in the ears of believing sons of men, sharers in my joy, conjoined with me in mortality, my fellow citizens and pilgrims . . . You have commanded me to serve them if I wish to live with you and in dependence on you. . . . So, to those whom you command me to serve, I will reveal not who I was, but what I have now come to be and what I continue to be. (C 10.4.6)

For Augustine, the confessions stem from his *diaconal* (i.e. servant) responsibilities: he must speak/write for the sake of his flock, for his fellow Christians, in order to move them toward God. Thus he prays: "Stir up the heart when people read and hear the confessions of my past wickednesses, which you have forgiven and covered up to grant me happiness in yourself, transforming my soul by faith and your sacrament" (C 10.3.4). Note, then, that there is an important impetus which I would describe as both evangelistic and pastoral: "silence" is not an option precisely because of this pastoral or diaconal imperative.

But in order for confession to "work," language (words, signs) has to be able to somehow "make present" that which cannot be made present; words need to be able to point to something which exceeds language, which cannot be reduced to language, viz. the interiority of a self which is not even present to itself – the secret of the God-relationship. Or, to put this another way, we need to be able to *speak* about something which nevertheless cannot be "thematized" (Levinas) or objectified because it is incommensurate with language. Now, it is not the case that some words are better than others; rather, it is the *use* of language which is at stake.

Because of the incommensurability of the private self and public language, the self cannot be made "simply" present in language. Rather, in confession, the self is present in words and yet also remains absent; it is made present in only an oblique (Derrida), indirect (Kierkegaard) manner. Recalling our consideration of his incarnational understanding of language above, Augustine also sees this use of words in confession as *incarnational*. For in the language of confession, one is able to span the distance between interiorities, able to manifest the depth of the self which, for the other, is absent, an essential secret – and yet it does not claim or pretend to comprehend the self's interiority or grasp this secret in a concept, publicizing the secret, as it were. In other words, as incarnational, and like the Incarnation, words of confession establish a connection between *transcendence* and *immanence*. Thus the strategy of "confession" resembles a kind of "appresentation": words are present to the other (in their sphere of ownness, we might say) and indicate or point to my thoughts and desires, which are "essential secrets" (see Figure 2). In this way, one is able to "tell the secret" without divulging the secret, able to express one's experience of and with God, while also honoring the singularity of that relation.

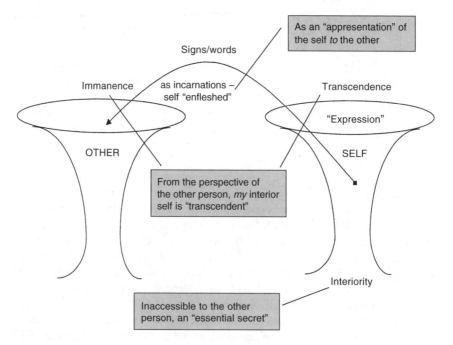

Figure 2 The strategy of "confession".

As in Levinas, it is precisely by means of language and "expression" that a relation is established with the Other:

> in its expressive function language precisely maintains the other – to whom it is addressed, whom it calls upon or invokes. To be sure, language does not consist in invoking him as a being represented and thought. But this is why language institutes a relation irreducible to the subject–object relation: the *revelation* of the other. (TI 73)

From the perspective of the other (the listener), in confession I am both present "with" my words, but also absent, in the sense that the words cannot fully embody or present the secrets of my heart. Thus there is a relation established, but not one that collapses the difference or separation between same and other; it is a relation which retains and respects the incommensurate.

Confession, as a strategy of incarnational expression, enables one to tell the secret without making it present, without divulging the secret. In confession, it is possible to say something; thus James J. O'Donnell describes the *Confessions* as "a trophy torn from the grip of the unsayable after a prolonged struggle on the frontier between speech and silence."[97] And that is why, he suggests, we find in Augustine such persistent concern with language:

> Behind this fundamental act of the self lay powerful and evident anxieties – evident on every page. Augustine is urgently concerned with the right use of language, longing to say the right thing in the right way. The first page of the text is a tissue of uncertainty in that vein, for to use language wrongly is to find oneself praising a god who is not God. The anxiety is intensified by a vertiginous loss of privacy.[98]

Augustine grapples – must grapple – with how to express the mystery of the self to others, a self that is a mystery even for him. In other words, to recoup this challenge as part of my thesis, Augustine must find a way to articulate that which is incommensurate with language. "Confession" is the response: in confession, which is literary and aesthetic rather than doctrinal and didactic, one is able to *indicate* the secret of the soul in such a way that the secret can be (ap)present to the other, but not fully disclosed (which would be impossible, since it is an essential secret).

Confession, I would suggest, is just what contemporary continental philosophy is looking for – or undertaking. As Carlson comments, "in light of the insistent conjunction between reflection on negative theological language and reflection on the finitude of human existence, one might rightly ask: do these contemporary approaches to the apophatic and mystical traditions simply mistake for an ever desired but unknowable God a desiring human subject that remains opaque to itself?"[99] Thus, like Augustine, what would be at stake would be a "negative anthropology." But insofar as we would speak, we must speak in the mode of confession. Derrida, of course, maintains – against Kierkegaard and Augustine – that the "secret" is that there is no secret, no pre- or a-lingual self, no depth which precedes constitution by signs.[100]

But when Derrida pens his *Circonfessions*, he is in fact attesting, I would argue, to a depth and opaqueness of the Derridean self which seems quite Augustinian – a depth which remains secret. The whole project of his *Circonfessions* is staked on being able to surprise G. with a secret: "one undecipherable secret per jar."[101] But would that not mean, first, *having* a secret, and second, divulging that which cannot be spoken? And so an (im)possible task: to speak about that secret, to avoid not speaking about that secret. Are not Derrida's *Circonfessions* themselves testimony to the possibility of confession? Indeed, in them we have testimony regarding the secret, but a bearing witness which does not divulge the secret – a speaking which neither concedes nor effaces the incommensurate.

Notes

1 Recall my discussion of the formal problem of incommensurability in the final section of Chapter 2.

2 Note that for Augustine, as for Husserl (and unlike Levinas), transcendence is characteristic of all things, though certain "things" (God, the other person) are uniquely transcendent, insofar as theirs is an "essential" transcendence which can never be made present, unlike, for instance, the back of the house, which is only "accidentally" transcendent. For a more detailed discussion of the transcendence of things *vis-à-vis* words, see below.

3 I am attentive to the peculiarity of such a formulation. For a similar suggestion, however, cf. Enrique Dussel's notion of "interior transcendentality" in *Philosophy of Liberation*, trans. Aquilina Martinez and Christine Morkovsky (Maryknoll, NY: Orbis, 1985), 39, 47–8. I have continued cautiously and hesitatingly to employ the term "transcendence" in connection with interiority in order to retain a semantic connection with the problem as developed by Levinas and Marion. The same "challenge of speaking" which they locate in relation to transcendence is repeated, for Augustine, Kierkegaard, and Heidegger, in the challenge of speaking "of" oneself.

4 For a discussion which problematizes Dionysius's relationship to "negative theology," see Jean-Luc Marion, "In the Name: How To Avoid Speaking Of 'Negative Theology,'" trans. Jeffrey L. Kosky in John D. Caputo and Michael Scanlon, eds., *Of God, the Gift, and Postmodernism* (Bloomington: Indiana University Press, 1999). (Prior to its publication, I refer to section numbers rather than page numbers.) There he suggests that "negative theology" is in fact a *modern* invention (I).

5 However, in the second half of this chapter I will suggest that Augustine does not (or could not, if we read him deconstructively) fall prey to Derrida's critique of Husserl in *Speech and Phenomena* because confession, though a mode of "expression," is nevertheless an *indicative* mode of expression – suggesting that there is *only* indication, which never makes interiority present, since that interiority is never even present to oneself.

6 "The limitations of human language," James O'Donnell notes, "are displayed by the paradoxes in which the divine nature compels Augustine to speak. . . . Human words used by humans fail in the presence of the divine, and whatever can be said is only approximation, and most human discourse fails to say anything of God at all, despite endless loquacious efforts." O'Donnell, "Augustine's Idea of God," *Augustinian Studies* 25 (1994): 26.

7 The contemporary reader must recall the fundamentally oral paradigm of Augustine's philosophy of language. Brian Stock emphasizes the orality of interpretation for Augustine in *Augustine the Reader: Meditation, Self-Knowledge, and the Ethics of Interpretation* (Cambridge, MA: Belknap Press of Harvard University Press, 1996), 26–7; on the oral

culture of late antiquity and the early medieval period, see Stock, *The Implications of Literacy: Written Language and Models of Interpretation in the Eleventh and Twelfth Centuries* (Princeton: Princeton University Press, 1983), 12–87.

8 Below (DM 10.31–3), the entire problem of signification will be taken up within the context of the Platonic doctrine of recollection.

9 Note, however, that many "things" can also function as signs, such as "that piece of wood which we read of Moses throwing into the bitter water to remove its bitterness," or the stone under Jacob's head while dreaming, or the animal which Abraham sacrificed on Mount Moriah (DC 1.2.2). In a sense, every thing *could* function as a sign, *except* God, the ultimate "end." This is also why God is the only "thing" ("if, that is to say, it is a thing" [DC 1.5.5]) to be enjoyed.

10 Book I takes up an exposition of things, and Books II–III provide an analysis of signs. All of this falls within the larger project of instructing pastors on *how* to teach their congregations (that is, it is a book on *method* not "doctrine," as older English translations suggested). The first three books are concerned with the "way of discovery" or biblical interpretation, while the fourth book takes up the "way of putting things across," viz. preaching or rhetoric.

11 Strictly speaking, spoken words are signs of things, and written words are signs of signs. Cf. Aristotle, *De Interpretatione*, I.i (trans. E. M. Edghill in *The Basic Works of Aristotle*, ed. Richard McKeon (New York: Random House, 1941). While gestures are also signs, words are the privileged example in Augustine.

12 Written letters are the paradigmatic example of signs pointing to signs; or in charades, when one raises two fingers to signify "two words," and then proceeds to gesture in order to get others to guess the first "word" (*verbum*), which would then be a sign of the thing itself.

13 With regard to this point, I would suggest that Derrida's "*il n'y a pas de hors texte*" is a fine French translation of what Augustine is describing in Latin.

14 Note the phenomenological impetus toward the "appearance" of "the things themselves."

15 This is also restaged by Kierkegaard in *Philosophical Fragments*. Elsewhere I hope to pursue the analogies between these reproductions.

16 I am not so interested in *solving* the paradox as *inhabiting* it and experiencing its tension. Jason Drucker, in "Teaching as Pointing in 'The Teacher,'" *Augustinian Studies* 28 (1997): 101–32, attempts to solve the paradox by making a distinction between "teaching" and "learning." On this account, the sign does not "teach" me anything (new), but I can nevertheless "learn" from it (insofar as it points me to the thing itself). While I will come to a similar systematic conclusion, I do not see the necessity for making this distinction (which does not seem operative in the text itself).

17 In terms of Husserl's phenomenology, the thing is not "presented" but rather "*ap*presented."

18 This is precisely the intent of Heidegger's "formal indication" – a philosophical concept which must be "completed" or "fulfilled" (*Vollzugsinn*) in one's *own* experience.

19 Derrida, *Parages*, 25, as cited by John D. Caputo, *The Prayers and Tears of Jacques Derrida: Religion Without Religion* (Bloomington: Indiana University Press, 1997), 47.

20 As suggested at the beginning of the chapter (following Derrida's lead), there is a certain ethics of semiotics at work here, an imperative of speaking well, a "proper" way for signs to function. It would be interesting to develop this account in dialogue with contemporary analytic epistemology which advocates a "deontological" account of knowledge, or even a "virtue epistemology" (Zagzebski). For Augustine, there is a way that signs *ought* to be employed, a duty we have in their use.

21 I employ the term "inauthentic self" to describe the fallen self in Augustine, in order to allude to the Augustinian character of inauthentic Dasein. I have considered this in further detail in my "Confessions of an Existentialist: Reading Augustine After Heidegger," *New Blackfriars*, 82 (2001): 273–82 (Part I); 335–47 (Part II).

22 Cf. also *De vera religione* 1.20.38–9: "The sin is evil, not the substance that is sinfully loved. . . . Vice arises in the soul from its own doing."

23 Cf. the discussion of Scheler's "Ordo Amoris" in Chapter 3 above.

24 For a discussion of the relationship between *signum, sacramentum,* and *mysterium* in Augustine, see Robert Dodaro, OSA, "*Sacramentum Christi*: Augustine on the Christology of Pelagius," *Studia Patristica* XXVII, ed. Elizabeth A. Livingstone (Leuven: Peeters, 1993), 274–80.

25 I am creatively appropriating here, not without parallel, Jean-Luc Marion's distinction between the "idol" and the "icon" in his *L'idole et le distance* and *God Without Being,* discussed above in Chapter 3.

26 *De Trinitate* 9.13, trans. Edmund Hill, OP, The Works of Saint Augustine I/5 (New York: New City Press, 1991).

27 Mark D. Jordan, "Words and Word: Incarnation and Signification in Augustine's *De doctrina christiana,*" *Augustinian Studies* 11 (1980): 177–8. This is also why, for Augustine, the Scriptures are a "privileged set of God-speaking words within the Christian community – he treats them as one of the highest instances of God-infleshing for us" (p. 178).

28 To again appreciate the incarnational paradigm here, let us allude to the same concern in Kierkegaard's *Philosophical Fragments.* How can that which is transcendent – the Wholly Other – be made known to the finite, human perceiver? It must appear within the finite, present itself within the sphere of immanence. But this appearance does not undo its transcendence. I will take up Kierkegaard's account in more detail in Chapter 5 below.

29 What I mean by this is that, in the Incarnation, God himself employs analogy, makes himself known "according to the mode of the perceiver," in terms that finite humanity can understand (and in this thought I follow both Aquinas and Kierkegaard). God exploits the "likeness" in the human being in order to make himself known in the Incarnation.

30 Anthony J. Godzieba, "Ontotheology to Excess: Imagining God Without Being," *Theological Studies* 56 (1995): 3.

31 Ibid., 3–4.

32 I have retained the use of the second person here since it is employed by Augustine in the Sermon itself.

33 The "word" in this instance will become the "inner word" in *De trinitate* (see below), which is in fact a "thought," a word uttered in the heart. This opens another question regarding the possible logocentrism of Augustine's account; in other words, would not Augustine be subject to the same critique as Husserl in Derrida's *Speech and Phenomena*? While I hope to pursue this matter elsewhere, it lies beyond the scope of my current concern. Allow me here just to say that I think there is a fundamental difference between Augustine and Husserl, insofar as for Augustine, the self cannot be made transparent to itself. There is a depth and mystery of the self such that it cannot be made fully present to itself (this is discussed briefly below).

34 What we might even refer to as an "appresentation."

35 Levinas must provide an account which permits some kind of "connection" across the space of "separation," otherwise the call of the Other would never be heard. He describes this as "metaphysical": "In metaphysics a being separated from the Infinite nonetheless relates to it, with a relation that does not nullify the infinite interval of separation" (TI 80). This is also why Levinas is very critical of "mysticism," which in its quest for "union" with God is actually seeking to overcome separation and close the distance between the terms. But is not the logic of incarnation precisely a kind of "relation without relation," particularly given the fact that Levinas himself emphasizes such a relation happens only in language? (TI 97, 194–5).

36 See DC 1.11.11: "Of this we would be quite incapable, unless Wisdom himself [the Word] had seen fit to adapt himself even to such infirmity as ours" (trans. modified). See also VR 16.30: "But in no way did he show greater loving-kindness in his dealings with the human race for its good, than when the Wisdom of God, his only Son, co-eternal and consubstantial with the Father, deigned to assume human nature when the Word became flesh and dwelt among us." The Incarnation reaffirms the goodness of creation.

37 The same theme of condescension can be seen in Kierkegaard's account of the movement of the god and the analogy of the king and maiden in *Philosophical Fragments*, 26–30.

38 It seems to me that currents in British theological discourse that want to appropriate this theme of Platonic "participation" as central to an incarnational theology (e.g. Milbank, Ward, Pickstock) fail to appreciate that Augustine's incarnational insight is his most *un*Platonic moment. For a succinct discussion, see their "Suspending the Material: The Turn of Radical Orthodoxy," the Introduction to *Radical Orthodoxy: A New Theology*, eds. John Milbank, Catherine Pickstock, and Graham Ward (New York: Routledge, 1999), esp. 3–4. This will be pursued further in Chapter 5 below.

39 David Vincent Meconi, SJ, "The Incarnation and the Role of Participation in St. Augustine's *Confessions*," *Augustinian Studies* 29 (1998): 68.

40 Ibid., 71.

41 If Marion is so close to Levinas, and Levinas is confessedly Platonist, what does this say about Marion's "Platonism"?

42 Here I would differ from Meconi, or at least Meconi's Augustine: for me, it is not just "fallen" humanity, but humanity as such – humanity as created and finite – which is incommensurate with the transcendence of God. That "no one can see God" is not a postlapsarian condition, but constitutive of finitude. And insofar as finitude is inherent to a good creation, the finite conditions of knowing are an aspect of even a "good" creation. (For a more sustained reflection on finitude as a creational good, see my *The Fall of Interpretation: Philosophical Foundations for a Creational Hermeneutic*, esp. chs. 5 and 6.)

43 Below, in the latter part of this chapter, we will consider the same affective goal of the *Confessions* as Augustine indicates in his *Retractationes*.

44 A kind of eloquence, that is, which differs from classical Latin rhetoric, but nevertheless does not violate its principles. Indeed, Augustine's point in much of the fourth book is to demonstrate the way in which the biblical authors do employ "our eloquence" (DC 1.6.10), but only unintentionally and not as a priority. But one can still learn eloquence from them; thus Augustine suggests that what North African preachers need to do is spend their time listening, not to teachers of classical rhetoric, but Paul, Amos, and Ambrose (4.6.10–7.21; 4.21.45–50) – though if you have the time, a little Cicero couldn't hurt (4.17.34–19.38).

45 Recall Heidegger's injunction, following suggestions in Aristotle's *Nichomachean Ethics*, that method and categories must be determined by the topic, not vice versa.

46 Will it not be necessary to rethink this notion of "referent" in this context?

47 In earlier work, I tried to get at the same matter of a non-objectifying discourse, particularly about God. However, in that context I described it as "evangelism" or "storytelling," particularly *good* story-telling, both in the sense of telling good stories, but also telling them *well* (see James K. A. Smith, "How To Avoid (Not) Speaking: Attestations," in *Knowing* Other-*wise*, ed. James H. Olthuis [Bronx: Fordham University Press, 1997], esp. 228–30). One may hear in that strategy echoes of a certain narrative theology and ethics, which I would not necessarily abandon but will not pick up on here. But I note this only to indicate that the problem and strategies are similar and continuous.

48 Godzieba, "Ontotheology to Excess," 18. For Godzieba, postmodernism, a continuation of modernity, simply instantiates the "Protestant principle" (Tillich) which protests any identification of divinity with finite mediations. (As such, would not the early Barth be a postmodern *par excellence*, and Brunner a "Catholic"?) Godzieba also seeks to sketch a "third way" very close to what I am arguing for here, a "third choice which refuses to say 'never' but which will never say 'always,' which denies both the absolute fit of the conceptual and its pure evacuation" (p. 18). My only reservation concerns his inclusion of Marion (along with Kasper) as an example of this third way, as I will discuss below.

49 First in *L'idole et la distance. Cinq etudes*. Paris: Grasset, 1977; Livre de Poche, 1991./*The Idol and Distance*. Trans. Thomas A. Carlson (New York: Fordham University Press, 2001), 249ff.

50 In *God Without Being*, "denomination" remains on the side of predication, naming (*noming*) as defining; in the later "In the Name," however, "de-nomination" is praise.

51 Thomas A. Carlson, *Indiscretion: Finitude and the Naming of God* (Chicago: University of Chicago Press), 201.

52 However, Marion still privileges silence in this context – not the silence of agnosticism (which is yet another idolatry [GWB 107]), of course, but an "agapic" silence, a silence which is silent "out of respect" (ibid.). But does silence respect such transcendence? Is not such a silence still an inversion of predication, and thus maintaining its violence as a horizon?

53 One would need here to consider the errancy (*destinerrance*) of the postal system of language, as Derrida does in *The Post Card*. I have done so in "How To Avoid Not Speaking," 218–28. The "errancy" in this case, however, is due to the postal system, not a lack of determination regarding the address(ee); in other words, errancy is not a matter of intention, but fulfillment.

54 See James K. A. Smith, "Determined Violence: Derrida's Structural Religion," *Journal of Religion* 78 (1998): 197–212; and *The Fall of Interpretation*, ch. 4.

55 Carlson, *Indiscretion*, 219.

56 Derrida, of course, does not have recourse to the "closed chambers" of prayer discussed by Augustine (DM 1.2), since for Derrida there is no interior word which escapes the chain of signification or language. Perhaps the only other possibility for a "pure" prayer would be instances of *glossolalia* – speaking in tongues – a mode of speech which precisely cannot be repeated. For relevant considerations, see Michel de Certeau, "Vocal Utopias: Glossolalias," *Representations* 56 (1996): 29–46; and Steven J. Land, *Pentecostal Spirituality: A Passion for the Kingdom* (Sheffield: Sheffield Academic Press, 1993): 111–12.

57 See Smith, "Determined Violence," 210–12.

58 Marion, "In the Name" (II).

59 Ibid. In a response to Marion's presentation of this paper, Derrida lauded this neologism: "denomination works wonderful [*sic*] in French, meaning at the same time to name and unname."

60 Ibid.

61 I think Levinas misses this distinction: he fails to appreciate the medieval attentiveness to the inadequacy of concepts and knowledge itself. For Augustine and Aquinas, "to know" does not necessarily mean "to comprehend."

62 See, for instance, Letter 147. I will take this up in detail below in Chapter 5, since this is a key text for Aquinas in his discussion of comprehension (*ST* Ia.12.7).

63 Carlson seems to misunderstand undecidability as "indecision," particularly when chiding Marion: "While Marion's phenomenology points powerfully toward the undecidable, he in fact seems nevertheless to have decided" (*Indiscretion*, 234; cf. 235). But decision is not opposed to undecidability; in other words, decision is not a deconstructive sin, but rather a necessity. Undecidability is the condition that *demands* choice, in spite of the fact that "all the data are not in." As such, undecidability is very closely linked to faith. I have tried to push this in a Kierkegaardian direction in my "Between Athens and Jerusalem, Freiburg and Rome: John Caputo as Christian Philosopher," *Paradigms* 10 (1995): 19–24. See also John D. Caputo, "The Good News About Alterity: Derrida and Theology," *Faith and Philosophy* 10 (1993): 453–70.

64 As such, Augustine's strategy of "confession" is in fact closer to Heidegger's "formal indication" than the strategy of "praise" discussed above. However, formally speaking, they are all the same insofar as they arise in the face of the same challenge: how (not) to speak of that which is incommensurable.

65 For Augustine, consciousness is intentional; however, the priority is not on perception (as in Husserl) but "love" as an intentional mode of consciousness. Recall the discussion above (Chapter 3); see also Arendt, *Love and Saint Augustine*, 18–19.

66 The same emphasis on the non-objectification of the self is found in Plotinus, *Enneads* 5.3.3. For a discussion, see Sara Rappe, "Self-Perception in Plotinus and the Later Neoplatonic Tradition," *American Catholic Philosophical Quarterly* 71 (1997): 433–50.

67 It is important to note that he confesses this in Book X, where the confessions are no longer of the past, but confessions about the present – the confessions not only of a convert, but a bishop. Thus we should not think that Christian conversion solves the mystery of self-knowledge. It is a start, not an end.

68 And it is precisely "his mind" which remains inaccessible (cf. Husserl on the essential inaccessibility of the other subject's consciousness in CM V).

69 Stock, *Augustine the Reader*, 110. Stock finds in these discussions an anticipation of the problem of "other minds." I am suggesting that, more uniquely, for Augustine the problem is *my own* soul.

70 SZ 43/41 (followed by a quotation from the *Confessions*). We should note this distinction, however: Heidegger seems to suggest that that which is "nearest" is not seen because we are not looking, whereas we will see for Augustine, the inability to see the self is more essential than accidental, issuing not from a failure to look but rather an inability to probe its depths.

71 This is the passage cited at SZ 43/41.

72 Cf. Descartes's response to his discovery of the idea of the Infinite within himself at the conclusion of the Third Meditation.

73 I say a "certain" Augustinian ego, since we have been bequeathed at least two: the Pascalian existential ego (which I am attempting to retrieve) and the Cartesian substantial ego (which I am attempting to deconstruct). The latter is the product of an uncritical development of Augustine's persistent Platonism, failing to realize that other (Christian) moments in his thought undermine these Platonic traces. Thus one can certainly find Augustine privileging a soul which would be present to itself; but this would also be the soul which scholarship has linked to heritage of the Greek "world soul" – a fundamentally unChristian notion. For my attempts to deconstruct these Platonic moments, see my "The Time of Language: The Fall to Interpretation in Early Augustine."

74 "I was no longer a baby incapable of speech but already a boy with power to talk," (C 1.8.13). For Augustine, words are only one kind of sign or mode of signification; gestures, written letters, and other things (*rei*) can function as signs. For discussion, see *De Magistro* (CSEL 77), 4.8–10; and *De Doctrina Christiana* (CCSL 32), 2.1.1–2.5.6, addressed above.

75 "He who is making confession to you is not instructing you of that which is happening within him. The closed heart does not shut out your eye" (C 5.1.1). "Indeed, Lord, to your eyes, the abyss of human consciousness is naked" (10.2.2).

76 Recall my discussion of language as an incarnational "mediator" above.

77 Again, note that for Augustine it is a hermeneutics of love which prevails (cf. DC, Book I). Only those who "love" will rightly understand the confessions: "To such sympathetic readers I will indeed *reveal* myself" (C 10.4.5, emphasis added). What is of importance here is that this "revelation" is a revelation of the self *insofar as it is possible*. The interiority of the self is structurally exterior to the other person, such that my interiority *per se* is inaccessible. And yet, it can be "revealed" *to a certain degree*, in a manner which retains the "difference" between self and other, preserving the incommensurability while at the same time bridging it.

78 Brian Stock notes an important aspect of this which we cannot pursue here: "If language, from which reading and writing derive, is definable through a community of speakers, then selves, souls, or minds, which depend on language for their human expression, have to have their communities too. . . . It is this intersubjective quality that makes Augustine's *Confessions* unique in the ancient literature of the soul, rather than the doctrine that the inner self is veiled, mysterious, or inaccessible. His story hovers between thought and the world before it enters the world in words that are intended to be interpreted by others" (*Augustine the Reader*, 16). What I am locating is precisely the tension between the public traffic of language and the inaccessibility of the self, which *is* found in Augustine.

79 For further discussion of the relationship between language and interpretation in Augustine, see my essay, "The Time of Language: The Fall to Interpretation in Early

Augustine," *American Catholic Philosophical Quarterly* 72 (1998), Supplement: *Proceedings and Addresses of the ACPA*, 185–99.

80 Søren Kierkegaard, *Fear and Trembling/Repetition*, ed. and trans. Howard V. Hong and Edna H. Hong (Princeton: Princeton University Press, 1983), 82.

81 The tragic hero is always Greek, whether Antigone or Agamemnon. This is because for Kierkegaard, Greece is the land of universals, whereas the promised land of Canaan – where they speak Hebrew – is the land of singularities. German, spoken by Hegel, is all Greek to him (and Heidegger!).

82 *Fear and Trembling*, 92–3.

83 Ibid., 59, 93.

84 "At every moment, Abraham can stop; he can repent of the whole thing as a spiritual trial; then he can speak out, and everybody will be able to understand him – but then he is no longer Abraham" (ibid., 115).

85 Ibid., 113. All that Abraham can say are those "famous last words": "God will himself provide a ram." But this is *ironic*, a saying which says nothing, does nothing to disclose the secrets of singularity (118–19). For a discussion, see Derrida, *The Gift of Death*, trans. David Wills (Chicago: University of Chicago Press, 1995), 59.

86 John D. Caputo, *Demythologizing Heidegger* (Bloomington: Indiana University Press, 1993), 202.

87 Cf. Derrida, *Gift of Death*, 100–1.

88 Indeed, one must question whether Kierkegaard's account would be possible apart from his biblicist presuppositions which guarantee that in Genesis, we have God's account of the story. This is why Levinas's reading of the narrative is more suspicious.

89 See my analysis above.

90 Kierkegaard, *Concluding Unscientific Postscript to Philosophical Fragments*, Kierkegaard's Writings XII, ed. and trans. Howard V. Hong and Edna H. Hong (Princeton: Princeton University Press, 1992), 78.

91 Ibid., 79, emphasis added.

92 Ibid., 78. For a discussion of Kierkegaard's strategy of indirect communication, taken up in dialogue with both Husserl and Derrida, see Roger Poole, *Kierkegaard: The Indirect Communication* (Charlottesville: University Press of Virginia, 1993), 200–32.

93 We must remember that this is not simply the "confession" of sins; Augustine is not "going to confession." It is important to here note the breadth of the notion of "confession" for Augustine. Reading him from a post-medieval (and Catholic) perspective, the reader is tempted to level this to a sense of confessing one's sin, what one does "in the confessional." (In *Sermon* 29, Augustine admonished those "who immediately beat their breasts when they hear about confession in the scriptures, as though it can only be about sins, and as if they are now being urged to confess their sins.") While this is true (who is more sinful than Augustine?), this seems to me one-sided; the richness of "confession" is better understood in terms of "witnessing" and "testimony" – giving an account of one's experience with God, "what God has done in my life."

94 Kierkegaard, *Concluding Unscientific Postscript*, 79. Kierkegaard consistently emphasizes the artistic and poetic aspect of indirect communication. It would be important to note, though I cannot pursue it here, the fundamental *aesthetic* moment of Augustine's *Confessions*.

95 Stock, *Augustine the Reader*, 16.

96 Ibid., 17.

97 James J. O'Donnell, *Confessions*: I, Introduction and Text (Oxford: Clarendon Press, 1992), xvii.

98 Ibid.

99 Carlson, *Indiscretion*, 4.

100 Derrida, *On the Name*, 22–31. For commentary on the notion of the "absolute secret" in Derrida, see also Caputo, *Prayers and Tears*, 289–91.

101 Jacques Derrida, "Circumfession," in Geoffrey Bennington and Jacques Derrida, *Jacques Derrida* (Chicago: University of Chicago Press, 1993), 248.

Part Three

TRAJECTORIES

In Part Three we return from the phenomenological excursion through the formal problem of incommensurability, having recouped resources in early Heidegger and Augustine, and now return to the orienting theological question within such a horizon. Our task is to sketch the phenomenological possibility of theology – not in deference to a "secular" phenomenology to which we must pay homage in order to garner the "right" to speak, but rather by sketching a radically Christian phenomenology of appearance and revelation. This will unveil a "logic of incarnation" as the condition of possibility for language in general, and theological language in particular.

5

INCARNATIONAL LOGIC
On God's refusal to avoid speaking

> We have to predicate [concepts] of a subject which they qualify, but
> which in its deeper essence is not, nor indeed can be, comprehended
> in them; which rather requires comprehension of a different kind.
> Yet, though it eludes the conceptual way of understanding, it must be
> in some way or other within our grasp, else absolutely nothing could
> be asserted of it.[1]

The problem of theology

Drawing on a classic formulation of the "problem of evil,"[2] I would suggest that this
book finds its origin in what we could describe as the "problem of theology" (see
Figure 3): if (1) God is Infinite, and (2) language – particularly conceptual language –
is finite, then how will it be possible to *speak* of God, since (3) speaking requires the
employment of language, and theology requires the employment of concepts?
Eberhard Jüngel tackles the same problem under the rubric of the "the problem of
the speakability of God," which he also describes as "the problem of theology."
Succinctly stated, it is the matter of "how one can talk about God humanly and not
miss his divinity in so doing."[3] Since there can be no such thing as an "infinite
concept," any speaking of God would seem to reduce God to finitude. And thus the
theologian is faced with either violating God's transcendence and the reduction of
God to immanence/finitude, or one must not speak of God, remaining silent.

Further, this same incommensurability attends not only our "talk about God" but
also the very possibility of God's self-revelation, insofar as any revelation must occur
in terms which must attend to the finitude of the receivers of such a revelation. This

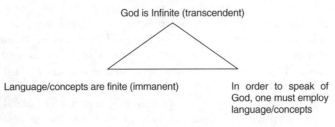

God is Infinite (transcendent)

Language/concepts are finite (immanent)   In order to speak of
God, one must employ
language/concepts

Figure 3 The problem of theology.

concluding chapter will thus argue that the "resolution" of this challenge for language – and more particularly theological language – is found in God's own "resolution" of this latter challenge in the Incarnation. The Incarnation is God's refusal to avoid speaking, and so the Incarnation functions as a paradigm for the operation of theological language which both "does justice" to God's transcendence and infinity, but at the same time makes it possible to "speak." In other words, it is the Incarnation that provides an account which affirms both transcendence and immanent appearance – both alterity and identity – without reducing the one to the other. We can thus return to the terrain mapped out in the first chapter and see the way in which both "kataphatics" (or theological positivism) *and* "apophatics" miss this incarnational paradigm: a kataphatics reduces God's transcendence to immanence, while an apophatics in fact "reduces" God to mere transcendence, precluding the possibility of revelation. This is because both of these strategies operate on the basis of a "differential ontology" grounded in a *mythos* of original violence, whereas the incarnational paradigm operates on the basis of a non-oppositional, analogical account of difference rooted in the Christian *mythos*.[4] If the question is how (not) to avoid speaking, we would conclude that by neglecting this incarnational paradigm, we end up with either a reductive "saying" which encompasses and grasps the Other, or we simply *avoid* speaking – a simple *not* saying. Without this incarnational paradigm, we are left with either an Arianism (kataphatics) or Docetism (apophatics). Only the Incarnation provides a *language* for the unsayable.[5]

But this specifically "theological" problem is a particular instance of a more general or formal problem which I have been pursuing, viz. how can we speak of that which is transcendent? Or more formally, how can one speak of that which is incommensurate with language and the order of conceptual knowledge? How will it be possible to conceptualize that which is non- or preconceptual – that which, simply, is otherwise than conceptual? Would not any "speaking" about this phenomenon be violent, in the sense that such conceptual/theoretical description would force non-conceptual modes of being into the parameters of conceptual thought? Would we not then be simply receiving more of the "same"?

After opening with this theological challenge (in the Introduction), and then formalizing the problem as the more general challenge of incommensurability (in Chapter 2), I have attempted to retrieve, in Augustine and the young Heidegger, strategies for grappling with this challenge which enable us to avoid (not) speaking. In this concluding chapter, I will return from our excursion into the formalized problem of incommensurability to the more specific problem of theological transcendence – on the one hand, the question of how (not) to speak of God, but on the other hand, the question of revelation. This is because I want to make the further – and perhaps audacious – claim that even the more formal, philosophical problem of language can only be resolved by recourse to an *incarnational* paradigm. More specifically, I will argue that it is the Incarnation which is both the paradigm and condition of possibility for the proper understanding of language in general and theological language in particular.[6] Not only is the Incarnation the condition of possibility for speech *about God* (*pace* Barth); it is the condition of possibility for speaking – or at least the condition of possibility for a proper understanding of language.[7] If we affirm that "we love, because he first loved us" (1 John 4:19), we can also affirm that we speak, because he has first spoken.

As such, the argument has a dual *telos*: more specifically, to develop an account of language which can undergird a theological method which "does justice" to God's alterity. But more generally, to sketch an incarnational philosophy of language rooted in the Incarnation as both paradigm and condition of possibility. Thus, in one sense I understand my project as an operation in "philosophical theology" or what we might even call "fundamental theology." In particular, my goal has been to open the philosophical space for speaking about God; even more specifically, mine has been a *phenomenological* project, seeking to make room for the possibility of speaking about God in the light of contemporary critiques leveled against phenomenology by Levinas, Marion, and others, which have been summarized above (Chapter 2). Having conceived my project in these terms, I do not, however, consider my project part of a classical "natural theology" which presupposes a neutral, objective "rationality"; nor am I attempting to clear the space for theology by means of a "secular" philosophy, as though one had to apologize to everyone in Paris (or at Penn State, for that matter) before one could speak about God. In fact, I am arguing that a *Christian* theology can only be possible on the basis of a *Christian* philosophy, a radically *incarnational* philosophy.[8] Even more radically, I am suggesting that it is the Christian confession and understanding of the Incarnation which ought to undergird a general philosophy of language.

In attempting to open "phenomenological space" for the possibility of theology, I do not mean to disclose an ontology which will function as a "corrective" to theology; in other words, my intention is not to crown phenomenology as "queen of the sciences," to which theology will become a handmaiden. On my account, theology is a second-order, reflective discipline which nevertheless operates on the basis of faith, reflecting on faith as its topic, with the goal of cultivating faithfulness. It is an inherently *ecclesial* task, irreducible to philosophy.[9] However, I do think that all questions of *method* are in fact *philosophical* questions, since they involve matters of epistemology and conceptual determination. When we consider the nature of concepts, or the possibility of transcendent knowledge, we are asking questions which go beyond the focused concern of theology as a science, but nevertheless concern theology at its very foundation. Where I differ from Heidegger is on his assertion that philosophy must be methodologically atheistic, bracketing all "commitments." As I have argued elsewhere,[10] this is to deny Heidegger's own insights regarding the presuppositions which accompany being-in-the-world and hence the impossibility of "objectivity." So instead, I would say that questions of theological method must be considered by a *Christian* philosophy, even a Christian *phenomenology*.[11] However, by a "Christian philosophy," I do not mean a covert theology (which would be a confusion of reflective responsibilities), but rather philosophical reflection which is grounded in Christian *faith* or *religion* – pre- or supratheoretical commitments which must be distinguished from the second-order reflection of theology.[12]

Our procedure has, in a sense, been circular: opening the question of language in terms of theological questions, then pursuing the more general, philosophical question of incommensurability and language, and now returning to the theological challenge in order to indicate that even the general problem of incommensurability is 'resolved' by an incarnational paradigm. My project, then, is to outline the phenomenological possibility of speaking of transcendence, particularly God, by indicating the incarnational logic which is the condition of possibility for language in general.

In order for this to be "phenomenologically possible," or to see the way in which the Incarnation is a paradigm for phenomenological appearance, I will first need to sketch an incarnational account of phenomenological *appearance* which makes it possible for the transcendent to "show up." In other words, it will be necessary to consider the conditions of phenomenological appearance and whether such conditions preclude the appearance of transcendence (as Marion argues [SP]), or whether the transcendent concedes to appear under such conditions (and if so, how and why). This will demand that we consider the question of *revelation*, first in the phenomenological accounts offered by Marion and Levinas, and then locating an alternative paradigm in Kierkegaard's *Philosophical Fragments*. Here I will argue that Marion and Levinas, in their insistence on an "absolute" and "unconditioned" revelation, in fact preclude the very possibility of revelation. In contrast, Kierkegaard's incarnational account of revelation is attentive to the "conditions" of revelation – not as external impositions upon God, but as created by the Creator, and thus conditions to which God condescends.[13]

Based on this, I will briefly recall the contours of incarnational *concepts* which will be the "tools" for speaking of God. In both of these moments of my incarnational phenomenology, I am operating within the horizon of Marion and Levinas's critique of phenomenology's understanding of the conditions of knowledge as that which violates and reduces transcendence. But at the same time I will be calling into question both their critique of phenomenology, and the viability of their own constructive proposals. As we will see, I think what they are both looking for (not necessarily what they *say* or *get*) is very close to my own incarnational account – which is not, of course, my own invention, but rather a retrieval of earlier, particularly patristic and medieval sources. Some might in fact hear in this incarnational phenomenology a revival of "analogy" – a heresy in Paris, to be sure. However, what I think will become clear is that "analogy" never really died in Paris – that, in fact, Levinas's and Marion's own proposal for the "revelation" and "manifestation" of the Wholly Other could only be possible on the basis of an incarnational or analogical account. This will open a discussion of analogy as an incarnational paradigm of language operation which can be retrieved in the current phenomenological milieu.

Finally, the incarnational paradigm operates on the basis of an affirmation of finitude, materiality, and embodiment. In this sense, I take it to be the very antithesis of the versions of "Platonism" which have dominated philosophy of language from the *Phaedrus* to the *Logical Investigations*. This claim, however, must be qualified, in light of Catherine Pickstock's and John Milbank's evaluations of the relationship between Platonism and Christianity – particularly Pickstock's careful arguments in *After Writing*. Thus the concluding section rehearses the perennial question of the relationship between Christianity and Platonism (and more specifically, the question of the continuity or discontinuity between the Platonic doctrine of *methexis* and the Christian doctrine of the *Incarnation*), sketching the contours for further discussion.

On (not) knowing the Wholly Other: a critique of revelation in Levinas and Marion

The problem of theology, and the formal problem of incommensurability, arise from the claim that the "Other" of which we speak is in fact *Wholly* Other – Infinite, heterogeneous, radically different, beyond (*au-delà*) our comprehension. The Wholly Other (*tout autre*) is not only different in degree, but different in kind – a difference of a completely different order or *genus*. Thus Levinas, when speaking of the alterity of the "face," emphasizes its resistance to determination:

> The face is present in its refusal to be contained. In this sense it cannot be comprehended, that is, encompassed. It is neither seen nor touched – for in the visual or tactile sensation the identity of the I envelops the alterity of the object, which becomes precisely a content. The Other is not other with a relative alterity as are, in a comparison, even ultimate species, which mutually exclude one another but still have their place within a community of a genus . . . The alterity of the Other does not depend on any quality that would distinguish him from me, for a distinction of this nature would precisely imply between us that community of genus which already nullifies alterity. (TI 194)

Any determination of the Other would happen in terms of the determining ego, which would straight away "nullify" the alterity of the Other. Then it would only be "other," not "Wholly Other."

The same holds true for Marion's account of God as Wholly Other or "Infinite": rather than succumbing to the phenomenological conditions of appearance, the "religious phenomenon" (as the "saturated phenomenon") displaces and over-whelms those conditions. As such, the religious phenomenon is an "absolute phenomenon" which precludes any analogical understanding:

> This phenomenon would escape all relations because it would not maintain any common measure with these terms; it would be freed from them, as from any a priori determination of experience that would eventually claim to impose itself on the phenomenon. In this we will speak of an absolute phenomenon: untied from any analogy with any object of experience what-soever. (SP 117)

As an absolute donation, the being-given *par excellence* (MP 588), the religious phenomenon (Gxd) is not subject to any horizon of perception, which would constitute a definition of the infinite, a compassing of that which cannot be encompassed. The saturated phenomenon is precisely the *un*conditioned: "Thus, in giving itself absolutely, the saturated phenomenon gives itself also as absolute – free from any analogy with experience that is already seen, objectivized, and comprehended. It frees itself therefrom because it depends on no horizon" (SP 118). Anything less, Marion argues, would not be Gxd, but only a "god," an idol of our own construction, created in our own image – the image of the same.

However, despite the utter alterity of the Wholly Other, it is imperative that it (the Face, Gxd) somehow "show" itself, make its presence felt – otherwise, the "Wholly Other" will be simply the truly Unknown, that which can be neither sought nor recollected. In other words, if the Wholly Other were *wholly* "Wholly Other," how would we know it even "exists"? How could any discourse concerning the Wholly Other – even about its being "beyond being" – ever be generated?[14] And more importantly, how could any *relation* with the Wholly Other be possible, apart from its appearing *in some manner*? This possibility is absolutely imperative, for it alone will be the condition of possibility for the ethical relation. If the Other, because of its alterity, could never appear for another, then the call to responsibility – resounding in the face – could never be heard (I could plead ignorance, as it were). Or if Gxd, because of his alterity, could never appear or be known by the creature, then the possibility of communion (even in love) would be precluded. Or as Jüngel considers,

> Justification implies recognition. Recognition, however, requires that the one who is recognized *permit* himself to be recognized. . . . To permit oneself to be recognized implies, in turn, that the one who is recognized knows the one who is recognizing. In the event of recognition, such knowledge is realized in that the recognizer must reveal himself if his recognition is to mean anything at all. No one can be recognized by a totally unknown person.[15]

In any case, the Wholly Other cannot remain *wholly* Wholly Other without denying the possibility of relation or connection. But for both Levinas and Marion – and in general, any theological perspective – such a relation is imperative. From this the question arises: how can the Wholly Other be "known" in such a way that will not deny its alterity? How can a relation be established with the Wholly Other which would not reduce it to the Same? What kind of "relation" would this be?

For both Levinas and Marion, the Other is not "disclosed" (which could happen only within and against a horizon) or "known" (since, for them, this would entail comprehension), but rather "revealed" or "manifested." Rather than being constituted by the perceiving ego, the Infinite reveals itself, from itself. In a central passage which warrants our full attention, Levinas sketches the way in which this "appearance" of the Other resists the totalization and domination of phenomenological conditions:

The manifestation of the *kath'auto* [from itself] in which a being concerns us without slipping away and without betraying itself does not consist in its being disclosed, its being exposed to the gaze that would take it as a theme for interpretation, and would command an absolute position dominating the object. Manifestation *kath'auto* consists in a being telling itself to us independently of every position we would have taken in its regard, *expressing itself.* . . . *The absolute experience is not disclosure but revelation*: a coinciding of the expressed with him who expresses, which is the privileged manifestation of the Other. (TI 65–6)

The revelation of the (Wholly) Other is an "absolute experience" – an experience in which the Other shows itself, from itself, on its own terms, rather than succumbing to the conditions of the constituting ego. In such a manifestation, the Other is both present and absent, "without slipping away and without betraying itself." This expression – which takes place in language (TI 195) – is that which makes possible a *relation* between the Same and the Other, "where the Other enters into a relation while remaining *kath'auto*" (TI 67). This, of course, must be a particular kind of relation, not a simple relation of appropriation or totalization which accompanies the relation of "knowing" (TI 48). Rather, Levinas argues, the relation based on the revelation of the Other is a "relation without relation" (*rapport non rapport*) (TI 80), "a relation whose terms do not form a totality" (TI 39), "a relation that does not nullify the infinite interval of the separation" (TI 80). Thus the relation with the Infinite – which is imperative – is a relation which is not a relation, a relation which does establish a connection, but does not erase the difference or incommensurability between Same and Other. Further, this relation is established on the basis of *language*, for in "discourse," "[t]he terms, the interlocutors, absolve themselves from the relation, or remain absolute within the relationship" (TI 195). In speaking, the Other presents itself, but not in such a way as to be appropriated or absorbed; rather, in "expression" the Other both shows itself and maintains its alterity.[16] It is this relation, then, which founds the freedom and responsibility of the "I" (TI 197); thus, the revelation of the Other is the condition of possibility for "ethics."

But still we must ask: in what way can the Wholly Other be *revealed*? Must not every revelation be *received*? What, then, will be the condition of possibility for the *reception* of such a revelation? Must not a revelation take place in terms that the ego can understand? Must it not be a revelation which is received *secundum modum recipientis recipitur*[17] – "according to the mode (condition) of the receiver"? This is where I would locate my critique of Levinas and Marion: any "revelation" can only be received, and must be received, insofar as the recipient possesses the *condition* for its reception – otherwise, it will remain unknown. If a friend wanted to "reveal a secret" to me, and revealed the secret in a note written in Japanese, the secret would remain a secret and unknown to me because, lacking the knowledge of Japanese, I lacked the condition to receive the revelation. So also with the Wholly Other: if the Wholly Other is to "appear" – and this is imperative for both Marion and Levinas – then it must appear in terms that the recipient of the revelation can understand –

otherwise, it will remain unknown, the "relation" will not be established, and the "revelation" will not take place. However, we should note three important qualifications in this regard: (1) this is not the same as saying that the ego dominates and determines the Wholly Other, as though it were an "invention" of the constituting ego. The movement remains one that privileges the intentional direction *from* the Other *to* the Same. (2) While the Other must reveal itself in terms of the conditions of the recipient, this does not constitute an imposition of those conditions upon the Other; rather, the Other gives itself, from itself, freely, without exploitation. In other words, as I have argued above (Chapter 4), it is a movement of *condescension*. (3) Such a revelation in terms of the conditions of the receiver does not deny or nullify the alterity of the Other, nor does its manifestation collapse its transcendence into finitude. While the Transcendent shows up in terms of the finite ego, it does not completely surrender itself to those conditions; rather, just as Levinas describes this paradoxical relation, the Other presents itself *while remaining Other*, showing up in the sphere of immanence without sacrificing its transcendence, neither slipping away nor betraying itself.

In giving itself, the Transcendent does not give up its transcendence, but rather reveals itself; in fact, if the Wholly Other did not give itself in terms of the conditions of the finite perceiver, there would be no revelation, only silence or ignorance. There would be no relation, only incommensurability without contact. While Marion and Levinas critique Husserl's account of the appearance of transcendence, insofar as it appears only within the conditions of knowing, I would argue that the Infinite *must* appear under such conditions, or remain simply unknown (which is not an acceptable implication for either of them). Thus both Levinas and Marion need to relinquish the notion that appearance undoes transcendence. Here, I think Jüngel's consideration of a "positive" concept of *mystery* is instructive: "Part of the structure of the positive concept of mystery," he argues, "is then, on the one hand, that it does *not* cease being mystery when it has been grasped."[18] This is in contrast to a "negative" concept of mystery which makes the mysterious unknowable only because of the finite conditions of the knower – almost an "accidental" mystery, if we could draw an analogy with Kierkegaard. This negative concept leads only to silence: "every word would be too much for God because every thought would be too little for him." Ironically, it is this negative sense of mystery which governs both rationalism and mysticism (or what I have described as kataphatics and apophatics), ending in silence regarding God.[19] The positive mystery, that which is a mystery in itself, not just relative to finite knowers, retains its mystery and otherness even in the moment it is revealed. Thus, "on the other hand, a part of the structure of the positive concept of mystery is that it is essential to the mystery that it permits itself to be grasped.... The mystery is therefore the subject of the process of letting itself be grasped: it *reveals* itself *as* mystery."[20] Revealing itself, it must reveal itself according to the conditions of the recipient; but in revealing itself *as* mystery, or *as* transcendent, it maintains its incommensurability.

In this matter of revelation "according to the mode of the perceiver," I am, of course, recalling an axiom of analogy, but also an axiom of the principle of incarnation, as developed in Augustine's account considered above. This problem, of how it would be possible to establish a relation with that which is wholly other, is precisely the challenge addressed by Kierkegaard in the early chapters of the *Philosophical Fragments* – and responded to by means of an incarnational strategy. Thus, before turning to a consideration of analogy in Augustine and Aquinas, I will follow Kierkegaard's incarnational account of the appearance of transcendence.

The appearance of the paradox: revelation in Kierkegaard

In many ways the problem we are grappling with – how it will be possible for that which is incommensurate to appear and be known – is a restatement of the Learner's Paradox, and thus a problem at least as old as Plato. From the lips of Socrates, responding to Meno, the problem is stated:

> Do you realize that what you are bringing up is the trick argument that a man cannot try to discover either what he knows or what he does not know? He would not seek what he knows, for since he knows it there is no need of inquiry, nor [would he seek] what he does not know, for in that case he does not even know what he is to look for. (*Meno*, 80e)

As Kierkegaard reformulates the question, "Can the truth be learned?" Plato's strategy is to *solve* the paradox: "No," he replies, "the truth cannot be learned; rather, it is recollected." In other words, nothing "new" or "other" is ever learned; in this philosophy of immanence, it is only what the soul already possesses – as self-sufficient – which can be "known," even though it may have to be recalled from its *Vergessenheit*.

In an attempt to displace this "Socratic" immanence philosophy,[21] Johannes Climacus undertakes an alternative, even opposite, strategy: rather than "solving" the Learner's Paradox by means of a self-sufficient soul (representative of modernity, to Kierkegaard), he thinks the second possibility – that something which was previously unknown could be learned, indicating a radical change and thus an instance in time which has eternal significance.[22] However, Kierkegaard concedes that if one is to genuinely "learn" that which is unknown, it cannot be something that one would even know to go looking for. How, then, will it be learned? It must, he says, be brought to the learner – it must be received as a gift. Thus, in contrast to the Socratic account of *recollection* whereby the truth is already possessed and so only *remembered*, Kierkegaard provides an account of learning that which is Unknown – wholly other – only on the basis of *revelation*,[23] a gift that must be *received*.

So, *if* the moment is to have eternal significance, *then* knowledge must not be a retrieval of what is already possessed, but rather the reception of a *gift*. Something new is given; something comes to be which previously was not – and it comes to be at a particular moment. In sum, if the "moment in time" is to have "decisive significance" – that is, if history is going to make a difference for knowledge – then the truth must be *learned*. But if the truth is going to be "learned," it must be a coming-to-know that which was previously *un*known, which was beyond or outside the learner's realm of knowledge. Or, to put it conversely, "if the moment is to acquire decisive significance, then the seeker up until that moment must not have possessed the truth, . . . indeed, he must not even be a seeker."[24] The (soon-to-be) learner will in fact be "outside the truth," even "untruth," and therefore will have forfeited even the condition to receive the truth.[25] The result is a radical *difference* between the "knower" and the unknown truth. If the learner is to come to know this truth, two things will be necessary: first, "the teacher must bring it to him, but not only that. Along with it, he must provide him with the condition for understanding it."[26] Thus, the unknown truth is given as a gift to the learner, and further, the teacher must provide the condition for its reception. But since the provision of the condition will in fact require a "transformation" of the learner, it must be the case that the teacher is God himself.[27] In fact, not only is God the teach*er*, his presence is in fact the teach*ing*.[28]

Moved by love, God, as the teacher, makes his appearance;[29] but here we locate the heart of the problem which interests us. How will God, who is unknown, wholly other, "appear" in a way that will make a relation with the learner possible? For if such a relation is not possible, then the learner cannot learn what was previously unknown, and we will be forced to concede the immanence of the Socratic. How will it be possible to bring about an understanding between[30] the two? Kierkegaard considers this problem in terms of a possible "equality" or "unity" which is not, however, a modality of sameness:

> The love, then, [of the teacher] must be for the learner, and the goal must be to win him, for only in love is the different made equal, and only in equality or in unity is there understanding. . . . Yet this love [between teacher and learner] is basically unhappy, for they are very unequal, and what seems so easy – namely, that the god must be able to make himself understood – is not so easy *if he is not to destroy that which is different.*[31]

According to Kierkegaard, in order for understanding to be possible, there must be a certain "equality" or likeness: in order to know another or understand someone, we must be "on the same level," as it were. But with respect to the relation between the teacher (God) and the learner (creature), there is "an intellectual difference that makes understanding impossible."[32] Thus the critical question becomes: will it be possible for the learner to come to know the god? Is not God so completely other, so radically different, so far above us, that it would be impossible to know him? Does not the incommensurability between the creature and the Creator indicate the impossibility of this relation? If it is impossible, then we are left only with the Socratic. How, then, would it be possible to establish "equality" between the teacher and learner *without*, however, *destroying the difference*?

As Kierkegaard argues, such an "equality" could only be made possible by a *descent* by God, and more particularly, by an *incarnational appearance* in which God will "show up" in terms that the finite knower can understand. "In order for the unity to be effected, the god must become like this one. He will appear, therefore, as the equal of the lowliest of persons."[33] His descent into history will constitute the only possible *revelation* of his transcendence which would make it possible for the learner to come to know the *un*known. In other words, "learning" can only happen on the basis of the Incarnation, for only when the wholly other gives itself in terms of the conditions of the learner is a relation between them made possible.

In fact, this thought itself – the thought of "Incarnation" – is a paradox which cannot be comprehended, and could not have been the invention of the learner.[34] This thought, which thought could not produce, is precisely that which impassions thought. It is so, but it is also the limit or frontier of thought – the point at which thought collapses; thus it is thought's torment and incentive. As such, thought wills its own collapse or downfall: "This, then, is the ultimate paradox of thought: to want to discover something that thought itself cannot think."[35] Thus, if God, as the absolutely different, cannot be thought, then *God* must make a leap, viz. the movement of incarnation: "if a human being is to come truly to know something about the unknown (the god), he must first come to know that it is different from him, absolutely different from him. The understanding cannot come to know this by itself (since, as we have seen, it is a contradiction); if it is going to come to know this, it must come to know this from the god."[36] This is a first movement which underscores the difference. But further, the paradox must "give itself" to be understood:

> How, then, does the learner come to an understanding with this paradox, for we do not say that he is supposed to understand the paradox but is only to understand that this is the paradox. We have already shown how this occurs. It occurs when the understanding [of the learner] and the paradox happily encounter each other in the moment, when the understanding steps aside and the paradox *gives itself*.[37]

The "moment" is the moment of passion, the moment of "faith" which is not a knowledge,[38] such that I can say that I have come to an understanding *with* the paradox (in the moment of faith), even though I do not "know" or "comprehend" it.

In summary (see Figure 4 below), according to Kierkegaard, the Wholly Other (the unknown) must appear in terms of the condition of the learner, if there is to be a relation between the two – if, in fact, there is to be a revelation. Thus the movement is one of (con)descent on the part of the Infinite, an incarnational movement of revelation whereby the transcendent reveals itself in terms of immanence, without thereby denying or sacrificing its transcendence. While showing up in the finite – the condition for the learner's understanding (of) God – the Infinite suffers no loss.

Analogy and respect: retrieving analogy in a French context

As for Levinas and Marion, so for Kierkegaard the establishment of a relation with the Wholly Other is imperative; but as he concedes (unlike Marion and Levinas, I think), such a relation, while not one of "knowledge," is only possible on the basis of a revelation, and such a revelation is only possible on the basis of a revelation

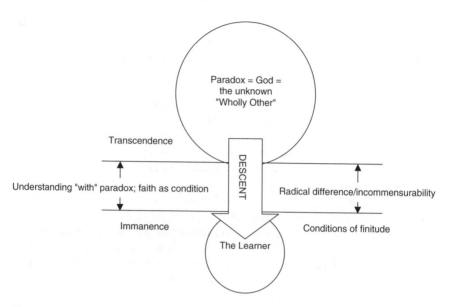

Figure 4 The incarnational appearance of the paradox.

"according to the conditions of the receiver" (*pace* Aquinas). Thus, ironically, the projects of Marion and Levinas become possible only insofar as they concede the possibility of an *analogical* account of the "revelation" of the Infinite, recalling a Thomistic axiom which Jüngel considers "indisputable."[39] My intention here is not to provide an exposition of the Thomistic doctrine, but only to suggest that my incarnational account of the appearance of transcendence, drawing on Augustine and Kierkegaard, follows a logic similar to that of analogy; or, conversely, analogy is an incarnational account of knowledge. Not only *can* the Transcendent appear in terms of immanence ("according to the conditions of the perceiver"), it *must* do so, otherwise it will not appear at all, nor could it be revealed or manifested apart from such conditions.[40] By invoking the Thomistic account of analogy, we should not forget that it was precisely such which stood at the heart of Husserl's account of the appearance of transcendence in the Fifth Meditation. Thus, by pointing to analogy as the necessary condition for any "revelation" of alterity, we deconstruct Marion's and Levinas's own critiques of Husserl's account.[41] Analogy is the condition of possibility, not only for phenomenology in general, but even the "limit" phenomenologies of alterity sketched by Levinas and Marion; this is because even these phenomenologies of revelation cannot displace that phenomenological (and Thomistic) axiom that what is "received" – whether a revelation or a gift – must be received "according to the mode of the receiver." Thus we are not surprised to see Derrida emphasize that "language never escapes analogy [*le langage n'échappe jamais à l'analogie*], it is indeed analogy through and through."[42] On my accounting, that is to conclude that language is incarnational through and through, that it never escapes incarnation as its paradigm and condition of possibility.

The incarnational filiation of analogy can be seen in Thomas's own discussion of "How God is Known by Us" (*ST* 1a.12), which is grounded in Aquinas's epistemological principle that all knowledge, as a matter of "reception," is possible only according to the mode or condition of the receiver: *quidquid recipitur, secundum modum recipientis recipitur* (e.g. *ST* 1a.75.5, 76.2.ad3).[43] Based on this principle, the question is: how will it be possible for us, as finite and conditioned, to know God, who is infinite and unconditioned? First, Aquinas notes that according to our "natural" powers, this is impossible:

> For knowledge takes place according as the thing known is in the knower. But the thing known is in the knower according to the mode of the knower. Hence the knowledge of every knower is according to the mode of its own nature. If therefore the mode of being of a given thing exceeds the mode of the knower, it must result that the knowledge of that thing is above the nature of the knower. (*ST* 1a.12.4)

However, this (im)possibility is overcome by grace, though I will concede that this is not quite an incarnational account, since here it seems to be a matter of "raising up" the human intellect to the level of the divine, rather than a movement of descent from the divine (ad3).[44]

But second, Aquinas considers the objection, akin to Marion's critique of the "screen of Being" (GWB 37–48), that "if God is seen through a medium [a horizon?], he is not seen in his essence. But if seen by any created light, he is seen through a medium" (*ST* 1a.12.5obj2). Aquinas's reply to the first objection now moves toward a condescensional account: "A created light is necessary to see the essence of God, not in order to make the essence of God intelligible, which is of itself intelligible, but in order to enable the intellect to understand" (ad1). The Infinite appears in terms that the created intellect can understand (that is, via a medium), otherwise it would fail to appear for a finite perceiver. Thus God, in himself and from himself, concedes to the conditions of human knowing in order to be made known.

Third, Aquinas, in contrast to modern accounts of knowledge, makes a careful distinction between "knowledge" and "comprehension," which will be crucial to any account of the appearance of transcendence which wants to also maintain its incommensurability. While God can be *known*, he cannot be comprehended by any finite intellect since "what is comprehended is perfectly known" (*ST* 1a.12.7); but since all knowledge is according to the mode of the perceiver, the finite creature cannot perfectly know the Infinite God. "Comprehension," in the strict sense of the term, denotes something being "in" something else, and "thus in no way is God comprehended either by the intellect or by anything else; for since he is infinite, he cannot be included in any finite being" (*ST* 1a.12.7). In order to unpack the distinction between comprehension and knowledge, Aquinas cites Augustine's letter concerning "The Vision of God": "It is one thing to see," Augustine writes, "it is something else to grasp the whole [i.e. comprehend] of something by seeing, since, indeed, a thing is seen when it is perceived as present in any way whatsoever, but the whole is grasped [comprehended] by seeing when it is seen, so that no part of it escapes notice" (*Epist.* 147.21). But the fact that God cannot be comprehended does not preclude knowledge of God altogether. Rather, it is possible for the Transcendent to appear – be known – when it reveals itself in terms of the conditions of the perceiver. Thus the God whom no one had seen, nor could see, at any time (John 1:18) was "beheld" (*etheasametha*) in that moment that "the word became flesh and pitched his tent among us" (John 1:14). Thus the analogical principle whereby the difference is known by means of the same is also a fundamentally incarnational principle, where the Infinite is known by means of a finite appearance, without losing its infinitude – "neither slipping away nor betraying itself."

In a sense, then, it is not necessary to "clear (phenomenological) space" for the appearance of transcendence; such transcendence must appear as any other phenomenon – according to the conditions of the finite perceiver. It will not be, as Marion suggests, a matter of displacing or overcoming these conditions, but rather understanding the possibility of the Transcendent condescending to such conditions without thereby undoing its transcendence. What I am contesting is Marion's and Levinas's assumption that appearance itself would constitute a violation of the transcendent; rather, in an incarnational account, we find an appearing which is not an appropriation, a giving which also remains a withholding – neither betraying itself nor slipping away.

This incarnational paradigm for revelation navigates a course between "correlational" theologies (of, for instance, Tillich, Rahner or McFague) and "revelational" theologies (of, for instance, Barth and von Balthasar). The former tend toward a reductive understanding of revelation which is in danger of reducing it to mere cultural manifestation; but the latter ignore the historical conditions of finitude which are the condition of possibility for the reception of a revelation. An incarnational account does justice to both of these poles. On this ground and in our critique of Marion and Levinas, we are only revisiting a celebrated early twentieth-century theological debate between Karl Barth and Emil Brunner. In this confrontation, Barth reacted to what he heard in Brunner as a "liberal" assumption regarding the possibility of a "natural theology" – which he found in both Catholic theology and, more importantly for Barth, German liberal theology. By privileging "natural" human experience, Barth argued, the Church stood in danger of being co-opted by reigning ideologies – a concern that proved only too true after Hitler's rise to power; so for Barth, questions about the relationship between transcendence and immanence involved questions of the relationship between nature and grace; and the latter ultimately was a question of the relationship between church and state. However, for our present purposes, what is most intriguing is Barth's reaction to a particular concept in Brunner's theology of revelation.

According to Brunner, Barth's dialectical theology concluded that, given the priority and sole sufficiency of grace (*sola gratia*), one could not assert even a point of contact between the divine and human since, for Barth, that would undermine their incommensurability, undoing the alterity of God as "Wholly Other." This was the fundamental point that Brunner wanted to contest: far from denying that there could be such a "point of contact" (*Anknüpfungspunkt*), Brunner argued that there *must* be such a "capacity" in order for revelation to occur – most specifically, the "capacity for words" (*Wörtfähigkeit*).[45] As Trevor Hart summarizes, "[w]e must, he argues, be able to speak meaningfully of a 'point of contact' (*Anknüpfungspunkt*) for grace in nature in some sense, else we are left with a revelation and a redemption which are floating in mid-air never actually *making* contact, and never, therefore, actually revealing anything to or redeeming anybody."[46] In other words, Brunner was making a point similar to what I have argued above, viz. that even if we want a theology that begins from revelation, that revelation must first be *received*, and there are conditions for that reception: all reception is according to the mode of the perceiver. Thus any revelation must be *given* in terms that are in some sense commensurate with the conditions for its reception by the receiver – in this case, finite[47] human beings. How could Barth reject this assertion?

Barth's passionate response and rejection of Brunner's thesis can be attributed to several factors, not least of which perhaps is a certain "talking past one another" due to a heated context for debate (a common problem in the history of theology – consider Augustine and the Pelagians). However, I want to focus on just three elements of his response and offer a critique. First, Barth is concerned that in Brunner's "formal" point of contact or *capacity* for revelation there remains a hint of a "material," natural knowledge of God which would not be revelational but the possession of a self-sufficient humanity – tantamount to idolatry (or what we might describe as a theology of immanence). Second, Barth sees the discontinuity of human and divine, and the human *in*capacity to secure salvation, emphasized as the chief significance in the doctrine of the virgin birth, so closely related to the theme of incarnation that we are pursuing. As Hart summarizes,

> The virgin conception at the beginning of God's entry into human flesh, just as surely as the resurrection at the end of it, speaks decisively of God's capacity to achieve his purposes in that which, by nature, has no capacity to realize the same ends. Mary, being a virgin (i.e. precisely *as* virgin, rather than considered more generally as a woman), is utterly unable to conceive a child apart from the creative act of God in her womb. . . . Human beings, sinful and fallen, have no "capacity" in and of themselves for God, no natural predisposition to hear and receive his Word. Again, the Spirit of God must come and create (*ex nihilo* in this respect) precisely such a capacity.[48]

While this metaphor is telling for understanding Barth's position, it also opens the door to critique. First, while the central truth here is certainly God's gracious initiative and activity, it does not occur without reference to the "conditions of the receiver." For if God really wanted to demonstrate the utter incapacity of humanity, and assert his own free (re)creative powers, should God not have impregnated a man? Is the capacity really created *ex nihilo*? Does it not begin with a created womb? In other words, is not Mary's (albeit virgin) womb nevertheless a condition for the birth of the Savior? Is not this matrix a condition of possibility – a "point of contact" – to which God concedes in his gracious and free operations?[49] So does not the doctrine of the virgin birth also assert the point we have been making: that "contact" between the divine and human does happen on the basis of conditions which characterize finitude? In emphasizing that Mary was utterly unable to conceive this child apart from the creative activity of God, Barth seems to confuse "capacity" with a "tendency" or "predisposition." So in his debate with Brunner, what is at stake is less whether there is a "capacity" for human beings to receive revelation but rather whether there is a natural "tendency" for them to do so. One could assert the former without concluding the latter.

This leads us to a final point with respect to Barth's critique of Brunner: if by "capacity" Brunner means something "active" and material, then Barth cannot go along with him. But if he means a "passive" capacity – a capacity to receive – then Barth and Brunner can be brought together.[50] The "active capacity" would constitute a "tendency" or "ability" which Barth rejects because it functions as the basis of a "bottom-up" theology which construes the divine in terms of the human – a strategy easily susceptible to a Feuerbachian critique; but the "passive capacity" would indicate simply a "condition," and it is this passive capacity which we are indicating as both (1) the condition of possibility for revelation of the Other, and (2) that which demands that any such revelation be analogical, i.e. incarnational. This is why Barth ultimately ends up affirming a version of analogy as the condition of possibility for theological language. But rather than an analogy of attribution which moves in an ascent from human to divine, Barth's concept of analogy is one of *condescension* much like we saw in Augustine. The event of revelation occurs, not because of a positive capacity of human beings to rise up to the Infinite, but because of a movement of the Wholly Other toward human beings, condescending to appear under the conditions of perception which alone would make the revelation revelatory. "What if," Barth asks, "God be so much God that without ceasing to be God he can also be, and is willing to be, not God as well? What if he were to come down from his unsearchable height and become something different?"[51] The revelation of the Wholly Other occurs precisely in God's being willing to become other, to concede to the conditions of human knowing. "If it is *not* impossible to speak of God," Hart concludes, "if speech of him, if theology is in fact a possibility for human beings, then for Barth it is so only because God himself spans the gap which creation posits and sin exacerbates."[52] Thus, while critical of the ascending movement of the *analogia entis*, Barth recognizes that the condescending movement of an incarnational analogy is the condition of possibility of theology, that is, talk about God. Our further claim is that such is the condition of possibility of language in general.[53]

Having outlined the conditions for the incarnational appearance of transcendence, allow me to briefly sketch an incarnational understanding of conceptual description. If the first is a matter of knowledge, even being, the second is a matter of "naming." I will not repeat here the detailed accounts of the "concept" which I have sketched in Chapter 3 (in terms of "formal indication" as an "iconic" concept) and Chapter 4 (in terms of "praise" as a non-objectifying mode of conceptualization). In both instances, the concept is to function as a pointer, an indicator of that which exceeds and eludes it. Nevertheless, and at the same time, that transcendent referent is referred to in the concept. Thus it is both present and absent, indicated but not grasped, given but not comprehended. The sign finds its "completion," however (seen in both Heidegger and Augustine) when the receiver is directed toward the experience of the thing itself to which the concept points. As Trevor Hart summarizes,

> We "know" how these human media refer beyond themselves as we are drawn into a relationship with the object to which they refer us, as we know him in faith, as the knowledge of God is granted us new every morning. Such knowledge cannot be pinned down, held onto, packaged, and handed on to others. We can only point to the human media faithfully in order to direct others to the reality of which we speak.[54]

Concepts, understood "incarnationally," will relinquish any attempt to grasp or encompass, and thus must be accompanied by a certain "humility" attentive to the play of signifiers and the elusiveness of transcendence. Such an employment of concepts will find its *telos* in an ethical methodological modesty which will avoid the pretentious claim of possessing and determining the divine, since such determinations are so often accompanied by a violence which seeks to also demarcate the rigid boundaries of the community. An incarnational concept, while "embodying" transcendence, denies any claim to domesticating or rigidly determining such transcendence. Rather, it opens itself to the Other.

This is why an incarnational account of concepts is concerned with the *ethics* of method: "concepts," understood as formal indications, do not "deliver" to us a privileged understanding or interpretation of the phenomenon, but rather a perspective or adumbration of its appearance. As such, the (theological) concept, which is grounded in the experience of that appearance, should not be considered "definitive" or "normative" in any strong sense of the word – since such definition is precisely what characterizes the conceptual idol.[55] The concept is merely a pointer – and a formal one at that – which directs others to find its fulfillment in the experience itself. Its task is not to play the role of a substitute for the Transcendent, but to direct the gaze beyond itself *to* the Transcendent, and be challenged by this Other. By understanding concepts in this "humbled" manner,[56] we would avoid their institutionalization and idolization, both of which are operations that tend to suppress difference within community, and too often do so in a violent manner. In doing justice to transcendence with an incarnational understanding of appearance and conceptuality, we will, it is hoped, do justice to others, respecting difference as part of an incarnational community.

The specter of Platonism: reconsidering participation and incarnation

If the Incarnation is God's refusal to avoid speaking, then this incarnational logic will be opposed to both an "Arianism" which would reduce the transcendent to immanence, as well as every "Docetism" which would construe such a revelation as only feigned – not a real condescension. The most challenging and persistent form of the latter has traditionally been described under the rubric of "Platonism" – an ontology which devalues the material, refuses condescension, and thus avoids speaking. The most rigorous apophatics, I would argue, remains a kind of *theologia gloria* insofar as it concedes this "Platonic" disjunction which refuses the possibility of incarnation.[57] And so we are left without speaking – with only silence.

Things might not be quite this simple. As I have already suggested above (Chapter 3), if we consider the *dis*continuity between Christianity and Platonism with Saint Augustine, we find Augustine pointing to the absence of the doctrine of Incarnation as the central theme missing from those "Platonic books" (C 7.9.14); on this register, the Platonic doctrine of "participation" fundamentally differs from the Christian logic of incarnation.[58] However we might like to construe this passage with respect to the question of continuity or discontinuity, we must at least concede that Augustine wants to point out *differences* between Platonism and the incarnational logic of Christianity. What he "did not read there" were precisely accounts of God's condescension (John 1:1–14, Phil. 2:6–11) and self-donation on the cross (Rom. 5:6, 8:32).[59] The question, then, is whether these differences result from a *deficiency* in Platonism ("completed" or "made up" by Christian revelation), or a more fundamental *opposition* between two worldviews. Thus recent theological movements have wanted to identify the two, even portraying Plato as a kind of "sacramental" or "incarnational" philosopher – even theologian. John Milbank first sketched a manifesto for rethinking ontology and social theory rooted in "Platonism/Christianity."[60] This identification of Platonism and Christianity was later solidified around the concepts of "participation" and "incarnation," as part of a vision for a Christianity as "radical orthodoxy" which is *both* "more incarnate" *and* "more Platonic":

> The central theological framework of radical orthodoxy is "participation" as developed by Plato and reworked by Christianity, because any alternative configuration perforce reserves a territory independent of God. The latter can lead only to nihilism (though in different guises). Participation, however, refuses any reserve of created territory, while allowing finite things their own integrity.[61]

So in contrast to Augustine (and yet, in the name of Augustine), who saw the logic of the Incarnation as that which distinguished Christianity from Platonism, these proponents of Radical Orthodoxy (particularly Milbank and Pickstock) wish to see this as the site of their communion. This project of identifying Platonic participation with Christian incarnation (the fund, as we have seen above, for a sacramental logic) is pursued most rigorously by Catherine Pickstock. As such, in what follows I will attempt carefully to engage her argument in order finally to argue that there is an important element of the Platonic ontology which she has overlooked in her analysis of the doctrine of participation – an element which points again to what I see as an incommensurability between Platonic participation and an incarnational logic.

Pickstock's position is unfolded through a reading of Plato's *Phaedrus* which contests Derrida's interpretation of this dialogue in his early essay, "Plato's Pharmacy."[62] At stake in this encounter between Pickstock and Derrida is an entire history of interpretation of the *Phaedrus*, even a history of the interpretations of the interpretations, which we could lay out as follows:

1. The *Phaedrus* concludes with a consideration of the difference and opposition between "dialectic" (i.e. philosophy) and "rhetoric" – a theme that has occupied the interlocutors since the inception of the dialogue, instigated by the young Phaedrus's love for that "lover of speeches," Lysias (*Phaedrus*, 228a–e). Following Socrates's prayer for Lysias's conversion to philosophy (257b), Phaedrus is haunted by the epithet leveled at Lysias, viz. that he was merely a "speech writer" (257c) – which is to say, a "sophist" (257d). While this pushes Socrates to question the criteria for what would constitute a "good" speech,[63] it ultimately leads to an allegiance between speech and the soul (271d) which then becomes the ground for a hierarchical relationship between speech and "writing" (274c–d). In opposition to Theuth and in league with Thamus's reply, Socrates concludes that writing, far from being a "potion" (*pharmakon*) to aid memory, in fact is a poison which fosters forgetting:

> In fact, [writing] will introduce forgetfulness into the soul of those who learn it: they will not practice using their memory because they will put their trust in writing, which is external and depends upon signs that belong to others, instead of trying to remember from the inside, completely on their own. You have not discovered a potion for remembering, but for reminding; you provide your students with the appearance of wisdom, not with its reality. (275a)

Writing signals the advent of something *exterior* to the soul, unlike speech which operates "from inside." Further, writing is implicated in a chain of signification which is not only exterior but also sensible and dependent upon others, insofar as any language must be characterized by a universality (there is no private language). As a result, the soul is drawn outside of itself, lured out of the interiority which is the site of truth to an exteriority which is a loss and forgetting.

Thus Socrates draws the analogy between writing and painting:[64] both are "silent" in the face of question because the "reality" which they represent remains *absent*. Writing thus signals the death of the author, the impossibility of the author's "presence":

> When it has once been written down, every discourse rolls about every-where, reaching indiscriminately those with understanding no less than

those who have no business with it, and it doesn't know to whom it should speak and to whom it should not. And when it is faulted and attacked unfairly, it always needs its father's support; alone it can neither defend itself nor come to its own support. (275e)

Writing is not only an orphan, but a bastard, inferior to "another kind of discourse, a legitimate brother." This is a discourse which is a kind of interior writing, which is to say, not a writing at all:[65] "It is a discourse that is written down, with knowledge, *in the soul* of the listener" (276a). This discourse, this interior writing, is in fact *speech*, "the living, breathing discourse of the man who knows." Writing is only an *image* of this plenary speech (276a). The philosopher, refusing to traffic in exteriority and images, also refuses to write (276c).

2. The second chapter in this history of interpretation of both the *Phaedrus* and the relationship between speech and writing is in the history of philosophy of language from Aristotle through Hegel to Husserl and Saussure. Affirmed again and again is this evaluation of writing as merely an image of a full speech, a copy of a copy, signifier of a signifier. Speech is the site of a pure reproduction of the soul's self-presence, whereas as writing is a representation of speech.[66] The tradition agreed that this is what Socrates taught in the *Phaedrus* and further agreed that Socrates was correct in this estimation of writing and its relationship to speech. So we will refer to this as the "traditional interpretation" of the *Phaedrus*.

3. Derrida's reading in "Plato's pharmacy" is the third chapter in this history of interpretation. In short, Derrida agrees with the traditional interpretation insofar as it bears on the meaning produced by the text of the *Phaedrus*; in other words, he thinks Aristotle, Husserl, and Saussure were – whether they read it or not – good interpreters of Socrates's portrayal of the relationship between speech and writing. But he now disagrees on the second count, critically questioning the supposed privilege of speech. All that "plagues" writing in Socrates account (derivativeness, exteriority, sensibility, mediation) also contaminates[67] speech, indeed contaminates language at its "origin". Thus Derrida argues that language itself, and hence speech, is constituted by a kind of "writing" – *arche-writing* – as its condition of possibility. As such, the hierarchical relation between speech and writing is called into question, along with the very idea of full presence which undergirds such an evaluation.

4. The final chapter in this history of interpretation is penned by Pickstock, who challenges not only Derrida's interpretation of the *Phaedrus* but also seeks to subvert the "traditional interpretation." Far from offering a "metaphysics of presence," she wants to show that "Socrates' preference for spoken rather than written language is not a defence of "metaphysical presence" but the *reverse*, an attack on presence." And further, she will claim that "Derrida's insistence on the transcendental *writtenness* of language is revealed to be, after all, a rationalistic gesture which suppresses embodiment and temporality."[68] In order to effect this subversion of the traditional interpretation, it will be necessary for Pickstock to account for an entirely different *ontology* in the *Phaedrus*, since the devaluation of writing (in the traditional interpretation) is rooted in a traditional reading of Plato's ontology which operates on a

"scale of being" that privileges "being" and "reality" and devalues "images" as mere "appearances," even deceptions. Writing, we will recall, was devalued precisely because of its sensibility and exteriority, and the latter are devalued, in this traditional reading of a Platonic metaphysics, because they represent a certain "fall" from Being itself, from Reality. Writing is merely an "image," and hence traffics in the illusion and deception which characterize the temporality and change of the sensible world.

But Pickstock's goal is to question this reading of Plato, to reconsider whether this is really a Platonic ontology.[69] In contrast to this traditional reading of Platonic metaphysics which concludes with an otherworldliness and devaluing of temporality and the sensible order, Pickstock capitalizes on the theme of "participation" in Plato as an indication of a world-affirming metaphysics, even what might be described as a "liturgical" or "sacramental" ontology.[70] In other words, in order to demonstrate that Plato affirms writing as a sacramental medium, Pickstock must show that Plato (particularly in the *Phaedrus*) affirms the sensible world, embodiment, and temporality. With this new understanding of Platonic ontology the space is opened for demonstrating that Socrates in fact offers a "doxological" account of language. The argument proceeds by first dealing with the relationship between the intelligible and the sensible as one of "participation," and then reconsidering the question of "exteriority" by reexamining the matter of intersubjectivity (recalling that writing "depends on others"). In this respect, Pickstock's strategy is *theurgical*, representing an alternative[71] Platonic tradition which can be traced through Proclus and Iamblichus. From the perspective of theurgical Platonism, dualistic forms of Neoplatonism (such as one that could be found in Plotinus) were in fact "unorthodox."[72] Thus Iamblichus, in contrast to Porphyry's construal of the embodiment as a contamination, asserts the "sanctity of the world" and hence, embodiment. As a result, Iamblichian Neoplatonism – which takes itself to be the rightful heir of Plato – makes liturgical ritual central to the philosophical life.[73] This stems from what Shaw sees as the central difference between Iamblichian and Plotinian Neoplatonism: the doctrine of the "completely descended soul" affirmed by Iamblichus in contrast to the view of the soul as "undescended" in Plotinus and Porphyry – where the question concerns whether the soul descends into the body.[74] "That the soul's ritual use of matter could itself bring about the salvation of the soul was certainly a new development in the Platonic tradition," Shaw observes, "yet despite its apparent unorthodoxy, there are elements in the dialogues that lend it support – most obviously the doctrine of *anamnesis*, the core of Plato's epistemology (*Phaedo* 75e; *Meno* 81cd)."[75] One could say, then, that Pickstock has picked up this Iamblichian hermeneutic and is reading the Platonic dialogues through a theurgical lens, making the case the Plato was more Iamblichian than Plotinian.

This theurgical reading can be seen in two elements of Pickstock's interpretation of the *Phaedrus*. First, Pickstock locates the key to a new understanding of Plato's ontology in the principle of *participation* (*methexis*): "in the *Phaedrus*," she observes, "Plato portrays the transcendence of the good, its beyond presence-and-absence, as a kind of *contagion*, for its plenitude spills over into immanence, in such a way that the good is revealed in the beauty of physical particulars."[76] In the dialogue, for instance, the philosophic lover loves young Phaedrus, that "beautiful boy," precisely because his beautiful physical visage is the catalyst for remembering the Form of beauty itself.[77] The philosopher thus can glimpse the transcendence of the good "in the mundane order, and is thus given to revere all physicality according to its participation in this spiritual sun."[78] From this Pickstock concludes that one finds in Plato a fundamental affirmation of materiality and the temporal order, since the transcendent is manifested in immanence. In fact, she determines that temporality and materiality, far from being distractions or obstacles to philosophical "knowledge," are for Plato the conditions of possibility for philosophical knowledge: "[s]uch temporality does not compromise that knowledge, but rather constitutes its condition of possibility for us: the good arrives through time, and therefore time is not merely a ladder of access which can be kicked away, its job performed."[79] In a moment, we will need to carefully consider this qualification, "for us."

Socrates's "more positive reading of physicality" grows out of "the strongly positive view of *methexis* (participation) in the *Phaedrus* [which] frees him from the charge of otherworldliness and total withdrawal from physicality, for the philosophic ascent does not result in a 'loss' of love for particular things, since the particular participates in beauty itself."[80] The "detour" through the material and sensible "remains in a sense unsurpassable." (Again, we will need to interrogate this qualification: "in a sense.") This does not mean, of course, that the philosopher is absorbed in the sensible; there remains a sense in which the philosopher neglects the "things below;" but it is not that the philosopher "turns away from physicality itself (for that would deny him access to the good), but that he neglects a *mundane apprehension* of physicality as merely immanent."[81] In other words, the philosopher sees "through" the material to the transcendent, whereas in fact it is the sophist who reduces the sensible to the merely immanent, shutting down the reference to transcendence.

This revaluation of temporality and materiality is the ground for a revaluation of "exteriority" or intersubjectivity. At stake here is the relationship between "inside" (soul) and "outside" (the world, others): is there a privileging of the interiority of the soul in Plato? Would the "going out" which is characteristic of language be a "loss" on this register? Does Plato seek to guard the static interiority of the soul from the contamination of exteriority in writing? Pickstock argues that, while Plato certainly distinguishes the two, he nevertheless seeks to establish a harmonious relationship between them, at times even privileging exteriority over interiority.[82] "An alternative reading of interiority in Plato," she suggests, "would be that it is open to the outside without any need for violation, since reception of the external is represented in the *Phaedrus* as ontologically constitutive."[83] In fact, she concludes, if we look at just what Socratic "knowledge" is about, we see that it indicates an *opening* to the outside, a being possessed *from without*, even a *purification* from without: "Because the Socratic self is in this way constituted from without, knowledge of the self, Socrates's ultimate epistemological goal, is knowledge of what is "outside" the self, which is the good and its mediations."[84]

With this revaluation of materiality, temporality, and exteriority, language – which is sensible, temporal, and "depends on others" – is seen as ultimately "doxological, that is to say, as ultimately concerned with praise of the divine."[85] A participatory ontology that affirms materiality and embodiment is the ground for a doxological and sacramental philosophy of language, analogous to the theurgical revaluing of liturgical embodiment. And it is precisely "through language, another kind of exteriority," that the soul is moved to reflection on the transcendent.[86] In contrast to the "immanentism" of both the sophists and modernity, Socrates offers a sacramental ontology, a doxological philosophy of language, and a corresponding liturgical understanding of the *polis*.

Before offering a critique of Pickstock's argument, it should first be recalled that her proposal for a "sacramental" and "doxological" account of language – by which the transcendent is "revealed" in immanence – bears deep structural affinities with what I have been describing as an incarnational logic. My critique is concerned with locating such an account in Plato. Here I have two principal reservations, which stem from a more fundamental reservation about the supposed continuities between theurgical Neoplatonism and Christian "incarnational" or "creational" accounts of being-in-the-world.

First, the equation of Platonic "participation" (*methexis*) with Christian "incarnation" seems problematic on several counts: (1) If that were the case, then we must wonder at Augustine's insistence that it was precisely a notion of "incarnation" which he could not find in those Platonic books.[87] If we follow Augustine's lead, I think we find justification to assert at least a fundamental difference, and perhaps a deep incommensurability between the two notions. While it is the case that one can see a "positive" role for materiality, embodiment and temporality in the *Phaedrus* (particularly when read with theurigcal eyes), I think that Pickstock avoids the question of the *origin* or *commencement* of materiality in Plato's ontology. This corresponds to the question of the "descent" of the soul in Neoplatonism: while Iamblichian, theurgical Neoplatonism affirms the complete descent of the soul into the body, and hence affirms the positive role of embodied liturgy in the salvation of the soul, it remains to be consider just what occasions this "descent" of the soul "into" a body. Is not this descent occasioned by a fall?[88] Is not embodiment the result of a certain "falling away" from the gods, from the authenticity of a soul's identity with the disembodied existence of the gods? And hence is not "salvation" precisely the achievement of *dis*embodiment (*Laws* 12.959a–d) – liberation from the "pollution" of the body (*Phaedo* 64a, 66b, 81a). In other words, while it may be the case that there is a positive role for materiality and embodiment in theurgical Neoplatonism, and perhaps even in the *Phaedrus*, the material has a role to play in recollection only due to the fact that the soul has, regrettably, fallen into a body and therefore materiality is necessary as a kind of *remedial* propaedeutic. On a Platonic register, the material world is constituted by a kind of "fall," which does make the sensible and temporal a "necessary" detour, but only given the fallen condition of the soul. On a radically incarnational or creational register, the material does not play a simply "remedial" role in a postlapsarian state of affairs, but rather an integral and essential role for creatures *as* created. The eschaton will not be without sacraments, precisely because a Christian eschatology affirms the eternality of the material.[89] We can see the contrast when we consider a Platonic "eschatology" whose *telos* is precisely the liberation of the soul from the "pollution" of the body (*Phaedo* 81b). "As long as we have a body," Socrates argues, "and our soul is fused with such an evil we shall never adequately attain what we desire, which we affirm to be the truth" (*Phaedo* 66b). This is why to be "re-embodied" is a punishment (81e–82c). So a participatory ontology only affirms materiality and embodiment as a kind of "necessary evil" based on a prior determination of embodiment as already constituted by a fall. In contrast, an incarnational ontology is based on a prior affirmation of the goodness of creation (Gen. 1:27) as an affirmation of the primordial and necessary goodness of materiality, not merely its remedial functionality. Insofar as Iamblichian Neoplatonism does not affirm bodily resurrection, we have a strong indication that there reamins a fundamental incommensurability between the Neoplatonic evaluation of materiality and that offered by an incarnational paradigm which begins from an affirmation of the goodness of creation (Gen. 1:31).

Second, Pickstock's reading of the Socratic self as constituted by an "openness" to exteriority as the condition of possibility for knowledge seems to run contrary to Socrates's own affirmations about the nature of knowledge as *recollection*. Hence her curious reading of Kierkegaard which undoes Kierkegaard's own opposition between Platonic "recollection" and Christian "learning,"[90] where she (not surprisingly) suggests the Christian form of liturgy is really only a supplement to, not a contradiction of, Platonic liturgy.[91] By suggesting that Platonic knowledge is a knowledge "from without," Pickstock cannot do justice to Socrates' affirmation that true "learning" is *not* a deposit made from some exteriority, but rather a recovery of that which is interior to the soul. Our authority on this score is nothing less than the *Republic*: "Education isn't what some people declare it to be, namely, putting knowledge into souls that lack it, like putting sight into blind eyes. . . . But our present discussion, on the other hand, shows that the power to learn is present in everyone's soul" (*Republic* 518b–c). In short, I think that Pickstock overreads Socrates on this score.

In the end, however, Pickstock's doxological or sacramental account of language parallels that which I have been describing as an incarnational account. The logic of incarnation, in contrast to the mere logic of participation, moves by condescension rather than ascension, and is rooted in a more fundamental affirmation of embodiment as an original and eternal good, rather than a remedial "instrument" of salvation whose *telos* is disembodiment. Thus the logic of incarnation is a logic of *donation*, a logic of giving. As such, it is the condition of possibility of revelation, and hence the condition of possibility of language, which is itself a donation. This incarnational logic subverts the differential logics of both kataphatics and apophatics which can only conceive immanence and transcendence as oppositionally related. In contrast, the logic of incarnation – as the condition of possibility for language – signals the possibility of a revelation (whether a word or Word) which is both present and absent, immanent and yet transcendent, spoken but not exhausted. In short, it is because of the Incarnation that we avoid not speaking.

Notes

1 Rudolf Otto, *The Idea of the Holy: An Inquiry into the Non-Rational Factor in the Idea of the Divine and Its Relation to the Rational*, trans. John W. Harvey (Oxford: Oxford University Press, 1950), 2.

2 If God is perfectly benevolent, and omnipotent, then whence comes evil? The three propositions, when affirmed together, constitute a contradiction, a logical impossibility. God's goodness would want to exclude evil, and God's omnipotence would be able to exclude evil. If God is both of these things, then why does evil exist? For a succinct formulation of this challenge, see J. L. Mackie, "Evil and Omnipotence," in *Philosophy of Religion*, 3rd ed., ed. Louis P. Pojman (Belmont, CA: Wadsworth, 1998), 186–93. See also David Hume, *Dialogues Concerning Natural Religion*, ed. Martin Bell (London: Penguin, [1779] 1990), X.

3 Jüngel, *God as the Mystery of the World*, trans. Darrell L. Guder (Grand Rapids: Eerdmans, 1983), 230. I will return to Jüngel's response to this problem in more detail below.

4 For an analysis of both the "differential ontology" of violence and the counter-ontology or "ontology of peace," see John Milbank, *Theology and Social Theory* (Oxford: Blackwell, 1990), chs. 10–12.

5 Cf. Sanford Budick and Wolfgang Iser, *Languages of the Unsayable: The Play of Negativity in Literature and Literary Theory* (New York: Columbia University Press, 1989), which included Derrida's essay, "How To Avoid Speaking."

6 I take this to be an analogue of Graham Ward's claim that "language is always and ineradicably theological" (in Ward, *Barth, Derrida, and the Language of Theology* [Cambridge: Cambridge University Press, 1995], 9), and a correlate of Catherine Pickstock's claim that "liturgical language is the only language that really makes sense" (though we would contest the supplemental claim that "the event of transubstantiation in the Eucharist is the condition of possibility for all human meaning"). See Catherine Pickstock, *After Writing: On the Liturgical Consummation of Philosophy* (Oxford: Blackwell, 1998), xv.

7 At stake here is whether the claim that the Incarnation is the condition of possibility for language is an *ontological* or *epistemological* claim. What would it mean to say that the Incarnation is the ontological condition of possibility for speech? Would that be to make the ludicrous claim that no one spoke before the Incarnation? Or that someone who rejects the Christian belief in the Incarnation is consigned to silence? Of course, this could not be the case; rather, it would mean that words function on the basis of a procedure of "enfleshing" the incommensurate which is inherent to the very structure of creation and the history of relations between Creator and creature, and is performed *par excellence* in God's becoming flesh (John 1:14). In other words, this would require the development of an incarnational ontology (the focus of my current research, results forthcoming). This would, by definition, be a Christian ontology which could only be determined by one with Christian commitments; in other words, an atheist, or scientific reductionist, would reject the notion of an "incarnational ontology" *tout court*. But their own ontology would also be grounded in particular pretheoretical commitments which the Christian would reject. So there is no such thing as a "neutral" or "objective" ontology.

The second aspect of the claim – the Incarnation as the *epistemological* condition of possibility for a proper understanding of language: by this I mean that any philosophy of language which does not look to the Incarnation as a paradigm of expression will err either on the end of immanence or transcendence.

8 I have criticized various notions of an "autonomous" philosophy and sketched the possibility of a Christian philosophy in my "The Art of Christian Atheism: Faith and Philosophy in Early Heidegger," *Faith and Philosophy* 14 (1997): 71–81. See also John Milbank, "Knowledge: The Theological Critique of Philosophy in Hamann and Jacobi," in *Radical Orthodoxy: A New Theology*, eds. John Milbank, Catherine Pickstock, and Graham Ward (New York: Routledge, 1999), 21–37.

9 For the most part, I would agree with Heidegger's own account of these matters in "Phenomenology and Theology." Ironically, on the matter of the faith-groundedness of theology, Marion and Heidegger are agreed.

10 For my critique, see "The Art of Christian Atheism: Faith and Philosophy in Early Heidegger," *Faith and Philosophy* 14 (1997): 71–81.

11 Marion's scholastic understanding of the relationship between a "revealed theology" and a "natural [philosophical] theology" – which would be a *phenomenology* – precludes the possibility of a Christian phenomenology (see MP). Thus he would maintain that the analyses of *Étant donné* and *Reduction et donation* are characterized by a certain "neutrality." (And while our projects have much in common, I have a suspicion that something similar is at work in Milbank, who consistently emphasizes that it is a *theology* which grounds social theory, for instance. This might be confirmed by the "turn" to Aquinas.) I hope to pursue these issues elsewhere.

12 In this regard, I follow Herman Dooyeweerd, *In the Twilight of Western Thought: Studies in the Pretended Autonomy of Western Thought*, Collected Works B/4, ed. James K. A. Smith (Lewiston, NY: Edwin Mellen Press, 1999), 79–116. As Dooyeweerd also notes, since both Christian and non-Christian philosophies are grappling with the same phenomenon – an intersubjectively shared "world" – the commitments of philosophy do not preclude dialogue. In fact, it is only when those commitments and presuppositions are realized that such dialogue is possible (pp. 36–42).

13 Recall our discussion of the same movement in Augustine's account of language in Chapter 4 above.

14 In other words, how could *Totality and Infinity* even be written?

15 Jüngel, *God as the Mystery*, 231.

16 We could repeat the same considerations in Marion, where Gxd, though Wholly Other, is revealed in the Eucharist (see GWB 139ff.).

17 Aquinas, *ST*, 1a.75.5.

18 Jüngel, *God as the Mystery*, 250.

19 Ibid., 246–52.

20 Ibid., 251. Cf. Otto's similar remarks on the "mystery" of the Wholly Other: "The truly 'mysterious' object is beyond our apprehension and comprehension, not only because our knowledge has certain irremovable limits, but because in it we come upon something inherently 'wholly other,' whose kind and character are incommensurable with our own" (*Idea of the Holy*, 28).

21 When we turn to Pickstock below, it will be of interest to recall that, for Kierkegaard, it was Socrates who represented "immanentism." Pickstock attempts to minimize the difference between Socratic recollection and Kierkegaardian "repetition" as indicated in the *Fragments* by appealing to her reading of Plato which finds an "erotic mediation of the good in the beauty of the physical world" (*After Writing*, p. 268). I think there are two problems with this: first, below I will challenge this reading of Plato as a "sacramental" philosopher; second, this mediation of the good in the physical world is not relevant to Kierkegaard's question, as we will see here. For Kierkegaard, the beautiful face of Phaedrus is only an *occasion*, whereas the encounter with the god (the teacher) is revolutionary. Pickstock's misreading of Kierkegaard on this point is further indicated when she draws attention to the similarity between Socrates and the apostles (p. 271); Kierkegaard, of course, is happy to concede the similarity. But what is really at stake is the qualitative difference between the apostles and the god (the teacher).

22 While the discussion begins with the question, "Can the truth be learned?" (*Philosophical Fragments*, p. 9), the question is posed in a different way on the title page: "Can a historical point of departure be given for an eternal consciousness; . . . can an eternal happiness be built on historical knowledge?" (p. 1).

23 Ibid., 11.

24 Ibid., 13.
25 Ibid. For Kierkegaard, one is untruth through one's own fault, a condition he describes as "sin" (p. 15).
26 Ibid., 14.
27 Ibid., 14–15. The Hong translation uses "the god" throughout the *Fragments*, as noted above; I have modified it here and in what follows.
28 Ibid., 55–6.
29 Ibid., 24–5.
30 Note, it is *not* a matter of how the learner will come to understand the paradox, as though it would be possible to comprehend it. For Kierkegaard, this would be precisely a relation which would destroy the difference between the two. Thus, he is careful to say that it is a matter of coming to an understanding "with" the paradox (p. 59).
31 Ibid., 25.
32 Ibid., 27.
33 Ibid., 35.
34 Regarding the latter point: at the end of the first two chapters, Climacus responds to an objector who claims that this "thought project" sounds just a little like the New Testament, making Climacus the shabbiest of plagiarists (pp. 21–2, 35–6). Climacus responds by conceding that the tale or alternative story he is weaving, though it has been told by many humans, could never have been *invented* by humans. That is, we have an idea of that which we cannot produce – and therefore it must have been *given* to us (an argument analogous to Descartes's account of the origin of the idea of the "Infinite").
35 Ibid., 37.
36 Ibid., 46.
37 Ibid., 59, emphasis added.
38 Ibid., 62.
39 Jüngel, *God as the Mystery*, 254.
40 I note this only because Levinas would draw a distinction between "appearance," which happens under the conditions of the constituting ego, and "revelation," which is the manifestation of the Other on its own terms.
41 I think this is also Dominique Janicaud's concern in *Le tournant théologique de la phénoménologie française* (Paris: Éditions de l'éclat, 1991), 30–2. With this we would seem to be asserting the opposite of Ward's insight that it is revelation which "enables us to recognize that our language is analogical. The analogical character of language is substantiated by God alone and, as that character appears, so we, as recipients, believe" (Ward, *Barth, Derrida, and the Language of Theology*, 15). But this contradiction would only be apparent, since I too am asserting that God's revelation in the Incarnation is the condition of possibility for language to function analogically. But unlike Ward, I am also arguing that such a revelation must be an analogical operation. (Perhaps this could be described as a dialectical relation.)
42 Jacques Derrida, *Speech and Phenomena*, trans. David Allison (Evanston, IL: Northwestern University Press, 1973), 13.
43 It is pertinent to note that in looking to Thomas's account of analogy, I am not attempting to rehabilitate a project of natural theology, which I have already rejected above. So I am not concluding from this that we can infer from creation to God by means of natural, unaided reason (which is why Barth asserted that Catholic [analogical] theology and liberal theology both operated on the same principles); however, I do think that the epistemological axioms in Aquinas's account of analogy must also be the conditions for the reception of any "special" revelation as well. Thus, I am sympathetic to Barth's critique of Aquinas's project for a natural theology, but would assert that the epistemological aspects of analogy are not inextricably linked to such a project. (John Milbank has recently challenged the common claim that Thomas engages in a project of "natural

theology" in the usual sense, emphasizing that even God's revelation *in creation* is still God's *revelation*. See Milbank, "Intensities," *Modern Theology* 15 (1999): 445–97. I hope to take up an analysis of this argument elsewhere.)

44 We will return to this movement of "ascent" in Aquinas's account of analogy in our discussion of Barth below.

45 Emil Brunner, *Natur und Gnade: Zum Gespräch mit Karl Barth* (Tübingen: J.C.B. Mohr, 1934), 11, 18–20.

46 Trevor Hart, *Regarding Karl Barth: Toward a Reading of His Theology* (Downers Grove, IL: InterVarsity Press, 1999), 152.

47 Barth, of course, would add "finite *and sinful*." I am sympathetic to wanting to take into consideration the "noetic effects of sin." However, the problem I have sketched is only exacerbated by the Fall, not introduced by it. Further, I have consistently argued against any conflation of finitude with fallenness in my *The Fall of Interpretation: Philosophical Foundations for a Creational Hermeneutic* (Downers Grove, IL: InterVarsity Press, 2000). I am sometimes concerned that Barth and Marion fail to make the distinction.

48 Hart, *Regarding Karl Barth*, 163, summarizing Barth's response in *Natural Theology*, 93–4 and 123ff.

49 And, of course, the womb itself is God's creation.

50 Hart distinguishes between these two senses of "capacity" as "capacity1" and "capacity2" (*Regarding Karl Barth*, 166–9).

51 Karl Barth, *The Göttingen Dogmatics: Instruction in Christian Religion*, Volume 1 (Edinburgh: T&T Clark, 1991), 136.

52 Hart, *Regarding Karl Barth*, 184. Ward makes the same observation: in rejecting any association with Bultmann and Gogarten's "dialectical theology," Barth was rejecting their project of founding the possibility of theology on a philosophical (i.e. existentialist) foundation or justification. He was "not rejecting an analysis of the human situation *vis-à-vis* revelation . . . He is only too aware that revelation can only be made comprehensible and makes itself comprehensible within the metaphysical structures of human thinking" (*Barth, Derrida, and the Language of Theology*, 95).

53 Though not drawing this conclusion, Hart (*Regarding Karl Barth*) is attentive to the fact "the problem of theological language provides a particularly clear instance of the problem of human language and its mode of reference to reality in general" (p. 192). Ward also notes that "insofar as in chapter 5 of the *Church Dogmatics* he is making a statement about language *tout court*, and insofar as Christian speaking about God can only be understood within a more general economy of representation, then his problematic is identical to that analysed in *Redesphilosophie* and Heidegger's ontology of Logos" (Ward, *Barth, Derrida, and the Language of Theology*, 103).

54 Hart, *Regarding Karl Barth*, 192.

55 I have discussed this in a slightly different context in my "Fire From Heaven: The Hermeneutics of Heresy," *Journal of Theta Alpha Kappa* 20 (1996): 13–31.

56 Again, as modeled in the humiliation of the Incarnation (Phil. 2:5–11).

57 Derrida's argument in HAS is analogous: what mystical theology offers us, he argues, is not the end of metaphysics, but a hyper-metaphysics, a "super-essentialism" (HAS 79).

58 In this respect, I am sympathetic with the argument of Michael Horton in his essay, "Eschatology After Nietzsche: Apollonian, Dionysian or Pauline?," *International Journal of Systematic Theology* 2 (2000): 29–62.

59 The allusions/references are Augustine's. See C 7.9.13–14.

60 Milbank, *Theology and Social Theory*, 290.

61 Milbank, Pickstock, and Ward, "Introduction," *Radical Orthodoxy*, 3.

62 Jacques Derrida, "Plato's Pharmacy," in *Dissemination*, trans. Barbara Johnson (Chicago: University of Chicago Press, 1981), 63–171.

63 Again, Socrates entreats: "convince Phaedrus, him of the beautiful offspring, that unless

he pursues philosophy properly he will never be able to make a proper speech on any subject either" (261a).

64 Cf. *Republic* 10.595a–605d.

65 Cf. Husserl's notion of a "transcendental writing" in *The Origin of Geometry*.

66 Tracing this through the history of philosophy from Plato to Saussure is Derrida's project in *Of Grammatology*. I have discussed this in more detail in ch. 4 of *The Fall of Interpretation*, 115–29.

67 This language of "contamination" is Derrida's; I call it into question in my *Pure Derrida?*

68 Pickstock, *After Writing*, 4.

69 This would also require another line of questioning which I can only note but not take up in detail, viz. the extent to which much of what is bequeathed to us under the rubric of "Platonism" is in fact *Neo*platonism. That is a significant question *if* there is significant discontinuity between Platonism and Neoplatonism. And even if there is, we must also consider to what extent the Platonic corpus gives rise to Neoplatonism. Further, one must be careful how Plato is read, particularly the role of "myth" in his thought. We will have to bracket these questions here, but my thanks to Mark Morelli for pointing out these issues.

70 What Pickstock refers to as a "sacramental" ontology is akin to what I have been describing as an "incarnational" ontology. In the end, it must be noted that Pickstock and I agree about the importance of an incarnational ontology; but we disagree as to the resources for its development. She finds it in Plato's notion of "participation," whereas I will argue that there is a fundamental difference between Platonic "participation" and Christian "incarnation." Further, whereas Pickstock undertakes a critique of Derrida in the name of a participatory ontology, elsewhere I have found resources in early Derrida for the development of an incarnational ontology. See my "A Principle of Incarnation in Derrida (*Theologische?*) *Jugendschriften*," *Modern Theology* 18 (April 2002): 217–30.

71 So any charge of "Platonism" must respond to the query: *Whose* Plato? *Which* Platonism? My thanks to John Milbank, Robert Dodaro and Wayne Hankey for pushing me on these issues, even if, in the end, we remain disagreed. For further discussion of such questions, see Endre von Ivánka, *Plato Christianus: La réception critique du platonisme ches les Pères de l'Eglise*, trans. Elisabeth Kessler, rev. by Rémi Brague and Jean-Yves Lacoste (Paris: PUF, 1990), 13–20, 425ff.

72 See Gregory Shaw, *Theurgy and the Soul: The Neoplatonism of Iamblichus* (University Park, PA: Penn State Press, 1995), 10–11. My thanks to John Milbank for pointing me to this significant source.

73 Ibid., 14–27.

74 Ibid., 11. Below I will return to ask, even of Iamblichus, just what occasions this "descent"?

75 Ibid., 24.

76 Pickstock, *After Writing*, 12.

77 "[W]hen he sees a godlike face of bodily form that has captured Beauty well, first he shudders and a fear comes over him like those he felt at the earlier time; then he gazes at him with the reverence due a god, and if he weren't afraid people would think him completely mad, he'd even sacrifice to his boy as if he were the image of a god" (*Phaedrus*, 251a–b).

78 Pickstock, 12.

79 Ibid., 13.

80 Ibid., 14.

81 Ibid., 15.

82 Ibid., 30.

83 Ibid., 28.

84 Ibid., 29.

85 Ibid., 37.

86 Ibid., 31.

87 Admittedly, we might have to deal with another question here, viz. what library constituted these "Platonic books?" Were these Plato's dialogues? Or were these the books of Neoplatonists? And if so, which Neoplatonists? Iamblichian? Porphyry? Plotinus? If the last, one could envision someone claiming that the notion of incarnation was not to be found in the (Plotinian) Neoplatonists, but that if he had only read the *Phaedrus*, Augustine would not have been so disappointed. But that would only push us once again to a question we have bracketed: whether there is such a *dis*continuity between Plato and Neoplatonism in this respect.

88 See Shaw, *Theurgy and the Soul*, 144–5. One finds what I consider to be disturbing suggestions in this regard in Augustine's commentaries on Genesis. For a critical discussion, see my *The Fall of Interpretation*, 139–46.

89 For a helpful analysis in this regard, see Michael Horton, "Eschatology After Nietzsche: Apollonian, Dionysian or Pauline?," *International Journal of Systematic Theology* 2 (2000): 29–62.

90 Recall our discussion of *Philosophical Fragments* above.

91 Pickstock, *After Writing*, 268–71. Her misreading of Kierkegaard stems, in part, from a confusion of the distinction between the "apostle" and the "Teacher" in *Philosophical Fragments*. Indeed, Kierkegaard does suggest that there is an analogy between human teachers ("learners" or "apostles") and the Socratic teacher. But there is a fundamental discontinuity between these human teachers – who can only be "occasions" – and the Teacher who is also the god, who provides both the object of learning and the condition for its reception. In so many ways, the contrast I am making between the Platonic and the "incarnational" is a replaying of this contrast established by Kierkegaard.

INDEX